# IRAQ

## FROM MANDATE TO INDEPENDENCE

First published in 1935 and reprinted now because of its current political relevance, this work concentrates on the events which led to the 1932 installation of Faisal as King of Iraq at the termination of the British Mandate.

Though it deals chiefly with politics at the time, the book also offers important insights into current developments in Iraq and their historical significance. Anyone interested in the future of Iraq and the Middle East at large will find this a compelling read.

# THE KEGAN PAUL
# ARABIA LIBRARY

Faisal ibn Hussain.

# IRAQ
## FROM MANDATE TO
## INDEPENDENCE

ERNEST MAIN

Routledge
Taylor & Francis Group

LONDON AND NEW YORK

First published 2004 by Kegan Paul Limited

Distributed by:
Extenza-Turpin
&
Columbia University Press

Published 2018 by Routledge
2 Park Square, Milton Park, Abingdon, Oxon OX14 4RN
52 Vanderbilt Avenue, New York, NY 10017

Fisrt issued in paperback 2018

*Routledge is an imprint of the Taylor & Francis Group, an informa
business*

**British Library Cataloguing in Publication Data**
A catalogue record for this book is available from the British Library.

**Library of Congress Cataloging-in-Publication Data**
Applied for.

ISBN 13: 978-1-138-86968-4 (pbk)
ISBN 13: 978-0-7103-0908-2 (hbk)

# FOREWORD

By LORD LLOYD OF DOLOBRAN, P.C., G.C.S.I., G.C.I.E., D.S.O.

THE history of Iraq during the past fifteen years is a history eloquent of great achievements too little chronicled and too little known. It is a story of foundations that were laid down with foresight and wisdom by Sir Percy Cox in the very wake of the advancing armies —foundations soon to be powerfully built upon by Sir Arnold Wilson and carried forward in face of intricate and ceaseless difficulty by the skill and devotion of Sir Henry Dobbs. It is a story, too, of the masterly work of Sir John Salmond and of Colonel Joyce— of the rare sympathy and knowledge of Gertrude Bell, and of the gallant heroism of officers like Leachman, Shakespeare, and a score of others, whose names will be remembered and honoured by the Arab of the Euphrates and of the Nejd long after they have been forgotten by people in England.

But this history of Iraq has more than an intrinsic interest. It relates to an experiment in statecraft of a kind never before attempted, the success of which is still in grave doubt. General Smuts' theory of the Mandate, born of the idealism of Woodrow Wilson and the realism of Clemenceau and Lloyd George, has in Iraq been worked out to its consummation. It was perhaps natural that the theory should in its application, inheriting the mixed motives of its parentage, accentuate that conflict between the two ideals of self-government and good government, which Lord Cromer, aptly quoted by Mr. Main in his preface, declared to be inherent in British policy in the East.

Mr. Main, for the first time, outside of official publications, tells the whole story of Great Britain's discharge of her mandate in Iraq. He has lived for some years in the country as an onlooker—and a newspaper editor at that—who sees most of the game, and his survey is therefore not only impartial but also substantiated by personal observation and experience. To give proper perspective to his subject he devotes an interesting chapter to the origins and conditions of the British connection with the Arabs during the war, and

3

emphasizes the misunderstandings that arose from the divided control of Anglo-Arab relations on the east and west of the Arabian peninsula respectively. Mr. Main, as is to be expected, supports the policy and methods adopted on the Mesopotamian side and is critical of the political activities with which Lawrence was identified. I think perhaps that his angle of vision has led him to underestimate the value of Lawrence's unique services and remarkable achievements during the latter part of the war, to which I can bear personal testimony, and at the same time to exaggerate his responsibility for the subsequent troubles in Iraq. The insurrection of 1920 was symptomatic of a far wider reaction, which accompanied the withdrawal of British troops from the Middle East and which had repercussions in India, Afghanistan, Persia, Turkey and Egypt as well as in Iraq. Nevertheless Mr. Main's thesis is interesting, and there is no doubt that the difficulties of the British officials in Iraq in the years immediately following the war were greatly enhanced by the failure of the British Government through preoccupation with other matters to decide between conflicting aspirations in the Middle East.

But it is with the subsequent period of the Mandate or of the treaties by which it was implemented that the bulk of the book is concerned. The exercise of the Mandate in Iraq, as interpreted by the British Government, involved the creation of a national administration with a representative constitution; British authority, at first supreme, gradually diminished as it was transferred with various checks and safeguards to the Iraqi executive until, with the admission of Iraq to the League of Nations, complete independence of British control was attained. The speed with which this process was carried out depended in theory upon the growing ability of Iraqi statesmen to handle their own affairs in consonance with the principles of progressive and enlightened government. In practice however it was influenced by many extraneous considerations. In 1923, for example, a press campaign in England advocating wholesale surrender of all our responsibilities in Iraq induced the Government of the day to accept a drastic, and as it turned out quite impracticable, curtailment of the period of the original treaty, which regulated the mandatory period. In 1926 this period was prolonged by twenty-five years in conformity with the condition imposed by the League of

# Foreword

Nations for the inclusion of Mosul within Iraq. In 1929, however, after constant agitation on the part of Iraqi politicians culminating in a sort of ministerial strike, the British Government promised unconditionally to recommend Iraq's candidature to the League of Nations, which resulted in the termination of the mandatory regime in 1932. The question that inevitably suggests itself is whether extraneous considerations of this kind have in fact been permitted to influence unduly the British Government's policy in Iraq, and whether all the responsibilities inherent in the Mandate were discharged before the Mandate was surrendered. It is when we turn to the chapter on Minorities and read of the massacre of the Assyrians by the Iraq troops at Simel that this question becomes most insistent. Mr. Main does not presume to answer this question—indeed it is a question that only the future can answer—but he provides the data on which an intelligent opinion can be based.

The prospect indeed holds some disquieting features. Apart from the Assyrian problem which is not yet solved, there are the Kurds in their inaccessible country still hardly reconciled to Arab government; there are the Shiahs of the middle Euphrates nursing religious and political jealousies; there is mutual disdain and lack of sympathy between tribesmen and townsmen; an Iraqi Air Force equipped with bombing machines and an Army willing, and apparently able with impunity, to brush aside civil control and to take the law into its own hands; there are headstrong, inexperienced and none too scrupulous politicians; worst of all, there is no King Feisal on the throne, with his unrivalled experience in the handling of Arabs of all classes, to manipulate and control these jarring elements.

But, the man in the street will ask, what does it all matter to us? The answer is that both British interest and British honour are involved. As to our interest, Mr. Main explains how Iraq has become a vital link in British imperial communications. Chaos in Iraq would sever that link and disrupt the whole system. To obviate such a disaster the Anglo-Iraq treaty of 1930 provides for the maintenance of British Air bases in Iraq territory; and so the Royal Air Force, to which in large measure the Iraq State owes its existence, is still available. Its mere presence may be enough to protect Iraq from any threat of foreign aggression, and it will no doubt have considerable moral effect on the maintenance of internal order, but its active employment for the latter purpose is not provided for, and in this connection Mr. Main raises a pertinent question. Active intervention, it is understood, will only be authorized if British interests are threatened. But what are British interests? Almost any serious rising in Iraq may constitute a threat to British interests, and should such a rising be directly occasioned by maladministration on the part of the Iraq Government, what will be the British attitude? A great responsibility will rest on the British Ambassador and Air Force commander to ensure that British forces are not used, even passively, as an instrument of misgovernment and that considerations of interest are not allowed to outweigh those of honour. During the mandatory regime British officials set up standards of security, justice, religious and political toleration, financial morality, health and education, which are described in the later chapters of this book. While it is not to be expected that those standards will be maintained in their entirety, their complete abandonment and a relapse into intolerance, tyranny or anarchy would be a disaster for which Great Britain would be answerable to the civilized world. This has been officially admitted. The British Ambassador explicitly assured the Permanent Mandates Commission of the League of Nations, when recommending Iraq's candidature to the League, that, should Iraq "prove unworthy of the confidence that has been placed in her, the moral responsibility must rest with His Majesty's Government."

The future fortunes of the Iraq State are therefore of peculiar concern to the British people. Hitherto detailed information of our dealings with that country has not been readily available, and it is impossible for us to appreciate where we stand without full knowledge of the facts. This knowledge Mr. Main has now placed within our reach, and I hope that many will profit by it.

LLOYD

30 PORTMAN SQUARE, LONDON
*March 1935*

6

# AUTHOR'S PREFACE

THE British Government, in the conquered territory of Iraq, proceeded in 1920 to face boldly the dilemma which Lord Cromer ten years earlier had said was inherent in British policy in the East. The Englishman as Imperialist, said Cromer, is always striving to attain two ideals which are apt to be mutually destructive—the ideal of good government, which connotes the continuance of his supremacy, and the ideal of self-government, which connotes the whole or partial abdication of his supreme position.

The history of Iraq outlined in the following pages is an attempt to deal faithfully with the change from conquest to political freedom experienced by the people of Iraq during the past dozen years. Living in the country during the later years of the Mandate and into the beginnings of autonomy, having already seen two kings on the throne, having myself occupied positions of complete independence and enjoyed, gratefully and impartially, the friendship of Arab, Kurd, Jew, Christian, and British (both service and civilian), I have tried to estimate fairly the achievement of this new freedom, with its backgrounds and its various reactions.

For many of the illustrations I am indebted to Miss Marjorie Armstrong and to Flight-Lieutenant H. F. Cardwell, R.A.F. For the transcription of the Iraqi national anthem (on the following page) I have to thank Flight-Lieutenant P. J. R. King, R.A.F.

BAGHDAD

7

IRAQI NATIONAL ANTHEM

# CONTENTS

# LIST OF ILLUSTRATIONS

# *Iraq*

## MAPS

# HISTORICAL INTRODUCTION[1]

FROM the earliest time down to about 600 B.C., the history of the country which is now Iraq is the history of Babylonia and Assyria. Before these two powers reached their zenith, their predecessors were the more ancient kingdoms of Sumer and Akkad, which for centuries had maintained their precarious civilization, holding out alternately against floods and drought. Indeed, it is a recognized fact that the ancient history of Iraq turned upon the struggle for the control of the water supply, and most of the wars and the battles and the rise and fall of kingdoms and principalities, have been dependent upon this.

Between Sumer and Akkad, from the earliest times, there was thrust forward a bastion maintaining the claim of the Elamites (who lived in central and southern Persia) to the great waterways of Mesopotamia, but in general the history of the country in these days is that of the balance of power, or the alternate defeat of Sumer and Akkad. Half-way through the third millennium B.C., the two great kingdoms came together, and the combined kingdom included, among other famous cities, the well-known Ur of the Chaldees and Kish. The joint kingdom continued to have a prosperous existence for about four centuries, when the famous law-giver Hammurabi, himself a descendant of invaders from the West, seized the power about 2000 B.C., and at a stroke made Babylon world-famous.

Hammurabi was one of the great progressive rulers of all times. His code of laws, largely extant to this day, shows a grasp of criminal, civil and commercial jurisprudence which has been excelled by few law-givers since his day. Under his strong and just rule Babylonia rose to affluence as the great emporium of trade between East and West. The city rose to heights of prosperity hitherto unknown, but its glory did not long survive the death of Hammurabi, for it was soon submerged under the tide of the Kassite invasion and for about 1,400 years remained in comparative obscurity.

During all this time the state of Assyria, based upon the town of Nineveh near Mosul, was gradually growing in strength and importance, largely perhaps because of its control of the headwaters of

[1] See chapter on Antiquities for a somewhat fuller account.

the Tigris. Between 700 B.C. and 600 B.C., Assyria was rising to its greatest power and its frontiers were stretching far to the east and far to the west. The ancient splendours of Babylonia were completely outshone, and the old city of Babylon, built by Hammurabi, was destroyed by the Assyrians. But between 600 B.C. and 500 B.C., the Chaldeans, who originated in the neighbourhood of the Persian Gulf, swept aside the Assyrian power on their way north and took its place for over half a century. Nebuchadnezzar of the Old Testament was one of the rulers at this period and he it was that rebuilt the Babylon whose ruins may be seen to this day. It was during his reign that the power of Babylonia extended to the Mediterranean, and his capture of Jerusalem was followed by the leading of the Jews into captivity, the Jews whose miseries are recorded in the pages of the Old Testament. It is certain that the Jewish colonies in Iraq to-day are very largely descended from these ancient captives.

But the time of native rule was drawing to an end, and in 539 B.C., the Persians under Cyrus moved westwards and destroyed the power of Babylonia. Persian influence remained paramount for two hundred years, the Persian armies crossing and recrossing the country, until Alexander the Great in his imperial conquests took Mesopotamia in his stride and brought the country under Greek influence. Alexander died at Babylon, where his war-hardened veterans filed past his deathbed so that he could give them his last benison. Greek influence continued in Seleucia—the city founded by one of Alexander's generals just south of Baghdad—but the Persians soon returned to the scene, the Parthians overthrowing Seleucia and establishing Ctesiphon, just across the river. Another wave of invasion from Persia followed, represented by the Sassanid dynasty, who about A.D. 200, brought Ctesiphon to its greatest magnificence, building the great tiled and jewelled arch, the ruins of which remain to this day. For nearly four centuries this state of magnificence continued: the country was prosperous, trade flourished, and the ancient canal systems were developed and extended.

Meantime in the south a new star had arisen. The Prophet Muhammad, born in A.D. 570, brought Islam into being as a great fighting religion and before a century had passed the Muslims had swept away the Sassanids. The whole of the Arabian peninsula

# Historical Introduction

came under Muslim control and the Caliphs took the place of the ancient rulers. The Abbasid Caliphs removed the capital from Damascus to Baghdad, and the City of the Caliphs, as it came to be called, reached its zenith of power and splendour. In this golden age of Baghdad visitors came to the city from all parts of the world, students were attracted to the famous city of learning on the Tigris, which was in fact a great university while Europe was still plunged in barbarism. The famous stories of *The Thousand and One Nights* tell of Harun ar Rashid, the greatest of these Caliphs, and of the glories and magnificence of the city at that time. The rule of the Caliphs continued for several centuries, although as was inevitable, there came a decline from this high eminence.

In the heart of Asia there were during those centuries great stirrings of the Mongol and Tartar tribes and in the middle of the thirteenth century of the Christian era, a great invasion under Hulagu Khan swept through Mesopotamia and wiped out the Arab Caliphs. Baghdad was sacked and pillaged. The victors piled the skulls of the vanquished outside the gates of the city. The great irrigation systems were destroyed. The country became the abomination of desolation. This was in A.D. 1258. Not until our own time did Baghdad begin to recover.

On a fine May day in 1453 the Turks swept into Constantinople, and one hundred years later, while they were pushing westwards into Europe, they were at the same time thrusting south from Anatolia and in 1534 Iraq came under direct Ottoman rule. Corrupt and inefficient, hampered also by the poor communications and the long distances, the Turkish rule was shadowy except in the towns; indeed, all that Constantinople worried about was the exaction of tribute from all the provinces. Whole belts of the country became from time to time independent, as and when strong tribal leaders arose. Insecurity even in the towns became a by-word, life was so cheap that murders could be arranged for a few pence. There was no effective law except the law that might was right, and until the time of the Great War the country was terrorized by a succession of robber barons who lived on plundering and blackmail.

From 1914 onwards the history of Iraq is generally familiar to most people. The British troops landed at the mouth of the Shatt-al-Arab as soon as Turkey entered the war. Their object was to protect

# *Iraq*

British oil interests in South Persia. They soon found it necessary to push north—meeting with incidental reverses, including the surrender at Kut—and finally entered Baghdad in March 1917, driving the Turks almost completely out of the country by the time of the Armistice some eighteen months later. A period of indecision followed. Most of the British officials were under the very distinct impression that the country would remain a British colony or protectorate. A change of policy prevailed, however, and after the Euphrates rebellion in 1920 had been quelled, the British more and more definitely decided to withdraw as soon as the Mandate which she was exercising on behalf of the League of Nations should become capable of termination by reason of Iraq's growth to political and administrative stature.

As the years passed, the British control was withdrawn, the officials remaining only as British advisers to the Iraqi officials who took their places. This tendency still continued, in a manner steadily becoming more and more intensive until September 1932, when the Mandate was terminated. On October 3rd Iraq was admitted to membership of the League of Nations and thus became independent.

TYPICAL SUNNI ARAB IN WINTER KIT

A BAGHDAD COFFEE-SHOP

# IRAQ

## CHAPTER I

### THE LAND AND THE PEOPLE

IRAQ, since time immemorial, has been one of the great highroads between East and West. Its people have watched for countless centuries the caravans faring forth from Baghdad to Aleppo and Damascus, to Mecca in the south and Samarkand in the north, to Persia, Afghanistan and India; they have watched the caravans returning. It has seen successive waves of conquest, with invaders and counter-invaders sweeping across from east to west and back again. It has its own dark history of crime, of ambition, of passionate love; through all the centuries the common people have carried on their commonplace existence and ensured the survival of civilization in the plain of the Two Rivers.

The Kingdom of Iraq lies between the southern frontier of Turkey and the head of the Persian Gulf. On the east it marches with Persia, and while its western boundary is coterminous with that of French-controlled Syria and British-controlled Transjordan, there is in fact no effective frontier in the inhospitable desert which stretches from the Euphrates into Syria. The total area of Iraq is 453,500 square kilometres and the country maintains a population of about 3,000,000. Physically the country may be divided into three parts: Firstly, there is the great plain of the two rivers; secondly, the uplands and foothills which begin to rise from the plain about two hundred miles north of Baghdad; thirdly, the highlands of the north and north-east.

The plain through which the two great rivers Tigris and Euphrates run for the greater part of their course, is the largest of these three divisions; it consists entirely of alluvial sediment brought down by the rivers. The northern edge of this great deposit may be roughly traced by a line on the map between Ramadi in the west and Khanaqin in the east. No stone exists in this plain. It is in fact the delta of the two rivers, which for miles in their course are higher than the surrounding country, which must be protected against floods by bunding. The foothills occupy the area lying between Khanaqin and Mosul and Khanaqin and Ramadi. The land surface here consists of rolling uplands of uncultivable gypsum desert in the northerly portion. Whereas the riverain plain does not exceed 150 ft. above sea-level at its highest, the uplands average about 1,000 ft. More fortunate than the plainsmen, the inhabitants here can engage in cultivation, with the result that the country to Western eyes looks more familiar and is indeed in places very beautiful. North of the uplands comes the highland region. The mountain ranges here exceed 10,000 feet and some of them reach as much as 15,000 feet. The climate here is the ordinary highland climate, a cold winter with heavy rains and snow, and a hot summer. There are many fine streams and the cultivation is varied.

Of the 3,000,000 population two-thirds are Muslim Arabs. The 90,000 Christians live largely in the north of the country, and Muslim Kurds to the number of about 500,000 inhabit the mountains in the north-east. One or two minor sects will be noted later. The people of Baghdad are predominantly Arab, but there are many wealthy Jews and Christians, mostly engaged in business. So too in Basrah. The Jews in the country total some 100,000.

Life in the desert is hard. Man depends upon water for his existence and upon the camel for his ability to reach it. The Baduin regulate their lives by the rains and the floods. In the deserts and plains the rainfall does not exceed six inches in the year and the rainfall is confined to the months of November, December, January and February. In the highlands of the north, stretching into Anatolia, the rainfall swells the rivers, which rise still higher after the melting of the mountain snows in early spring, with the result that the Tigris and the Euphrates come down in heavy flood. At Baghdad the Tigris rises by from 20 to 23 feet; the Euphrates, which comes down a little later, rises about 15 feet. The flooding in the past has not been scientifically controlled,[1] but the overflowing streams, ensuring a rich but transient vegetation, have had a vital influence on the politics and history of the country.

The deserts, the rivers, the hills all have their own peculiar people and problems.

[1] See chapter on Irrigation.

# The Land and the People

The deserts of Iraq stretch north-west, west, south-west, south, and east from the valleys of the Tigris and the Euphrates. To reach Aleppo, Damascus and Jerusalem the great Syrian desert must be crossed. Nowadays this is an easy journey and regular motor services are maintained. No adventures need be expected, apart from punctures or, in the wet season, being bogged. Great stretches of the desert are simply rolling downs of gypsum or gravel. Here cars can attain great speeds, the only danger being the occasional hidden hole or depression. But there are also enormous areas of alluvial soil which rain quickly turns into glutinous mud, and there are numerous patches of deep, soft sand into which cars run at their peril. The Syrian desert is crossed normally in about twenty-four hours. Halfway, at Rutbah Wells, the only water-hole on the route, there is a comfortable rest-house, or hotel, at which clean beds and excellent meals can be obtained. It lies two hundred miles from any other water and is one of the wonders of this part of the world.

The journey in the hot weather can be stifling; in the cold weather it is bitterly cold. The Syrian desert rises to 2,000 feet above sea-level and the usual desert climate prevails—great heat in the summer and intense cold in the winter. The traveller will see from time to time Baduin tribes on the move, or in their encampments. These are collections of black hair tents identical with those of Abraham and other patriarchs of the Old Testament. Camels, asses, sheep and goats are the wealth of these wandering communities, apart from gold and silver, or the individual jewellery and adornments worn by the women or stowed away in the Shaikhs' treasure-chests.

Their life is hard. As season succeeds season they migrate, with all that they possess. In the summer, when the sun burns up everything, they move either to the rivers or to the permanent water-holes. So great is the congregation of tribespeople at such places that great political and diplomatic skill is frequently called for in order to maintain the peace. In the winter, when the rains bring out all the vegetation of the desert, the tribes move out farther afield. It is in this season that raiding normally takes place, for with the extended grazing provided by the rain, greater mobility is possible and the camel-riders, two to a camel on a raid, can make long journeys with ease and security. But raiding is dying out, partly owing to greater Government control in the desert, partly because modern weapons make it really too dangerous a sport. In the old days there were few casualties, but now with machine-guns on armoured cars, as some of the big shaikhs have, there would be many.

The desert is instinct with politics. Each tribe has its own place in the scheme of things and its own circuit of movement from grazing-ground to grazing-ground. Although the desert seems to be trackless, yet there are ancient well-defined tracks from town to town, from village to village, and from water to water. Urgent news is brought by quick camel-riders; the general gossip of Arabia is carried from bazaar to bazaar by pilgrims, wandering men, traders, and by the Solubba, a curious tribe of tinkers and hunters who move freely through the tribes.[1] News travels fast in the desert and the shaikhs are invariably well informed about the balance of power in Arabia, whose stars are waning and whose in the ascendant. Their "desert news service" is also most complete on the mercantile side —the prices of live stock, gold and motor-cars. The coffee-shops in the small desert towns are a veritable whispering gallery in which no secret of Arabia is long respected.[2]

The law of the desert is simple, indeed primitive. The scriptural "eye for an eye" is still the rule. The blood-feud persists and one murder must be expiated by another, committed by a near relative of the first victim on some member of the aggressor tribe. True, the principle of blood-money is also applied, and frequently the giving of a woman in marriage from the one tribe to the other may settle the dispute. But in principle the ancient law holds. It is administered by the shaikhs in tribunal and is as rigid in its application as any modern code. The shaikhs are chosen for their capacity, a son not necessarily succeeding his father. The Arabs have a very

[1] The Solubba are popularly supposed to be Muslimized descendants of the Crusaders (their name is derived from the Arabic word for "Cross"). Other theories give them a gipsy origin. They are beneath the notice of the true Badu, who despises them so much that they do not come within the scope of the blood-feud. This explains the security with which they move about in the peninsula. They possess much live stock, particularly a breed of large white asses.

[2] It is not so long since the first indication of an impending raid was given to the British intelligence service by the sudden frenzied buying of camel-saddles in a town five hundred miles away.

# The Land and the People

strong sense, not of democracy it is true, but of personal equality. The humblest man in the tribe has free access to the shaikh's council tent; Lawrence records that the "manner of the British officers toward their men struck horror into my bodyguard." The Arab in this way has more independence than, say, the Hindu, an indirect product perhaps of his faith.

The way of life among the Arabs is patriarchal, the honour of the women being jealously guarded. A woman's lapse from virtue means death at the hands of her father or brother. If she is a wife her husband hands her back to her family, who do the rest. This rule is almost universal. In the towns the more civilized codes of law are taking its place, but in the desert there is no truckling to new-fangled justice—the woman caught in adultery, or circumstantially guilty of it, is killed.[1] The women are seldom educated, even in reading and writing. They marry early—all that is asked of them is the ability to produce sons, and to milk, bake, make butter and cheese, and weave mats and clothing. The meals prepared by the women are frugal—rice, unleavened bread, eggs, chicken, hare, gazelle or bustard when game can be caught, lizards and jerboas (in the case of the more despised tribes). On greater occasions a sheep is slaughtered and roasted whole in an earthen oven. It is brought in on a flat tray, surrounded by high piles of rice and by smaller trays with chickens and other delicacies. Honoured guests are helped by the host who tears off with his fingers tasty morsels for them. Others may help themselves and when all have eaten till they can eat no more, they give up their places to the next in importance, going out to where the slaves or serving-men are waiting with spouted jugs to pour water upon the greasy hands of the feasters. At no time is there any privacy for anyone. Everything is common knowledge; the desert Arab, like the child, is not so much inquisitive as interested in the affairs of others. This is a characteristic of the urban Arab too; sometimes he carries it too far, and his Jewish and Christian neighbours vie with him in this respect. The native clerks in banks and other business firms think nothing of disclosing in the bazaar their customers' business affairs. In the case of the banks indeed many clerks are in the pay of various brokers and others who for different reasons may wish to know

[1] See Chapter XII.

the private affairs of some of the banks' customers. But in large part the desire to find out about one's neighbour is not so much dishonest as just naïve.

Murders in blood-feud or in revenge for honour besmirched, are counted for merit. Thieving is rampant, for the desert Badu, like the soldier, will pick up anything that may help him in his hard life. The Badu, too, is venal to a degree and a relatively small price will buy him. He is often treacherous, judged by Western standards,[1] and while he has plenty of *élan*, he lacks the power of sticking to a job or holding to some unpleasant task. He is apt to kill the goose that lays the golden eggs. He is hospitable in the extreme, but in the case of strangers his laws of hospitality demand only hospitality for a few days, after which the stranger, unless asked to remain, must take his departure and the risk of his erstwhile hosts becoming his enemies. The Badu has an acute sense of his rights; his sense of his duties and responsibilities is not so acute. His sense of honour is keen, and so is his pride.

The Badu too, is lazy. As soon as he can settle by fresh water he simply sits down and sleeps or waits for food to be brought to him by the women. The desert life is so hard that this is no doubt a natural reaction. The Badu's only enjoyments are physical. He has evolved no art-forms; his music is primitive in the extreme, his literature (apart from the Koran) is the narration of simple stories and ballads, more often than not bawdy, around the camp-fires or in the tents. His sexual life is completely devoid of civilized inhibitions. He will have two or three wives, and, if a man of wealth, even more—not simultaneously, for divorce of the earlier and older ones is a matter of no difficulty. The Koran lays down precepts as to when marital intercourse is not permitted, but apart from such occasions the Badu regards the sexual act just like any other of the physical functions. He sees nothing romantic in it; it is to him neither ennobling nor degrading, but just impersonal. Sons are desired; if daughters come instead, then shame is on the mothers.

The young boy grows up in surroundings which to the Western eye seem unhealthy. If he is of wealthy family he is surrounded

---

[1] In her famous memorandum of February 1919, Miss Gertrude Bell quoted the then Naqib of Baghdad as saying "It is the nature of every Arab to confide to the authorities the doings of all other Arabs."

in childhood by female retainers, all anxious for favours to come. Most boys in wealthy families are thus early initiated into habits of vice, and they get further opportunities if they are wealthy enough, or near enough, to go into Damascus or Baghdad. The boy is normally married[1] by the time he is seventeen or nineteen, and it is often found that any smartness of brain which he showed as a youngster begins then to disappear. Until about forty he may be said to be in the prime of life, but he goes down the hill fairly quickly and most Baduin of fifty or fifty-five are old men. Aphrodisiacs enjoy a ready sale in the bazaars.

It is from this desert stock that the Arab of Iraq has sprung. Numerically the pure desert stock is relatively small and there is at work a constant tendency to settle which blunts the sharp line that otherwise could be drawn between the nomad and the townsman. The nomad's tent is first anchored down by sheltering piles of brushwood. Then it becomes a reed-hut and finally a mud-hut. The townsman likes to see the tribesmen settled, thus fixing him where he can be found, but the police say it makes for an increase of petty crime, especially in hard times. Economically the free nomad may become a settled serf, the shaikh a feudal overlord. In the towns the harder virtues of the desert become softened into luxury and easy living; on the other side, weaknesses that the desert does not allow to survive exist in degenerate form; overall, the facile "smartness" of the townsman replaces the steadier, starker virtues of the tribes, and education comes in to widen the rift still more, for few of the children of tribespeople or cultivators go to school.

There is no prostitution except in the towns. It is controlled by police regulation, based on the Muslim ideal of safeguarding the family and the position of women. All prostitutes are licensed and registered, and pay a tax; if any "unofficial" woman is found engaged in prostitution in a private house, she is at once put on the register and removed to the official brothel-area, where she comes under police discipline and is subject to weekly medical examination. Most of the licensed prostitutes in Iraq are Iraqi or Syrian Christians and a smaller number are Jewesses; there are also Muslim women, usually widows[2] or discarded wives, of the lower

[1] See Appendix C for marriage customs in Southern Iraq.
[2] It is a disgrace for a woman to outlive her husband.

classes. There is no solicitation in the streets; the unregistered women have pimps. Homosexuality is rife, both among the idle women of the harems and among men. Sodomy is a penal offence, but in practice it is almost impossible to get a conviction in the courts.

Middle-class functions in the towns of Iraq to-day are carried out mainly by the Jews and the Christians, although with the post-war spread of education an educated Muslim middle-class is rapidly arising. In pre-war days the Christian and Jewish communities maintained their own schools, but the Muslims, except for the sons of the aristocracy, remained in the mass illiterate.[1] There is thus a great gap between the aristocracy and the labouring classes, with nothing to fill it except a few officials and lawyers, the older of them Turkish-trained. The townsman and the tribesman for centuries have hated each other; one of the most complex problems that Iraq has to face lies in the distrust between the towns and the tribes.

The Arab by temperament cannot build up a business over a long period. He always wants quick results. This is largely because there was no real security in Turkish days. But apart from that, the Oriental does prefer ups and downs (being an optimist he expects more ups!) to a steady but to him dull progress.

The family maintains its ancient tyranny over the individual. It is more than the family interest which is the dominating power even in the so-called individualist West. It is natural that man should strive for the interests of his family, but this healthy tendency is in Iraq carried to extremes which tend to militate against the efficient running of the state and of commerce, particularly the former. Government service is the goal of education in Iraq. The young effendi as a rule has his eye upon the civil service. This is all to the good, but the civil service so far has no corporate tradition and it is in this field that the tyranny of the family must be broken. It is probably natural that his father or mother or elder brother should be unwilling that some individual clerk should take up a new post in another town. But it is essential that such influences should not be allowed to interfere with movements in the civil service. This tyranny of the family is at work from the

---

[1] In the religious schools the *Mullahs* teach only reciting the Koran; some of them cannot even read.

CARRYING HOME FIREWOOD

OUTSIDE A FELLAHEEN VILLAGE; COMMUNAL BAKING OVEN
IN FOREGROUND

boy's birth until his death. At every crisis in his career, whatever the interests of his own future may dictate, the views of his family are his first consideration.

There are reasons for this. Until the past decade, communications were so bad and the country so insecure that to send a youth to the other end of the country made him almost as inaccessible as if he had gone to Europe or America. Moreover, the corrupt exactions of Turkish officials and the blackmail of the robber barons who studded the countryside tended to keep families together as a means of self-defence. A newly married couple in the old days never set up a house of their own. This centripetal tendency within the family is thus a force to be reckoned with. There are, however, signs that it is being gradually undermined and no doubt big changes will be seen when the older generation has passed away. Many young Arabs would like to see their wives going about in Baghdad unveiled, as they would in Syria or Turkey or Europe, but they dare not face the disapproval of their families. In practice, a Baghdad woman or girl[1] may be, and usually is, unveiled when travelling abroad, but as soon as she returns to Baghdad, on goes the veil again, except at parties and the like at which no Muslim men are present. But times are changing rapidly and by the time the next generation comes along, the family will begin to be relegated to the background.

The social system is feudal. An aristocratic family has whole families of retainers, virtually domestic slaves, who have grown up with the family and whose children will follow them. In the case of cultivators, the retainers are entitled by law to a certain share in the fruits of their toil, so that while socially the structure is feudal, economically it represents a form of profit-sharing. But this is established by custom and not by law; and as yet there is little sign of a fixed wage in farming. But the past decade has seen rapid changes and a new society is arising in the towns.

Along the rivers are the great cultivating landlords and their *fellahin*. On the Tigris and the Euphrates their principal crops are cereals. On the Shatt-al-Arab, centred on Basrah, are the great date-gardens, the export of fruit from which is an important source

[1] Baduin women and unmarried girls enjoy much greater freedom than townswomen.

of revenue. Social conditions among the cultivators, as might be expected, are advanced or retarded according to their distance from the nearest substantial town. The *fellahin* are as a class probably the most numerous in the country. Their condition has remained unchanged for centuries, although the easier communications and the increased security during the past ten or fifteen years have introduced an important modifying influence. If this has meant nothing else, it has meant that the strength of the government can be surely and swiftly brought to bear where and when required. In pre-war days there were great stretches of country, notably the Muntafiq (from the Euphrates to the Tigris, between Kut and Nasiriyah), where the Turkish writ did not run, where no official dared show his face, and where no taxes were paid. To-day this is no longer the case. The powers and influence of the shaikhs have tended to decrease with the growth in strength of the central control. As the Government has grown stronger, the individual *fellah* sees less and less necessity for tribal unity and so is less and less ready to stand tyranny on the part of his shaikh, which to his forefathers was tolerable because protection went with it. The Government is not yet strong enough to carry on without the shaikhs, although this is its aim. The gap between townsman and tribesman is thus in Iraq much wider than it is, for instance, in Egypt, even though it has been narrowed by easy and safe communications.

The cultivators, whether recently settled or the descendants of former generations of settlers, live frugally, but they are improvident and lazy. The date-packers for instance make enough in the two or three months of the season to keep them in idleness for the rest of the year, and they are typical. Their needs are few, and when the worst comes to the worst the odd job will always produce the few pence necessary for the next day or two. Their religion teaches them that Allah will provide; this kills all will even to live. A family of *fellahin* can exist on about a penny a day per head. They will have a meat meal not more than once a week, if that. Rice, flat-bread, dates and an egg or so are all they ask. The more necessary luxuries, such as tea, sugar, cigarettes, must of course be bought in addition; one reason why the *fellahin* suffered from the slump in grain prices during the past few years was that they had grown so accustomed to these that the luxuries had become costly necessaries. Large numbers of the *fellahin* are in debt, consisting largely of pay drawn in advance.

In the south of Iraq there are great stretches of marsh and shallow water, the Hammar Lakes, which extend from the Euphrates to the Tigris. Here exist, in the most primitive conditions, the so-called Marsh Arabs. For miles and miles huge reeds grow from the water and obscure the sky. It is the wildfowler's paradise. The Marsh Arabs, skilful watermen, have their own "paths" through these forests of reeds, pushing their sharp-prowed boats through on their journeyings to and from the various islands which stud the lakes and on which they have their homes. Their livelihood depends on their fishing and on their water-buffaloes and small live stock. They are of a low standard of intelligence.[1] They use a few words and sounds which are non-Arabic and they may indeed be a survival of the early peoples of the country; the boat which they normally use, the *mashhuf*, is identical with the models of four thousand years ago which have been unearthed in the tombs at Ur, only a few miles distant.

The Arab's religion is that of the Prophet Muhammad. He venerates Christ as a prophet and all the rest of the long list stretching back to the Old Testament times, but Muhammad was the last Prophet of God and there will never be another. Like all the fighting faiths, there is nothing of meekness or humility in Islam. There is but one God to the Muslim and He is all-pervading and omnipresent. There are, it is true, religious observances in the mosques, and there are certain big festivals in the Muslim calendar. But the Muslim carries his religion with him into his daily life. At prayer-times one can see praying men anywhere in the streets. All the vicissitudes of life are provided for in the Koran, which indeed is the *fons et origo* of Muhammadan jurisprudence. Free-thinking is beginning to show itself in the towns and particularly among those younger men who have been to Europe. But among the tribes the old faith exercises its sway to the point of fanaticism.[2]

Such then are the Arabs of the deserts and the alluvial delta.

---

[1] During the great four-yearly cholera epidemics in Southern Iraq the British medical officers have found that many of these marsh-people do not know even the names of their parents.

[2] For the Sunni-Shiah schism see chapter on the Holy Cities.

# *Iraq*

Going northwards and eastwards from Baghdad into the foothills, Turcoman and Kurdish physical types begin to make their appearance. They are more robust than the Arab; they are in fact mountaineers and not plainsmen. The Turcoman is no more than a central Asian type, the Kurd is a definite and clear-cut racial type. He is Aryan, while the Arab is Semitic. The Kurds are highlanders occupying the mountains in the north-east of Iraq and their homeland is cut by the political frontiers of Iraq, Persia and Turkey. They are a hardy, brave and cruel race, full of intelligence, and make first-class guerrilla fighters. They are said to be treacherous, but most of the British officers who have served with the Kurd are strongly predisposed in his favour. The Kurds provide most of the coolies in Baghdad and the big towns. They possess a strength and a stamina which the Arab of the same class, possibly through malnutrition,[1] does not possess and all the heavy carrying work is done by them. They are a musical race, with highland pipes like all mountaineers, and are excellent stage actors and mimics. They will be discussed more fully in the chapter on Minorities.

The mountains too have their nomads. These tribes, neither Arab nor Kurd nor Persian, move twice a year on their great migrations. They spend the winter in the plains of Iraq for the high Persian plateau is then snow-covered; the summer they spend on the plateau, for the Iraqi plains are then burned up. This involves a tremendous migration every six months. The whole tribe moves —men, women, children, babies, cattle, horses, asses, sheep, goats, dogs, and all their household impedimenta from the tents downwards. Everything has to be moved across rivers and rushing torrents. In the spring precipitous mountains over ten thousand feet high, must be climbed in order to reach the grazing on the plateau. In the autumn the descent has to be made to the plains. By the time a man is fifty he will have performed this great mountaineering ordeal a hundred times. It is an ordeal which eliminates all but the fittest; in addition to the actual trekking and climbing, the nomads must at all times be ready to defend themselves against marauders.

---

[1] When the Iraqi Government in 1931 forbade the practice of bringing Persian coolies to Basrah to unload and load ocean-going steamers, the Port Authorities had first to feed their new Arab coolies in order to bring them up to the required standard of strength and endurance.

28

# The Land and the People

The indigenous Christians in Iraq are relics of the old schismatic divisions of the Eastern communion. Most of the sects have archiepiscopal or episcopal sees, with prelates residing in Mosul. The chances of the war turned out unluckily for them. The Assyrians,[1] for instance, whose homeland was in the Hakkiari country, fought for the Russians against the Turks and now find themselves with neither home nor political independence. They are a fine fighting race. The men are clean, virile fellows and make excellent soldiers. Remnants of the Armenian race are dotted here and there in refugee camps where they have remained since the war. They do not count for much. Other Christian communities include Jacobites, Chaldeans and Syrian Catholics, as well as some Maronites. From the Chaldeans most of the hotel-keepers and waiters in the country are recruited.

One of the strangest religious sects, in this country of many sects, is the Devil-worshippers or the Yezidis. These Devil-worshippers number about thirty thousand. Most of them live in the Jebel Sinjar, on the frontier with Syria, but their chief shrines are at Shaikh Adi, a little to the north of Mosul. It would perhaps be more correct to call them Devil-Propitiators. They fear Satan rather than worship him, and prayers and offerings form their tribute. Satan is to them the greatest of the fallen angels, who after his repentance was given the earth to rule for ten thousand years. As this happened about six thousand years ago, he still has about four thousand to run. His name, Shaitan, is a veritable name of fear—so much so that the Devil-worshippers will use no word beginning with the sound *sh*. Even the very ordinary Arabic word *shatt*, meaning river, is tabu; their chiefs similarly, are never called shaikhs but are Amirs or Mirs. I remember one of them calling on me in Baghdad one day. In the approved style he sent up his card—a piece of tissue paper, like cigarette paper, with a crude rubber-stamp impression of the Sacred Peacock and below, in English from the left and Arabic from the right, his name followed by his title "Amir of the Yezidis." Ostensibly he came to pay his compliments to a representative of the generous and just British race; actually his object was to find out what could be done to help him to prosecute his claims to the principal chieftainship of his sect.

---

[1] See Minorities, p. 139.

29

# *Iraq*

For there are several claimants to this sacred—and lucrative—
post. The Yezidis worship the Devil in the form of the Sacred
Peacock, of which there are seven known bronze images. One is
kept at the principal shrine at Shaikh Adi; the other six are peri-
patetic and the control of them is a valuable property. Less important
objects of veneration are the white bull; the sun, moon and stars;
and the black serpent. The white bull is sacrificed annually—a
strange relic in our time of the Mithraic religion with which students
of Roman history are familiar. The bull is sacrificed at a Sun Temple,
north of Mosul, which is decorated with astronomical signs, and
has outside the entrance a representation of the black serpent, which
is associated with their faith. Jesus is venerated by them, but he
comes far behind Satan. The Peacock, i.e. Melek Taos, represents
the principal object of their faith, and Melek Isa (Jesus) is a poor
second. They believe in both the Christian Testaments and also
the Muslim Koran. Satan to them stands not so much for Evil, as
for Power, which explains the fact that their religion stands for
propitiation rather than worship. One of their religious tenets is
a rigid refusal to accept education, even the barest rudiments of
the three R's. For this reason alone they must have a dwindling
place in a state that is rapidly being modernized. To this must be
added the fact that they are shrinking in numbers, in spite of the
protection afforded by their isolated position.

Another sect in Iraq that is dwindling are the Mandaeans or
Sabaeans. They number less than five thousand, and one of the
reasons for their steady diminution is that when one of their women
marries a Muslim or a Christian she leaves her religion as well as
her community. These marriages are fairly frequent, for the Mandaean women are unveiled and are normally good-looking. The
visitor to southern Iraq is familiar with the Mandaeans—they are
the silversmiths, known as Amarah-workers, who work in the
bazaars making trinkets of silver with designs inlaid in antimony.
The origin of these people is unknown. One legend makes them the
descendants of the Queen of Sheba's subjects; another makes them
a pre-Christian sect of worshippers of John the Baptist. Neither of
these beliefs has scientific basis. What is certain is that ablution is
a vital feature of their religious belief—not baptism in the sense in
which we regard it, but immersion in the element which gives life.

# The Land and the People

For this reason their little communities are to be found along rivers, as immersion must follow all the pollutions of daily life, as well as major breaches of conduct, even formal breaches that may be committed in ignorance by their priests or leaders. They sleep lying north-and-south, and the dead are buried facing the north. The holiest among them are vegetarians. All are pacifists. All hold that a devout acceptance of their creed will avert disease or illness. They have no political ambitions and are a minority that sets no problems for the Arab Government.

The Jews are the one considerable section of the Iraqi nation not yet described. It is tolerably certain that they are the descendants of the Jews taken captive at Jerusalem by Nebuchadnezzar and brought to Babylon as slaves for clearing the canals of the silt which the floods brought down every year.[1] Like their co-religionists everywhere they have maintained their purity of race and the wealthy families have conserved their inheritances by inter-marriage. They have made themselves an integral part of the nation. Both in business and in politics they have played a big part. Anti-Zionist feeling is strong among the Muslims of Iraq. The first Lord Melchett, then still Sir Alfred Mond, was the centre of a riot in February 1928 when he visited Baghdad. He had been studying Zionist progress in Palestine, and his object in visiting Iraq was concerned with the chemical side of agriculture in which he was interested. The Jewish community in Baghdad decided to do honour to such a famous co-religionist, and at once rumours were started that Lord Melchett had come to Zionize Iraq. On arrival he was greeted by hostile demonstrations and the riots called for special government measures for the maintenance of order. These were dropped later. In August 1929, when the Wailing Wall disturbances broke out in Jerusalem, mass meetings were held in Baghdad protesting against the British policy in Palestine and also against the progress of Zionism. Special editions of the Arab newspapers were published, telegrams of condolence and protest hummed across the wires. But the Jews in Iraq were not molested.

In former times all men wore the flowing robe or *abba*, covering a garment like a nightgown, called a *dishdasha*. The Arabs wore headcloth and headrope, the Jews and Christians the *tarboosh* or

[1] "By the waters of Babylon we sat and wept."

fez. The younger generation to-day, especially in the towns, are wearing European clothes, with the Iraqi hat, the *sidara*.[1]

Muslim women of good family are rarely seen out in the streets. All Muslim women, except of the working classes or of the tribes, are veiled in public. Jewish and Christian women mostly wear European dress. Many of them as they walk out in the evenings wear bright salmon-pink stockings revealing heavy anklets worn underneath them. The younger ones may wear European hats; the older wear silk scarves or cloths over the head. In the case of some of the Christian women, they wear a broad flap that comes down over the eyes like a visor, and their robe-like garments are of bright pinks and yellows.

The climate of Iraq is trying but not unhealthy. In the north it is an Alpine climate, hot in the summer, with heavy snows in the winter. In the plain of the two rivers and in the desert the winter is as cold as a British winter. Snow has been known in Baghdad, but this is abnormal. The temperature once or twice every winter, however, falls below freezing point, even as far south as Basrah. The whole of the annual rainfall occurs in the winter months—in the plains not exceeding six inches and usually being less than that. The alluvial plain then becomes mud and except on macadamized roads all traffic ceases till the surface hardens again. The summer is intensely hot. On the lower Shatt-al-Arab the shade maximum in July and August approaches if it does not exceed 130 degrees Fahrenheit. In those months the night minimum is never much more than seventy and it is this variation of fifty or sixty degrees in the twenty-four hours that makes the great heat tolerable. Everyone sleeps on the flat-roofs of the houses, or at least out of doors.

Insect pests abound in the hot weather. Mosquitoes are common, especially in the marshier parts of the south, and there is much malaria, to which the population does not become immune. The sand-fly is also found everywhere. Sand-fly fever is common, and it has been established by researches in Baghdad, carried out by British scientists, that it is one definite species of sand-fly that transmits the local variety of the Oriental Sore known as the Baghdad boil, which takes about a year to run its course and then

[1] See p. 39.

THE SHRINE OF THE YEZIDIS AT SHAIKH ADI, NEAR MOSUL.
NOTE THE BLACK SERPENT BY THE DOORFOST

KURDS IN THEIR MOUNTAINS

# The Land and the People

leaves a permanent unsightly scar. The house-fly in its various subspecies is to be found everywhere, and, thanks to the primitive sanitation and hygiene among the masses, is the cause of much of the dysentery and of the eye and skin diseases which are rife.

Dust storms are frequent in the hot weather, especially if the previous winter has had little rain. The least breath of wind sets the desert sand in motion. What on water is a cat's-paw sets the tiniest particles scurrying over the surface of the ground until some obstacle checks them. On the middle Euphrates the desert is thus in continuous movement. When the wind rises, it carries the sand particles into the air in clouds. A heavy dust-storm is like a London fog and hangs overhead like a pall. The fine particles penetrate everywhere. The closest-fitting windows and doors cannot keep out the dust. These dust-storms when continuous are most trying. In the southerly parts of the country the dust usually comes with a north or west wind. The south wind, blowing up from the Persian Gulf, brings humidity to the atmosphere and lassitude to the people. The air seems to hang, sodden, over everything; there is no movement of any kind and one simply sits and sweats. In this kind of weather a man will leave his bath, dry himself, and in a trice is as wet with perspiration as when in the bath. "It was a toil to be," says Coleridge, and that is the southern Iraq late summer climate in a nutshell.

No one, unless compelled to, goes out in the sun. The Arab's clothes are excellent hot-weather clothes. The head-cloth protects the head and nape of the neck; the cloak is frequently rolled up and carried on the head, with part falling over the neck, thus giving additional protection. When the sand is blowing, and the sun is thus obscured, the Arab winds the free ends of his head-cloth over his nose and mouth, and brings the upper flap on the forehead down over the eyes, which thus look out through a narrow slit like a visor.

The houses are built for the summer. They have thick walls—in the north built of stone, in the south, where there is no stone, of mud or dried brick. Most houses are of only two storeys above ground, owing to the difficulty of finding a foundation for heavier weight. Nearly every house has a vaulted underground or semi-underground room or rooms in which the family eat and sleep during the hot afternoon. The prevailing insecurity in former times, coupled with the Muslim seclusion of women, determined the architectural style. Each house is built round a central courtyard.[1] As a rule every window in the house is barred and there are generally few windows below the first storey. The walls are high and the single door is of heavy wood, usually teak, studded with iron knobs and having a formidable lock. Most doors have a peep-hole, for the better examination of the stranger who knocks. During the last few years houses of the open villa type have been constructed in the suburbs of Baghdad and other towns. They have barred windows and sturdy doors but do not present the same "fortress" appearance as the houses of the traditional style.

In the old days of insecurity in the Middle East every man carried his shot-gun. The rifle took the place of the shot-gun, and to-day, even where there is comparative security, the rifles still remain. There is a system of licences to carry arms, under which all arms in the country are registered, but it cannot be pretended that the register is in any sense complete. The official figures show a steady annual increase, but this does not mean that every year there are more firearms in the country; it merely means that more of the existing firearms are being registered, perhaps through police discovery or because informers have given the owners away. The object of the Arms Regulations is officially declared to be "to make the possession of arms an expensive luxury and so discourage the practice of carrying them." In effect it is merely a revenue tax which is grossly unequal in its incidence and cannot in practice be effectively collected. It has done practically nothing to disarm the population. The population, it may be said, refuse to disarm; indeed since British control of the police ended, the price of rifles in the bazaars has gone up, showing that the demand for them has increased.

The capital of Iraq is Baghdad, a city of some 300,000 inhabitants on the Tigris. Baghdad is an interesting, fascinating, but squalid city. The old town, on the left bank, is a maze of narrow alley-ways; the new town is partly a similar maze, but a fine new town-planned area is being built. The extensions, north and south, of the old town on the left bank, are also more or less town-planned. During the

---

[1] At Ur the excavations have proved that the houses of four thousand years ago were of the same architectural type as the Arab houses of to-day.

# The Land and the People

past half-dozen years there has been much building, due as much to the world "flight from money" since the exchanges lost their stability, as to any confidence that the present degree of security in the country will be maintained.

Baghdad is a great trading centre. Both native and European firms, mainly British, carry on business as importers and exporters; new businesses, European in origin and meeting European needs, have been developed since the war. These will be dealt with fully in the chapter on Trade and Industry, but here may be noted one industry that has had a marked social influence. The Baghdad Races have been one of the most flourishing institutions in the country. Strictly under British control, with a Turf Club whose rules and standards are as rigid as those of the Jockey Club, the races are now chiefly supported by the Arabs. The extreme Nationalists, on the specious plea that racing has a bad influence in that it encourages betting, but in reality trying to aim a blow at the foreigner, have tried to stop the racing, but its popular backing is such that this will prove difficult. Moreover, the export of pedigree Arab horses to India is a lucrative business, and organized racing in Iraq has undoubtedly helped to maintain the pure-bred standard. The race meetings take place on Saturdays and Sundays during the cold weather, and the members' enclosure is a popular rendezvous, particularly in March and April, when the social season is at its height and the big races are run. The Horse Show also takes place at this time and is extremely popular. The riding by the Arab cavalrymen and policemen is amazingly good and the Arab horses, although small judged by thoroughbred standards, put up a good display of pluck and speed.

The weather during these two months is beautiful, although by the end of April it may be beginning to get a little warm for those normally accustomed to northern climates. At the same time it is possible to walk about the town in comfort, visiting the bazaars and other places of interest. The bazaars are not so extensive as those, say, of Cairo, but at the same time are more unspoiled and the native brass and copperware, silks, carpets and the like, are cheaper. The main bazaar runs from Exchange Square in the direction of the Tigris; immediately opposite, on the other side of the street, away from the river, is the fruit and grain market, which is still worth a visit. The bazaars with their constantly changing kaleidoscope offer countless opportunities for artistic photography.

The evening entertainments in Baghdad are not very varied. The cinemas are popular; the usual Hollywood and Elstree pictures are shown, with occasional Arab films from Egypt. Cabarets of the European type were suppressed in 1933. The reason given was that the artists—European or Levantine girls such as one sees in all the cabarets in the Near East—"take money out of the country." The real reason was a strange mixture. There was Arab puritanism in it as well as anti-foreign sentiment. The artists were foreigners and most of the people who visited the cabarets, and certainly all who spent big money there, were Europeans. There was the further coincidence that the cabaret-proprietors were invariably Christians, and the Christians in Iraq will invariably tell you that no Arab likes to stand by and watch a non-Arab making money. The closing of the cabarets meant considerable financial loss to the community. Whatever money the artists may have taken out of the country, this was certainly only a portion of what was spent and thus circulated through the town. The Iraqi in general has not grasped the principle that money is useless unless it is in circulation. The closing of the cabarets caused—as also would the stopping of the races— big losses to wholesale and retail business people, shippers, the national revenue, taxi-drivers (and through them car-dealers and the oil distributors), and the host of waiters and menials, whose wages were suddenly cut off.

Not all the evening entertainments, however, were stopped. The Arab theatres were allowed to continue. These are maintained by Muslim proprietors and are frequently run in connection with hotels and the larger coffee-houses. These entertainments are provided by Arabic women singers and dancers, whose performances are exotic and strange to Western ears and eyes. The music[1] is shrill and quavering and the instruments normally used are the zither, fiddles of various sorts, and drums of different varieties, shapes and tones. The drums are usually waisted cylinders. They are tucked

---

[1] While on the subject of music it may be stated that the Arab is given to singing songs, often love songs, as he walks along. He sings in a high falsetto, with many quarter-tones and grace-notes. It is interesting, too, to realize that the Arab does not whistle.

under one arm and the performer beats a tattoo with his fingers on the parchment which covers the top. The drummers, who begin as small boys, acquire great dexterity and their performances as a rule are no less interesting than the somewhat monotonous singing and swaying of the women dancers. They pound or thump their drums with their muscular fingers, bringing all kinds of varieties and changes of rhythm into their music and frequently working themselves up into a state of considerable exaltation. The dancing is static rather than dynamic. It is mostly symbolic and an expert dancer by her sinuous movements and gestures can move a whole audience to a state of great excitement. The public audiences are normally entirely composed of men.

Outside Baghdad the principal towns are Basrah, Mosul, Kirkuk, Amarah, Kut, Nasiriyah, Hillah and Sulaimani.

Basrah, the port of Iraq, is decaying but attractive. It is a straggling place consisting of three townships—Ashar, Basrah City and Margil. Ashar is the business centre, on the Shatt-al-Arab. Here are the banks and the chief business houses. Here too is the headquarters of the provincial government. Basrah City is declining in importance and many of its bazaars are closed. Both these are old towns with narrow streets and overhanging houses. Margil, where the port headquarters and the railway terminus are,[1] is a new town, of up-to-date bungalows laid out in a garden-city. The European community in Basrah live (with few exceptions) in Ashar or Margil. In the summer the climate is hot and humid, but the numberless creeks afford ample scope for picnics and outings. The small passenger craft of Basrah is the elegant and picturesque *bellum*—a gaily-painted gondola-like canoe, paddled or poled by two boatmen. Basrah's *bellums* are a most distinctive feature of the river scene. It was from Basrah that Sindbad the Sailor set out on his voyages. In the middle ages the city was a notable seat of learning. Its period of bursting prosperity came with the Great War, when it became the British base and its inhabitants simply coined money. Those days have gone, and Basrah's prosperity is once again entirely dependent upon the date-growing for which it has been famous for centuries.

Mosul, a fine open town, is the most important town in the

---

[1] See chapter on Railways, Roads and Rivers.

north. The population here is mixed—Arab, Kurd, Turcoman and Christian—the architecture different from any that the southern part of the country can show. Its streets are also wider and opener. Mosul is a busy centre. It is the central emporium for the northern highland region, and though the railway does not reach it, it is on the through railway route from Baghdad to Europe. All kinds of Christian sects deriving from the various Eastern churches have archbishops or bishops in Mosul, and just to the north-east of the town is the central shrine of the Yezidis, or Devil-worshippers. Across the river from Mosul is the site of ancient Nineveh, the whole of the countryside being associated with the name of the Prophet Jonah. Arbil[1] is a town of lesser importance lying to the north-east.

To the south of Mosul lie the oilfields. West of the Tigris is the new and undeveloped concession of the British Oil Development Company. The lands to the east of the river are reserved for the Iraq Petroleum Company, whose producing field is at Baba Gurgur, a few miles north of Kirkuk. Here about forty wells are ready for production and here is the landward end of the great pipe-line to the Mediterranean. The country is, as it were, saturated with oil. Near Baba Gurgur is still to be seen the "burning, fiery furnace" of the Old Testament, where Shadrach, Meshech and Abednego walked unscathed because the Lord was with them. The "burning, fiery furnace" is a little hollow in the arid foothills from which natural gas escapes to the surface in blue, lambent flames. The fire is perpetual and some have thought that the fire-worship which spread over Persia may have originated in this neighbourhood. Kirkuk is a mixed town. The older part is perched on a bluff, with narrow streets and alley-ways. The newer portion is partly squalid and tortuous, partly town-planned, with wide streets and gardens. It is a thriving place, thanks to the pipe-line activities.

Amarah and Kut, both on the Tigris, are important agricultural centres. They came into prominence in the world war but have since relapsed into their earlier obscurity. Nasiriyah, on the Euphrates, is a comparatively modern town, with well-laid out streets and bazaars. Hillah, also on the Euphrates, is the centre of an important agricultural region. Sulaimani, in eastern Kurdistan, was formerly

[1] See p. 230.

# The Land and the People

a storm-focus. Latterly, however, with the development of roads and motor transport it has been more settled. It is a marketing centre for this part of Kurdistan, and also has trade relations with Persia. South of Basrah is the quaint desert town of Zubair, a Sunni stronghold in a country of Shiahs. It is a Holy City of the Sunnis and is a great centre for desert news and trade. Owing to the difference in the Customs duties imposed respectively by Kuwait and by Iraq, Zubair's chief industry at present is smuggling. In the west of the country lies Ramadi, the principal passport office for the desert-routes; in the east the frontier station into Persia is Khanaqin, in the producing field of the Rafidain Oil Company; an off-shoot of the Anglo-Persian.

Such in brief is the country of Iraq, such the people who live in this new state. It was King Faisal's hope and avowed object to unify the different religions and sects so that they should all become *Iraqis*, all subjects in the same state, and not Arab or Jew, Christian or Kurd. To this end he devised the national hat known as the *sidara*, very like the old British Royal Flying Corps cap. But whereas Riza Shah in Persia, and the Ghazi in Turkey, could at a stroke put all Persians, and all Turks, into uniform headgear, no such uniformity of mind existed in Iraq and there was no possibility of compelling the independent-minded desert Arabs, or the cultivators, or the Kurds, into wearing any hat they did not like. Many of them, too, cannot even grasp the idea of uniformity. The *sidara* has therefore come to be the mark of the townsman. Officials are compelled to wear it, and the younger generation in the towns have generally adopted it. It is this question of unity of sentiment among the Iraqis that is to-day so difficult. In the East men are prone to conceal their thoughts, but to anyone who has lived in Iraq, it is clear that for many years to come there will be diversity of interest and of sentiment as between the different sections within the state.

# CHAPTER II

## BRITISH IMPERIAL COMMUNICATIONS

BAGHDAD has come back to its old importance as the junction of the great roads to the East. Indeed, Britain's interest in Iraq is largely, almost entirely, dictated by the necessity of keeping her Indian communications open. Now that flying has become a normal means of communication, and even of troop movements, now that motor transport has brought the journey across the Syrian Desert within a day's compass, the Suez route has lost a certain amount of its value to Britain. At the same time, and by the same token, the old land routes between the Mediterranean and the Persian Gulf via Baghdad are recovering their ancient importance which they enjoyed before the opening up of the Cape route to India.

Until the British troops in the war captured Palestine and Mesopotamia, the whole of the area from the Levant to the Persian frontier and from the highlands of Anatolia to the Arabian Sea was Turkish. It is true that the coasts of the Arabian Peninsula were under other influences, chiefly British, and it is also true that Arab Nationalist movements had been making some headway. But in general the Middle East, as far as the Persian Gulf, was "Turkey in Asia." All that the Ottoman wanted was his quota of troops and his taxes on produce and on foreign trade. These assured, the Government in Constantinople had little further interest in the more distant and backward parts of its Asiatic dominions. Its *valis* or governors had one and one only further interest—namely, to increase their personal fortunes at the expense of the inhabitants.

The future of Mesopotamia, Syria, and Palestine (with Transjordan) was decided at Paris. Woodrow Wilson insisted on their ultimate freedom, and invented the Mandate as a device to ensure their tutelage in statecraft until they were ready for liberty. In Syria, French influence, a relic from the times of the Crusades, was dominant, although there it was British troops accompanied by Lawrence's Arabs that won through to Damascus in October 1918. In Palestine there were numerous foreign interests, mainly of religious origin. British interest in the Holy Land had steadily

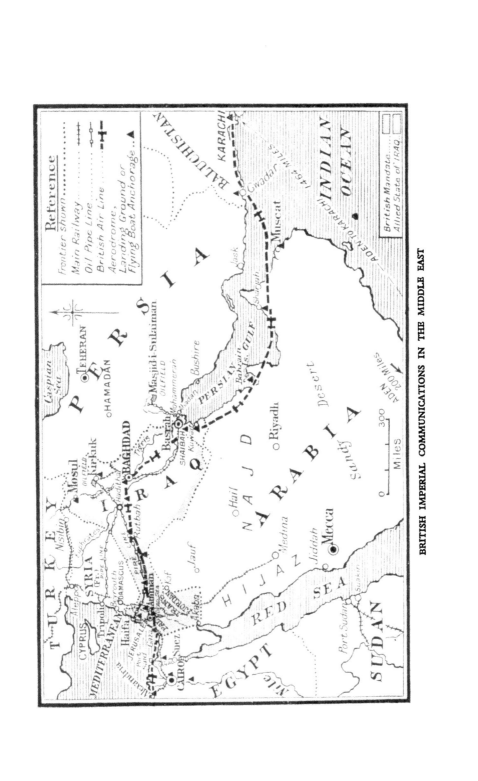

BRITISH IMPERIAL COMMUNICATIONS IN THE MIDDLE EAST

grown during the war, due to the vital necessity of keeping open the road to the East by the Suez Canal and the Red Sea. In Mesopotamia British influence was strong in Baghdad and in Basrah, which dominated the head of the Persian Gulf and therefore covered the British-controlled Anglo-Persian oilfields, and safeguarded, through the century-old operations of the British Navy in the Gulf, the flanks of the sea route to India.

As will be shown more fully later the idea of the Mandate did not appeal to the European Powers concerned in the idealistic way in which Wilson regarded it; "protectorate" was a more familiar idea in the Old World. But the settlement finally provided for "Mandates"—to be exercised in Syria and the Lebanon by France, and in Palestine (with Transjordan) and in Mesopotamia, soon to be called Iraq, by Britain. The principle, as laid down by Wilson, provided for the exercise of a Mandate—under the League of Nations, which set up for the purpose a Permanent Mandates Commission—by the Power which by reason of its experience and its geographical interests was best able to exercise it. Thus Wilson's ideals and Anglo-French *Realpolitik* were made to coincide; thus Britain in 1920 took over the control of the two springers of the great arch leading to India.

In the case of Palestine and Transjordan, the political situation remains essentially unchanged. There is constant friction, to a greater or less degree, between Jew and Arab. Each of the two sides maintains a press which is frankly propagandist; Britain is an effective control as between the two. Year by year the British High Commissioner, or his counsellor, visits Geneva to sponsor the annual reports which the British Colonial Office presents to the Permanent Mandates Commission of the League, and on which the British representatives may be examined and cross-examined by the members of the Commission, many of whom on behalf of their Governments have axes to grind. Meanwhile Palestine remains prosperous, one of the few bright spots in a world of depression. Such progress as she is making is due almost entirely to the Western methods introduced by the Zionists; before many years have passed the harbour developments at Haifa and the establishment of oil-refineries there will mean the growth of a purchasing power, at present non-existent, similar to that which

# Iraq

has populated with steady-going artizans the Anglo-Persian oil area in South-West Persia.

In the case of Iraq the Mandate ended in October 1932, when Iraq became independent and entered the League of Nations as a constituent member, in full and friendly alliance with Great Britain by virtue of a treaty,[1] negotiated in 1930, which came into force on the expiration of the Mandate. Except that the Arabs are now in full executive control in Iraq, the passing of the Mandate has so far made little essential difference. The country still depends on Britain for its defence. Within recent years, two insurgent Kurdish chiefs were reduced with the help of the British Air Force, and could not have been reduced without it.[2] If the Persians, for instance, wished to seize Basrah; if the Wahhabis under Ibn Saud, who is greatly impoverished through the failure of the Hajj in recent years, wished to repeat their century-old Puritanic exploit of looting the enormous wealth of the Shiah Holy Cities in Iraq; if the Turks were minded to recover Mosul and the oilfields—the Iraqis, as in their quieter conversations they will frankly admit, would be unable at present to defend themselves. Iraq has no defensible frontiers except in the northern mountains—and the Arab soldier, generally speaking, is no mountaineer. Moreover, the Iraqi Air Force is still in swaddling clothes.

By letting Iraq go, Britain has to some extent sacrificed British trade interests there, but she has removed any danger that might have arisen from hostile nationalism. There is a tendency in Iraq to impose heavy taxation upon those goods and services which the Iraqi does not normally use; in other words, the foreigners are being taxed more heavily than the Iraqi, in spite of the fact that the average foreigner in the country spends more money and is a bigger employer of labour than the average Iraqi. Nor is it any means certain that the British Embassy in Baghdad is so fully alive to this tendency as it might be. So far as hostile nationalism is concerned, the danger might have disappeared had Britain after the war made up her mind and declared resolutely for a protectorate. But the adoption of the Mandate policy not merely encouraged the

[1] The text of this treaty will be found in Appendix A.

[2] For full description of the work of the British Air Force in preparing Iraq for independence, see Chapter VI.

42

honest and sincere Nationalists, but stimulated all the place-hunters in the country, so that by 1923 or 1924 it was impossible to go back.[1]

In any event, however, Britain has still safeguarded her communications with India, provided Iraq remains strong. Under the 1930 treaty the British Royal Air Force will remain in Iraq, but by 1937 all depots and stations must be moved west of the Euphrates. The present headquarters of the R.A.F. Iraq Command are at Hinaidi, a few miles south of Baghdad, and there is a bombing squadron based on Mosul—both on the Tigris. The new headquarters are to be at Dhibban, near Lake Habbaniyah, about fifty miles west of Baghdad, on the right bank of the Euphrates. At Basrah the present flying-boat and bomber bases will remain as a link with the Arabian coast and with the British naval division operating in the Persian Gulf. The present disposition of the Royal Air Force from the Mediterranean eastwards is as follows:

*Mediterranean Command:* Malta.
*Middle East Command:*
  (a) Egypt—Aboukir, Alexandria, Heliopolis, Helwan, Ismailia, Khartum;
  (b) Transjordan and Palestine—Ammam, Ramleh, Sarafand.
*Iraq Command:* Hinaidi, Basrah, Mosul.
*India Command:* Karachi, Lahore, Ambala, Peshawar, Kohat, Risalpur, Quetta.
*Aden Command:* Aden, Khormaksar.
*Far East Command:* Singapore, Kai Tak.

The R.A.F. "bridge" is thus strongly constructed, particularly as the desert is now not only fully surveyed, but is also studded with dumps and landing-grounds. Until recently the trans-desert motor communications were concentrated upon the Baghdad–Damascus route. Within the past year or so the British Government has been trying to develop the Baghdad–Amman–Jerusalem route, thus ensuring that the western end is under British control in Palestine instead of under French control in Syria. For there seems no early possibility that the Palestine Mandate will come to an end. Palestine thus is the western springer of the British arch from the Mediterranean to India. Whether from Egypt or from Cyprus, the new air and land route to the East starts from Palestine.

[1] See Chapter IV for a fuller discussion of this point.

43

# *Iraq*

The other springer of the arch is the Arabian side of the Persian Gulf. Down that side of the Gulf British influence is now consolidated. The sloops of the Persian Gulf Division of the East Indies Squadron continue the century-old work of keeping order on the pearling banks, dispensing justice, and generally showing the flag in those inhospitable waters. It is no easy task. When one of the sloops was detailed to report on Elphinstone Inlet as a proposed permanent anchorage for naval ships, the visit of inspection was paid in the month of August, with the humidity such that the visibility was only about a hundred yards. Not a soul was to be seen on shore; even the native Arabs cannot live there in the summer and retire to their hot-weather villages in the hills behind. Many of the engine-room staff went down with heat-exhaustion, and the "survivors" brought the ship out at half-speed.

Such is the summer climate at the southern end of the Persian Gulf, where the British sloops for generations and the R.A.F. for five years have done magnificent service to British Imperia linterests. For many years now the shaikhs of the key principalities of Kuwait, Bahrain and Muscat have been under British protection; but it is only within the last year or two that the shaikhs of the Trucial coast (Northern Oman) have been coaxed into the fold, with the result that British air communications between Basrah and India are now flanked by friendly Arab potentates, until the sea-jump from Sharjah to Gwadar in Baluchistan sees the fliers once again in British territory. The extension of this air route across India and farther has increased the Imperial importance of the Palestine–Basrah–Oman bridge.

Over all hangs the smell of oil. The Anglo-Persian Company renewed its concession in 1933, but a keen fight has been going on for the oil which is known to exist on the Arabian side of the coast. At Bahrain the concession—providing for royalties at the rate of just over five shillings per ton produced—has gone to a subsidiary of the Standard Oil Company. On the Hasa coast the Standard Oil Company is busy. In Iraq, one small company, a subsidiary of the Anglo-Persian, is now producing, while two much bigger concerns have yet to make a start. The Anglo-Persian Company, in which the British Government is a major shareholder, has a 23¾ per cent holding in the Iraq Petroleum Company (with American, Dutch, and

French interests equally represented, the balance of 5 per cent being held by the original concessionaire), and appears to be in complete control of the administration on the spot. Soon the pipeline from Northern Iraq to the Mediterranean will be working, with one terminus, as insisted on by the French, on the Syrian and another on the Palestine coast. This latter terminus is at Haifa, which within ten years is bound to become one of the great ports of the Mediterranean, and in all probability an important British naval base. The other big company, the British Oil Development Company, is still prospecting.

There has been, for some considerable time, talk of a Haifa–Baghdad railway. Such a railway would greatly help in the consolidation of British influence in the Middle East, especially in the event of a hostile Russo-Turkish alliance. A Haifa–Baghdad–Basrah railway would tend to cut out the Suez route; it would open up the Iraqi and Persian markets to the West; it would become the new passenger route to India—once the Baghdad–Basrah railway was relaid on standard gauge. The projected railway would follow the line of the pipe-line—Haifa–Tiberias–Haditha—thence turning south-east to Baghdad. Already a great trans-desert telephone has been constructed under British auspices.

France, from her position in Syria, is showing a good deal of jealousy of these developments of British policy, some of which she did not foresee during the war-time negotiations. It is true that the French appeared to triumph when they drove Faisal from Damascus in 1920, but his dynasty is now firmly established in Baghdad, and in so far as it owes the maintenance of its position to Britain, to that extent it is bound to carry Iraq in the wake of British policy. Of that policy a strong Iraq is a vital part—as a buffer between British Imperial communications and any possibility of pressure from or through Turkey or Persia—and in the nature of things no one will derive more benefits from a strong Iraq than the Iraqis themselves. Iraq's steady progress towards independence and strength added to the French difficulties in Syria. The Syrians rightly consider themselves a more advanced people than the Iraqis, and they did not understand why they should not be regarded as equally ready for independence. It may be that before long France will be willing to give up the Syrian Mandate on condition that she retains full control of the coast. Already French jealousy is apparent in the efforts she has made to attract Iraqi and Persian transit trade to Beyrouth, where the French have promised both these Governments free port facilities—the implication being that the French fear the rise of Haifa.

There remains one aspect for consideration—the views and aspirations of the Arabs. The overland British route to the East is straddled by the Arab peoples. They claim to be the rightful inheritors of Palestine, they govern Iraq, they rule the coast from Basrah to Muscat, as well as the whole of Central Arabia. There has been much talk of "Arab union" or "Arab confederation." The Arab is a great talker.[1] Whether sitting in a coffee shop or in an editor's chair, there is nothing he likes so much, nothing at which he is such an adept, as political speculation. Now the idea of a great Arab confederation has fired the imagination of the politicians in all the Arab countries, and this idea is one that must be carefully watched by Britain. It must always be borne in mind that the forcing-house of the war brought Arab nationalism to fruition long before it could otherwise have reached this stage. Some of the Arabs themselves feel that they may be moving ahead rather fast; it is certain that the great mass of them, illiterate as they are and devoid of political consciousness, have no interest in anything except being allowed to carry on their lives in their own way and by their own ancient methods.

A further point to be noted is that the very nature of the Arab himself will militate against any form of union or even of federation. The Arab's nature is to be independent and distrustful—frequently even of his relatives. The desert life is a hard life, and through countless generations it has not left many of the finer characters except family affection and hospitality. Suspicion it breeds in large measure. Who knows what enemies may lie behind the next sand

---

[1] There are, in fact, departmental regulations which forbid Iraqi Government officials to receive their friends during office-hours, owing to the waste of time that ensues. If you call on business, the first thing the official does, is to ring for coffee. It is in the fine Arab tradition of hospitality, but clearly it can be abused. For the Arab comes slowly to the point. A man who calls on even urgent business will sit for a very long time uttering trivialities before beginning his devious approach to the subject. To rush a discussion is impolite.

dune or in ambush in the next *wadi*? Four hundred years of Ottoman rule merely intensified this secrecy and suspicion in which the Arabs had lived and worked. Frankly, it is almost impossible to imagine any gathering of Arab representatives who will not give individual promises or take individual action in diametrical opposition to what they have unanimously and solemnly decided in council half an hour earlier.

Some Iraqis used to argue for a joint Syro-Iraqi kingdom under the late King Faisal. This project might have had the support of influential elements in Syria anxious to see the French getting out. But many Iraqis, perhaps seeing more clearly, argued that union with Syria would be a mistake. Iraq is no doubt potentially richer than Syria, but the Syrians are more advanced than the Iraqis, and union would mean that the Syrians would simply move across to Baghdad and pick up the best jobs, returning in due time to their own pleasanter country. Such a prospect naturally does not commend itself to the Iraqis, who are looking for advancement themselves. At all events, the death of King Faisal put an end, for a time at least, to all talk of such union. So far as the Arabs in Palestine are concerned, they are too much occupied with their Jewish question to be really interested in any schemes for union. Transjordan scarcely counts. Abdullah its ruler, is an elder brother of the late King Faisal, and of recent years there has been no love lost between him and Ibn Saud, who ejected his family from Mecca. Ibn Saud counts for a great deal in any speculation on Arabia's future, but his country is terribly backward—it is only recently that acute economic distress and financial stringency induced him and his advisers to abandon their age-old objection to foreign industrial concessions. In any case, the freer Arabs of Syria and Iraq are by no means certain that domination from Mecca would be good for a united Arab "nation." The Gulf shaikhs realize fully that their influence is stronger as it is to-day than it would be as minor members of an "Arab League."

There is thus no immediate likelihood of Arab union. The Baghdad and Damascus newspapers have been from time to time full of the idea, and no doubt certain leaders and others, on both sides of the desert, are supporting it, with their eye on the main chance. But it is not yet within the sphere of practical politics.

# Iraq

British relations are cordial with all the Arab rulers on the Mediterranean–Oman route. The Indian political service, the navy, the army, and the air force have all contributed to this result. France, Germany, and the United States are all watching closely the consolidation of the new British bridge to the East.

Of the countries constituting this bridge, Palestine is to-day the most prosperous and the one with the brightest future. She has agriculture and industries and manufactures; in the Dead Sea are valuable chemical resources; the coast has two good ports, one of which will soon become a first-class port. In addition, Palestine's invisible exports, the money spent by tourists, have been considerable even in these years of slump. When the world depression comes to an end, and Haifa with its harbour and oil-refineries attains its full development, Palestine should be prosperous indeed. One of the secrets of Palestine's success, apart from British administration, is the fact that the returning Jews have put things on a European or American basis. Other Middle East countries have progressed in their own way; Palestine has gone ahead on Western lines, and the native Arab has had no share in this. Arab nationalism in Palestine is very real and very conscious of itself, but its mainspring is its hostility to Zionism; it is not constructive, and even in its destructive criticism it often wanders far from realities. Both in natural resources and in industrial and commercial development Palestine is the "promising" land.

Syria is peopled by a clever race, who since the Crusades have been closely connected with the West, particularly with France. In Damascus she possesses the flower of the Arab world—that lovely city which the Prophet himself would not enter lest he spoil his delight later in Paradise. Syria's trade is considerable, and when the pipe-line begins work the port of Tripoli will handle the French share of the total production. But economically Syria can compare neither with Palestine nor Iraq. She is relatively poor, and it is becoming more and more evident that France's chief interest is in controlling the coast and the mountains immediately behind it.

Iraq is the only portion of the former Ottoman territory that has achieved independence. The British community in Iraq are apt to say that the efficiency of the administration will diminish. The Arab reply to that would be that if their administration remains at

TYPICAL HOUSE-EXTERIOR, WITH STUDDED DOOR, AND NO
WINDOWS BELOW THE FIRST FLOOR

THE INTERIOR VERANDAHS AND COURTYARD OF OUR PLEASANT HOME
IN BASRAH

a standard which satisfies them, that is all that is necessary. So far as Britain is concerned, she is satisfied that it is to her interest to have a strong, friendly and peaceful Iraq on the flank of the new route to the East, and she has decided that she can ensure this more cheaply by encouraging Iraq's self-government than by enforcing a protectorate.

# CHAPTER III

## LAWRENCE AND THE ARABS OF IRAQ

THE policy, the personality and the money of T. E. Lawrence exercised a decisive influence upon the future of Iraq. Lawrence and his school of thought wanted independence *pur sang* for the Arabs. Others, no less competent judges, emphasized that any new Arab states that might come into existence, whether independent or not, must possess economic unity and therefore must be given scientific frontiers. From 1917 onwards the two ideas came into even sharper opposition; for a time in 1919–20, when the air was full of Woodrow Wilson, it seemed as if Lawrence's main preoccupation was to find thrones for his Sharifian allies, the sons of King Hussain. But by that time the diplomatic machine—aided by the *Realpolitik* of Clemenceau—was regaining control of the situation, and the Middle East, which to Lawrence was the be-all and the end-all, resumed its place and relative importance, as a pawn in the bigger game.

The sentimental influence which the desert and the desert people exert upon some Westerners is remarkable. Lawrence by temperament was strongly affected by it, but if it had stopped at that his authority and fame would not have equalled that of one or two other "Lawrences," who on the eastern side of the desert did work comparable with his, but of whose achievements, even names, the public at large have heard little. Leachman, for instance, was a legendary figure on the Mesopotamian side of the desert, where for years, even before the war, he had been out-Lawrencing Lawrence.

Gerald E. Leachman, who when he was murdered held the rank of Lieutenant-Colonel, C.I.E., D.S.O., in the Royal Sussex Regiment, had a long and distinguished pre-war record as a traveller in Arabia. He reported to the Mesopotamia Expeditionary Force early in 1915 as Political Officer. He was in Kut, but was sent out by Townshend, who thus deprived himself of services which might have stood him in good stead at the time of the surrender.[1] From that time onwards

[1] Lawrence, curiously enough, comes into this picture. He was despatched with Aubrey Herbert to negotiate a panic-offer by the British Cabinet of £2,000,000 to the Turks provided that the Kut Garrison of thirteen thousand

# Lawrence and the Arabs of Iraq

Leachman's life was spent not as a paymaster among allies but among hostile or troublous tribesmen. His name was known throughout the length and breadth of Arabia. His extreme mobility, which made his legendary fame, caught the fancy of the Arabs; his indomitable will and inexhaustible energy forced their admiration, wholehearted if at times reluctant. Hundreds of parents called their children by his name. He was murdered in cold blood by a recalcitrant shaikh in August 1920 but his name and reputation still live throughout Arabia.[1] A contemporary was E. B. Soane, a banker who became a great political officer and administrator. His line of country was Kurdish rather than Arab, his work was every whit as important as that of Lawrence, if less flashy.[2] He died at sea in 1923; and who has heard of him? So too with a dozen others, expert linguists and travellers, men who were before the war in the political service *de carrière* and knew Arabia like a book. They had no money to disburse, and thus aroused no cupidity among the Arabs—whose cupidity, especially of gold, needs little arousing and rapidly grows insatiable. There was, for instance, Captain W. H. I. Shakespeare, C.I.E., an officer of the Indian Political Department, known throughout Arabia as "Skaishpeer." This experienced and much-travelled officer was sent out, before the Turkish war began, to get into touch with Ibn Saud, who in the early months of 1914 had begun to turn against the Turk and whose star, if Britain had but realized it, was already rising. Shakespeare was sent to ginger up Ibn Saud and he was able to report, in January 1915, that Ibn Saud was with Britain. But in the same month, in an inconclusive battle at Jarrab[3] between

officers and men were liberated on parole. This poltroon offer, which the Turks declined, was not published in the British Press.

[1] See footnote on p. 75 for Leachman's splendid work during the 1920 rebellion, when he kept the Upper Euphrates calm without an anna to spend on bribes.

[2] See A. T. Wilson, II, p. 83: "He played on . . . their personal honour. He scorned to excite cupidity with gold, as was done during the war in western Arabia: he knew well that men do not respond for long to such a stimulant, which has to be administered in ever-increasing quantity and brings demoralization in its train."

[3] See Philby, *Heart of Arabia*, I, p. 386: ". . . judged by its results, the battle of Jarrab was one of the decisive battles of the Arabian theatre of war, and the death of Shakespeare, followed as it was by the abandonment of all attempts to use Ibn Saud for the furtherance of our campaign against the Turks, put an end once and for all to the hopes of Arab co-operation

Ibn Saud and his then rival, the pro-Turkish chief Ibn Rashid of Hayil, Shakespeare was killed. Had fate not thus ordained that at one stroke Ibn Saud should be temporarily checked and this trusted officer killed, the British Government at that early stage would have been bound to recognize Ibn Saud as the principal power in Central and Southern Arabia, and the idea of raising the Sharifians would not have occurred to anyone. For the ambitions of Ibn Saud and Hussain were mutually incompatible, and the subsequent years have amply proved which was the abler and the stronger ruler.

But speculation is vain. The thread of accident that runs through human affairs put the control of the Mesopotamia Expeditionary Force into the hands of the Government of India, which looked to its own interests and could not see beyond the Persian Gulf. The Palestine campaign was the affair of London, and by 1916 the mixed success of the Mesopotamian campaign had begun to load the dice in favour of the Arab Bureau in Cairo, which had got largely into the control of dilettantes and scholars in whose hands the moulding of policy seemed increasingly to lie.

It was thus easy for Cairo in 1915 and 1916 to exercise inordinate influence upon British war policy against the Turks, and the irony of things finally saw to it that the scandalous mismanagement of certain aspects of the Mesopotamian campaign appeared to justify, in the eyes of the British public, its Cinderella-like relegation. Added to all this, Lawrence gradually became a figure of romantic mystery, soon to grow into a legend. Finally he himself set the seal upon his reputation by emerging as one of the great writers of English prose.

What are the facts?

Kitchener had come from Egypt and the close association that had always existed between Cairo and Mecca led him to exaggerate

in the war which were not to be revived until eighteen months had elapsed, and were then revived in a different quarter with such remarkable results. It was left to Lawrence and the army of the Hidjaz to accomplish what in other circumstances—with a little better luck, and a little more imagination on the part of the authorities responsible for the conduct of the Mesopotamian campaign—might have been accomplished by Ibn Saud and Shakespeare. Under the star-spangled vault of the Arabian sky he lies as he fell on the field of Jarrab—a true friend of the Arabs as every Arab knows in Central Arabia."

the importance of the Amir Hussain, who controlled the Holy Places. In the autumn of 1914 he approached the old man—"that very difficult person," as even Lawrence called him—and thus began "the MacMahon correspondence." Sir Henry MacMahon was Acting High Commissioner and through him Kitchener sounded Abdullah, Hussain's second son,[1] as to the attitude of the Sharif his father in the event of a war between Turkey and the Allied Powers. On the day that Turkey entered the war, Hussain was assured that there would be no international intervention in Arabia. This was scarcely acceptable to the old man and in due course (1915) he demanded that Britain should guarantee the independence of all Arab lands in return for his revolt against the Ottoman. The lands he referred to covered the whole of the peninsula, the northern "boundary" being latitude 37, including therefore Palestine, Syria, Iraq and Southern Kurdistan. This of course was mere bazaar-bargaining, and in due and seemly manner Britain declined to agree. But by the autumn Britain was offering an assurance that, subject to safeguarding French interests in Syria and British interests in Mesopotamia, she would support Arab independence in the southern portions of the enormous area he had delimited.

When Turkey joined in the war, Ibn Saud's position was clear. He was anti-Turkish and pro-British, all he wanted being a British treaty to secure him against any unlucky turn of fortune's wheel. Hussain's position was not so simple, as the Hidjaz railway brought the Turks to his doorstep—the Turkish garrison remained in Medina until the war ended. According to the fatuous "biography" of King Faisal written by Mrs. Steuart Erskine, Hussain began by flirting with both sides. She quotes the full authority of King Faisal for this.[2] According to her statement, when the war broke out the Young Turk Party were trying to plot against Hussain in the Hidjaz. The documents, by a process not unusual in Arab countries, were all handed to Hussain, who then sent his third son, the Amir Faisal, to Constantinople in order to present the documents to the Grand Vizier and so get the conspiracy scotched (*op. cit.*, p. 40). This was in April 1915, when he was already in communication with Kitchener. Faisal's *real* object (*op. cit.*, p. 40) was to study the

---

[1] Now Amir of Transjordan.
[2] *King Faisal of Iraq*, by Mrs. Steuart Erskine, pp. 38 et seq.

situation in Syria, where Damascus was the centre of an Arab nationalist and anti-Turk movement. At Constantinople Faisal obtained official support against the Hidjaz plotters, but (p. 43) when he also discovered that the Turks "were at that moment carrying their archives and their treasures into Anatolia I decided then to join the extremists and to return at once to Mecca to help my father to save Arabia. . . . My father agreed, moved by the sufferings of the Arabs and at the same time hoping to assure their political future." Hussain already had the first British undertaking. Satisfied by now that the Ottoman power in Arabia was gone beyond recall, he put his demands to the Allies high.[1] But the statement quoted goes on to say (*op. cit.*, p. 45) that on returning to Damascus in the month of September 1915, Faisal found that the Turks had the Arab nationalist movement well under their thumb. It was doubtless this news that persuaded Hussain that his demand for the 37th degree of latitude had better be forgotten. Not until May 1916 did Faisal return to the Hidjaz and a week later the Hidjaz revolt began. All that Hussain really wanted, or hoped to secure, was complete independence in his own corner of south-western Arabia, British support against his rival Ibn Saud, and as a corollary the unfettered control of the great pilgrim revenues.

The attitude of the French, it is important here to note, was a vital factor in the situation. The war in Europe was not going well; France had century-old interests in Syria and the Lebanon; she was inclined to think that Britain, by withholding troops from the French front, might begin to build up an impregnable position in the Middle East and so present the ultimate peace negotiators with a *fait accompli* of colonial advantage. The French view therefore was one of which Britain was bound to take account. The Gallipoli evacuation, too, with its release of thousands of Turks, was a further factor that had to be considered.

Lawrence, studying the progress of the war, had come to the conclusion that, to enable the British campaign in Palestine to go through to its end, Arab irregulars must be raised to work on the flank. Cairo from the start had been thinking in terms of Mecca, and so it comes about that Lawrence begins his *Revolt in the Desert* by describing how he went down to Jiddah with Storrs to make

[1] See *supra*, p. 53.

a start with his new Anglo-Arab "alliance" and how he found his heaven-sent Arab leader in Faisal. Lawrence's idea was to develop an Arab guerrilla movement, working up the Hidjaz railway and harassing the Turks on the right flank of the British thrust from Egypt across the Canal into Palestine. His implements in forging this new British arm were his persuasive powers, his electric personality and his gold—a crescendo of arguments which no Arab born could resist.

Opportunity, it is said, comes but once to a man. If it is true, then Faisal owed his career to his friend Lawrence, but for whom he would have remained a simple Amir in the Hidjaz. Hussain himself was too old to take the field in an arduous campaign. His eldest son Ali had responsibilities, as the eldest son, which would keep him in the south near the capital. What of Abdullah, the second son? Lawrence met Abdullah soon after he landed, riding on a white mare, the mark of Arab nobility. The rebellion of Hussain had been hanging fire for some time and Lawrence suspected, as he has recorded, that its lack was leadership—"not intellect, nor judgment, nor political wisdom, but the flame of enthusiasm that would set the desert on fire." Even as they talked, Lawrence decided that Abdullah was not his man.

What of Faisal, the third son? The name Faisal means "the flash of the sword in its downward stroke," and Lawrence was soon to put him to the test. Lawrence's description of the first interview is historic.

A lengthy camel-ride brought him to Faisal's camp. A slave with silver-hilted sword was on guard, and Lawrence was led within to an inner court, on whose farther side, "framed between the uprights of a black doorway, stood a white figure waiting tensely for me. I felt at first glance that this was the man I had come to Arabia to seek—the leader who would bring the Arab Revolt to full glory. Faisal looked very tall and pillar-like, very slender, in his long white silk robes and his brown headcloth bound with a brilliant scarlet and gold cord. His eyelids were dropped; and his black beard and his colourless face were like a mask against the strange, still watchfulness of his body. His hands were crossed in front of him on his dagger."

Faisal was then, in 1916, thirty-one years of age. He looked older, as Lawrence says. His hollow cheeks were deeply lined and puckered with reflection. "His nature grudged thinking, for it crippled his speed in action. . . . In appearance he was tall graceful and vigorous, with the most beautiful gait, and a royal dignity of head and shoulders. Of course he knew it, and a great part of his public expression was by sign and gesture. . . . His personal charm . . . made him the idol of his followers. One never asked if he were scrupulous; but later he showed that he could return trust for trust, suspicion for suspicion." Here, says Lawrence, was "offered to our hand, which had only to be big enough to take it, a prophet who, if veiled, would give cogent form to the idea behind the activity of the Arab revolt. It was all and more than we had hoped for, much more than our halting course deserved. The aim of my trip was fulfilled." In this way then, for better or for worse, Faisal's destinies were linked with those of Britain.

Lawrence's electric personality had convinced the Meccan leaders that they might soon be rulers in the pleasant land of Syria, and in their own country where their writ ran they had no difficulty in organizing a force which by July 1917 had taken them to Akaba. In all probability that would have been their limit, but for the lure of Damascus held before the leaders and the money and loot promised to the rank and file.

More strange than his powers of persuading the Arabs was Lawrence's success in persuading the British Command to place enormous sums in English gold at his unfettered disposal, and to accept his guerrilla assistance on the flank. Such a supply of money was necessary if the Arabs were to be persuaded to move at all to help the British arms. At the first interview with Abdullah, to which reference has just been made, Lawrence in the first pages of *Revolt in the Desert* tells how Storrs and Abdullah "talked about money." Later, when he joined Faisal and his levies he refers to the Sharif's payment to each man of two pounds a month and four for a camel —"nothing else," he records, "would have performed the miracle of keeping a tribal army in the field for five months on end." Before long he is writing, "Profitable rumours excited the army" and these, trickling round the desert, brought in a great array of minor tribal chiefs, all anxious to liberate the Arabs—at a price to be paid by the British. Indeed the only day on which a full muster of the Arab

INFORMAL ABLUTIONS,
ASHAR CREEK, BASRAH

BASRAH'S BELLUMS

STREET SCENE,
MOSUL

allies could be counted on was pay-day. In his Chapter XIV Lawrence analyses the psychology of the great fighting shaikh Auda: "I suggested that Auda's present expenses in hospitality must be great; would it help if I advanced something of the great gift Feisal would make him, personally, when he arrived? Auda saw that the immediate moment would not be unprofitable; that Feisal would be highly profitable: and that the Turks would always be with him if other resources failed. So he agreed, in a very good temper, to accept my advance." Thus Lawrence on his Arabs. In his Chapter XII he describes his "comic interview" with Allenby, at which he asked the Commander-in-Chief for "stores and arms and a fund of two hundred thousand sovereigns to convince and control his converts." This conversion and control of the Arabs in the task of liberating the Arab races turned out to be even more costly, for in Chapter XXV he goes down to tell Faisal that Allenby had "put three hundred thousand pounds into my independent credit." But money to Britain mattered little in those days, and the military stalemate in Europe was such that any possibility of movement elsewhere was to be encouraged. Even the military suspicion of his free-lance methods melted or was brushed aside. But in point of fact, had Lawrence never existed, had the Arab revolt against the Turks, which had started locally and in a small way before Lawrence hitched it to the British arms, never gone beyond the area of the Holy Places, the collapse of the Central Powers in 1918 would still have put Allenby into Damascus and Aleppo before the end of the year. It is true that Lawrence and his Arabs did work of great value, their railway-cutting and other exploits making them important auxiliaries. But in 1916–17 it was not foreseen that as the major struggle developed, the military situation in the Middle East at the end of 1918 would still have been the same, Arabs or no Arabs, Lawrence or no Lawrence.

But later developments would have been vastly different. The Arab Bureau in Cairo never gave sufficient attention to the other facets of the Arab situation. They had little interest in the ferment that was going on in Central Arabia or on the Mesopotamian side of the desert.

What Lawrence did therefore was to start tendencies and release forces which are not yet worked out to their end. He raised problems

infinitely more difficult than those he solved. His ideas had much
to do with the Sykes–Picot agreement of May 1916, in which the
British negotiator was Sir Mark Sykes, that strange romanticist
who flitted from campaign to campaign as a half-official, half-
unofficial free-lance. By this agreement Syria (with Mosul[1]) would
go to France after the war, Baghdad and Basrah to Britain, the
territories to the south would be independent Arab. This did not
in the main conflict with the British undertaking given to Hussain
in the middle of 1915, with which he had apparently been satisfied.
By July 1917 the now-organized revolt in the desert saw the Arabs
in Akaba, and Lawrence exercising himself to ensure their persever-
ence to Damascus.[2] In Iraq General Maude had already entered
Baghdad (March 11th) and had issued a proclamation, drawn
up by Sir Mark Sykes, a turgid even ridiculous document, an
essential point of which made Basrah British and Baghdad Arab—
at complete variance with the Sykes–Picot agreement of a few
months earlier.

Young in his book *The Independent Arab*, in keeping with his
thesis, suggests (p. 275) that the announcement that the Baghdad
*vilayet* was to be an Arab state meant that "His Majesty's Government were already beginning to realize that direct British administration was incompatible with the satisfaction of Arab ideals." But
in March 1917 the situation was purely military. The people of
Mesopotamia were accustomed to the idea of victors keeping what
they had won. Others thought, or hoped, that the Turks might
return. In the west Lawrence and Faisal had not even reached
Akaba. In March 1917 there was no Arab demand for an Arab
state in the Baghdad *vilayet*. The only Arab nationalists who counted
were Faisal's officers, and their immediate interest was with Law-

---

[1] More than half Kurdish.

[2] Philby, *op. cit.*, I, p. 226. "The dream of an Arabian Empire under his
own rule was in those days a pet obsession of King Hussain, but he (has)
lived to realize that those castles were built in the air to be shattered, not
so much by those who resisted his ambitions from the beginning as by the
son (Faisal) to whom he had entrusted the command of his northern army,
and who from the day of Akaba (July 1917), if not before, had determined
to carve out a kingdom for himself independently of his father's schemes."
It is of interest to quote Lawrence's authority (*Revolt in the Desert*, Chap.
XXIX) for the fact that the Arab officers' commissions were issued by
Faisal and not by Hussain.

rence and their eyes were on Syria and Damascus. Towards the end of 1917, having been given such a definite lead by the Sykes proclamation which General Maude issued, these officers, who were already bound by a "Syrian Covenant," drew up a "Covenant of Iraq," in which they pegged out their claim to a possible new distribution of British political bounty. It may indeed have struck some of them that British subsidies would be available in Iraq on the same scale as that to which they were accustomed on the other side of the desert.

The new year brought Woodrow Wilson into the Middle East. His Fourteen Points were given to the world on January 8, 1918. The Twelfth Point referred directly to the Ottoman territories and appeared (in the words of A. T. Wilson[1]) to "substitute nationality, religion or race as the basis of Government in the Middle East in the place of ability and power to govern." It stated that the nationalities then under Turkish rule should be assured an undoubted security of life and an absolutely unmolested opportunity of autonomous development. This principle did not square with the British agreement with Hussain, or the Sykes–Picot agreement, or General Maude's proclamation, or (in a different way) the Balfour Declaration (November 1917) favouring the establishment within Palestine of a national home for the Jewish people. The Woodrow Wilson ideas, however, spread like wildfire and Arab nationalism received such a stimulus as it had not known from the days of its sketchy beginnings in the years before Enver and Talaat seized the reins of power on the Bosporus.

In the summer the Arab officers of the "Syrian Covenant" presented a memorial to the British Government and were told that in regard to the areas in Arabia which were free and independent before the War, and areas emancipated from Turkish rule *by the action of the Arabs themselves during the war*, the British Government recognized the complete and sovereign independence of the Arabs inhabiting those areas and supported them in their struggle for freedom.[2] This was in June. It was about this time that Faisal,

---

[1] Now Sir Arnold Wilson, M.P.
[2] Author's italics. See Young (*op. cit.*, p. 277), who remarks that whoever drafted this reply could never have dreamt that within five months the Arabs would have taken part in the capture of Aleppo, five hundred

who, as we have seen on page 53, had begun by flirting with both sides, began to wonder whether he was backing the wrong horse. A Turkish emissary came down from Damascus, and with him Faisal entered into negotiations, although he was still Lawrence's ally as he had been for months and was still in receipt of British *largesse* as he had been for over a year. Liddell Hart in his *T. E. Lawrence* (pp. 317-18) tells the story how Faisal promised the Turks that he would forsake the British side "if the Turks would evacuate Amman and hand over the province to the Arabs." The bird in the hand was clearly worth two in Damascus! It is strange to reflect that had things gone badly with Britain and her Allies in that summer of 1918 Faisal might, in spite of Lawrence, have taken that plunge—it is a fascinating speculation. But the German structure in the West was soon to start cracking. The Turks were soon completely on the run, both in Syria and Mesopotamia. Allenby was in Aleppo on October 26th. The British Command in Baghdad received orders on November 2nd to occupy Mosul under the terms of the Armistice with Turkey, which provided for the cessation of hostilities on October 31st. Faisal was still an Ally of the British. He had had a narrow escape.

The sixteenth clause of the Armistice provided for the surrender of all Turkish garrisons in the Hidjaz, Asir, Yemen, Syria and Mesopotamia to the nearest Allied commander.

What was a "garrison"? and was Mosul in Mesopotamia? These two questions suddenly became urgent, and they were boldly solved by General Marshall, in personal discussion with the Turkish commander in Mosul, whom he "persuaded" to move all his troops out of the *vilayet*. This put Mosul under British military control, and from now on the name Iraq came into use as the name of the territory comprising the Basrah, Baghdad and Mosul *vilayets*, whereas the old Greek term Mesopotamia strictly referred to the

miles away; and adds: "When I saw this document for the first time in the Foreign Office, it at once became clear to me why the Arabs had made such superhuman efforts to win their race with the British cavalry into Deraa, Damascus, and Aleppo. . . . I understood, too, for the first time why I had so often been asked, after the fall of Damascus, who had really taken the city. Was it the British army or was it our Lord Faisal?"

plain of the two rivers, that is Basrah and Baghdad only. Thus the beginning of 1918 saw the whole of the area covered by the Sykes–Picot agreement in British military occupation. In Iraq a British Civil Administration had been functioning *pari passu* with the advance of the troops. In Syria an autonomous Arab government under Faisal, with British advisers was set up in October, financed (according to A. T. Wilson) by the British Treasury at the rate of £150,000 a month—a continuation of the Lawrentian theory of *largesse* to which Faisal's Arabs were now beginning to think they had a prescriptive right.

The centre of gravity was now rapidly changing. The soldiers had ended their tasks, the armies had become mere custodians of law and order, and the diplomats and politicians were getting to work. In the Middle East the protagonists were Britain and France. Since the days of the Crusades France had been interested in Syria. British influence was well established in Lower Mesopotamia. The event of the war had, for all immediate purposes, put an end to Germany's thrust towards the Persian Gulf, and it appeared to open up new prospects for Italy and Greece in the Levant. The Sykes–Picot agreement, by giving Mosul to the French, had inserted a buffer between the British on the Tigris and Euphrates and any Russian conquest around Van. But the two revolutions of 1917 had caused Russia to disappear from the scene, Italy was encouraged to look for her chief war-gains at the head of the Adriatic and in Tirol, Greece had her eyes directed upon Smyrna and the Islands. Britain and France had big fish to fry and the Middle East became of secondary interest. To Lawrence the independence of the Arabs was still of prime importance. He felt that Britain still had a duty to his Sharifian friends, and he was to become more and more resentful of British policy as he saw his promises to the Arabs being modified one by one.

The Arabophile school found support in the doctrinaire theories of Woodrow Wilson. The great public enthusiasm for these theories, due in part to the nervous reaction from the intensive discipline and the repressive strain of four years of war, forced the realists in France and Britain to issue, on November 8, 1918, the document which has come to be known as "the Anglo-French Agreement."

# *Iraq*

It was published in London, Paris, Cairo and New York and ran as follows:

The end which France and Great Britain have in view in their prosecution in the East of the war let loose by German ambition is the complete and definite liberation of the peoples so long oppressed by the Turks and the establishment of national Governments and Administrations drawing their authority from the initiative and free choice of indigenous populations.

In order to give effect to these intentions France and Great Britain are agreed to encourage and assist in the establishment of indigenous Governments and Administrations in Syria and Mesopotamia, which have already in fact been liberated by the Allies, and in countries whose liberation they are endeavouring to effect, and to recognize the latter as soon as they shall be effectively established. Far from wishing to impose any particular institution on these lands, they have no other care but to assure by their support and effective aid the normal working of the Governments and Administrations, which they shall have adopted of their free will. To ensure impartial and equal justice, to facilitate economic developments by evoking and encouraging indigenous initiative, to foster the spread of education and to put an end to the divisions too long exploited by Turkish policy—such is the rôle which the two Allied Governments assume in the liberated territories.

This document took its place in the series of undertakings given to the Arabs. It promised a "free choice," but in fact no free choice was possible. Palestine was an Arab country, but the war-necessity which had forced the Balfour Declaration made it impossible for the Arabs to bar the entry of Jews from abroad. No "free choice" for non-Arab minorities was at any time likely, nor has it in the event been granted anywhere. The declaration was in fact an attempt to do lip-service to the doctrines of Woodrow Wilson while Clemenceau and Lloyd George were getting on with the business. Lawrence's advice was that three Arab states under the Sharifian brothers[1] should be set up—Syria, Upper Mesopotamia and Lower Mesopotamia. Economically and geographically Iraq is one: any division, into Upper and Lower, with duplicate courts and governments, would merely have doubled the financial burden upon the

---

[1] The eldest of Hussain's four sons, Ali, was not in the running, being the heir to the throne of the Hidjaz. Hussain, his father, abdicated in October 1924 under pressure of Ibn Saud's attacks, and Ali reigned less than a year, then leaving Ibn Saud completely master of the Holy Places. He went to live in Baghdad and died there in February, 1935.

people—unless of course it was expected that the British bounty would continue.

The essential point was that no "free choice" government that might be set up in those regions could be certain of maintaining order unless backed by a European Power. Without such backing, the setting up of Arab amirates or kingdoms would merely have extended the anarchy, always endemic in Arabia, to the more advanced northerly provinces, which under the Turks had at least been fairly orderly and in which traders had been able to count on a modicum of security and economic stability. Moreover, it is not clear what Woodrow Wilson had in mind when he spoke of the "initiative and free choice of indigenous populations." It is not possible to obtain any democratic political judgment in Arabia, partly because of lack of education and political consciousness, partly because of the secular cleavage between townsmen and tribesmen. At the most, all that can be obtained is the judgment (seldom unanimous) of the feudal oligarchy or of the priest-hood. Neither is democratic in the Wilsonic sense, but they form a sounder basis for politics in Arabia than do Western democratic doctrines.[1]

As far as Iraq was concerned, the Acting Civil Commissioner, A. T. Wilson, argued that Lawrence's three-state solution was impracticable and that Iraq (Basrah, Baghdad and Mosul) should form one state. He attacked the "diplomatic insincerities" of the Declaration which, he said, placed "a potent weapon in the hands of those least fitted to control a nation's destinies." He emphasized the almost entire absence of political, racial or other connection between Iraq and the rest of Arabia and argued that the problem of Iraq should be settled independently of Arab problems elsewhere. This, in the pull-devil-pull-baker game at Versailles, was impossible. A. T. Wilson argued that Iraq neither expected nor desired this Woodrow Wilson independence. In December Clemenceau and Lloyd George, meeting in London, reached an agreement the details

---

[1] Miss Bell, writing to her father on November 28, said: "The Franco-British Declaration has thrown the whole town (Baghdad) into a ferment. . . . On two points they are practically all agreed, they want us to control their affairs and they want Sir Percy (Cox) as High Commissioner. Beyond that all is divergence."

of which had been under discussion for many weeks. The British
Prime Minister demanded a British administration in Palestine
and the transfer of Mosul (which the Sykes–Picot agreement had
put in the French sphere) to the British. According to H. W. V.
Temperley, in his *History of the Peace Conference*, Clemenceau
agreed—on three conditions. These were that France should obtain
a share in the oil which might be produced in Mosul, that Britain
in these matters should support France against Woodrow Wilson,
that if the newly fashionable Mandates were established, France
should have that for Syria and the Lebanon—including Damascus,
Aleppo, Alexandretta and Beyrouth.[1]

It was now manifest that the territorial assignments in the Middle
East had definitely become pawns in the game. Lawrence was
disgusted, the Arabs were thrown back on the old Arabian pastime,
in which they were experts, of fishing to the best profit in the
troubled waters.

In Syria, backed by the subventions from the British Treasury
and helped by British advisers, Faisal's Arab administration had
settled down to work. The British Foreign Office, well aware of
the pressure which Woodrow Wilson was exerting in order to
force his League Covenant, with its Mandate articles, upon the
Allied peace-makers, was bound to meet France half-way. The
major Anglo-French problems were European—the problem of
reparations and the problem of the new map. It soon became clear
to Faisal and his entourage that in their own interests they must
prepare a second string to their bow, against the possibility, the
probability, that the British Government would in the end decline
to maintain them in Syria against the French. Apart from the
political aspect, this possibility had a financial aspect which appeared
to them most alarming. For if the Arab Government in Syria disappeared, there would disappear with it the British subsidy—if
for no other reason than that the French would reasonably object
to the continued British financing of the Arabs who then, disgruntled

---

[1] The oil agreement was concluded in the following April. So far as
Iraq was concerned France received a 23¾ per cent holding in the Turkish
Petroleum Company (now the Iraq Petroleum Company) and agreed to
British control of the pipe-line to the Mediterranean. This has now been
modified, and in addition to the British pipe-line from Kirkuk to Haifa,
France has her own bifurcation to Tripoli.

THE SELLER OF NUTS

THE CUPPED
HAND OF THE
BEGGAR

FRUIT STALL

at having the prize removed from their grasp, would be in the mood for subversive propaganda. The French too, could not but observe that, in spite of the earlier friendly arrangements between friends, Britain was already in possession of what had been agreed on as theirs: and, instead of the French being in Syria, Britain was financing there an Arab administration that in the nature of things was anti-French.

The efforts of Faisal and his Arabs were directed, therefore, towards retaining their hold on Syria and on the British subsidy, and at the same time preparing for the rainy day by pegging out a claim upon Iraq. A number of Faisal's officers were Arabs from Iraq, mostly Baghdadis, and while they might prefer Syria, both for its amenities and because it was the bird in hand, their desire to see a free Iraq was an honest one. The late Sir Henry Dobbs has referred to them as "adventurers,"[1] but this is perhaps scarcely fair, though they were nothing if not realists. No doubt had the position of the Arabs in Syria been secure, these men might have shown less immediate interest in Iraq, but the establishment of a permanent Arab administration in Syria would not have eased the task of a British administration in an Iraq protectorate. As will be seen later, many of the troubles that arose later in Iraq were fomented directly from Syria, where the Arabs already saw their power slipping; had they been allowed to establish themselves in Syria, the very fact might have stimulated national feeling (and the place-hunting instinct) among the Iraqis, chiefly among the politically minded Baghdadis.

At the beginning of 1919 the Baghdadis around Faisal sent to the British Government a memorandum in which they welcomed the Anglo-French declaration of the previous November as establishing that no part of Iraq was to be under British rule. This

---

[1] Sir Henry Dobbs is reported (*Near East and India*, February 23, 1933, p. 148) as having told the Royal Empire Society that these officers were "devoted adherents of the Amir Faisal, and it was largely the return of those experienced and determined adventurers that moulded the minds of the Iraqi public towards the subsequent acceptance of the Amir Faisal as their ruler." At the same meeting, Jafar Pasha, the Iraqi Minister in London and one of the officers referred to, retorted that they were not adventurers. He said that they "worked during the most difficult times [and] were, and are, animated by a sincere desire to work for their country to attain the glories of its ancient past."

arrived when London and Paris were still exercised by the great
primary questions of the peace, and both Foreign Offices were
regarding the Middle East as of secondary importance. In Iraq,
the strong man on the spot was developing the policy of an efficient
administration and he was left alone because the twin origin of the
Mesopotamian campaign persisted. Apart from the twofold control
by the Indian Government and the home Government, perplexities,
if nothing worse, arose from the conflicting temperaments of the
two Secretaries of State, Lord Curzon at the Foreign Office and
Mr. E. S. Montagu at the India Office. One result of this chequering
of politics and personalities was that so far as Iraq was concerned,
no progress appeared to be made until the early summer of 1919,
when a plan took shape for an administration, in which the Arabs
should have a share, covering five provinces in the plains of
Mesopotamia, an Arab province of Mosul, and beyond it a fringe
of autonomous Kurdish states with British political officers. About
this time A. T. Wilson was reporting the arrival in Iraq of "emissaries financed by the Arab Government in Syria," itself financed
from London, who engaged themselves "in arousing prejudice
against the (British) administration in Iraq, both on religious and
political grounds, in almost every division.[1] A. T. Wilson blames
the Foreign Office for failing to give him a lead and thus making
impossible any definite public statement on the future of Iraq.
While this indecision made the task of the trouble-makers easier
than it otherwise would have been, it was dictated by the tangle of
major problems that were being dealt with in Europe—problems
in which the future of Iraq and its three million people inevitably
played an inconspicuous part, though naturally those on the spot
saw things in a different perspective.

By June the Iraqi officers in Syria had redoubled their efforts to
secure Baghdad if they must lose Damascus. For the Versailles
Treaty, with the League Covenant, was now all but complete, and
they saw that the run they had had for their money was nearing its
end. It had been a good one. At the beginning of June the Chief
Political Officer of the Egyptian Expeditionary Force received a
letter from Faisal, who had hitherto shown no direct interest in
Iraq's affairs, complaining of the severity of the British administration

[1] A. T. Wilson: *Mesopotamia: A Clash of Loyalties*, p. 123.

66

in Iraq and suggesting that this severity was alienating the population. The letter went on to argue that the establishment with British help, of an Arab Government in Baghdad, should be expedited and to point out that the longer the delay the more difficult the ultimate change-over would be. Young (*op. cit.*, p. 287) records that he thought at the time that this letter was the handiwork of Lawrence and that Lord Curzon "thought that it savoured of impertinence." Later in the month Faisal's Baghdadi officers formally demanded that a national government should at once be set up in Iraq. The future of the Mosul *vilayat* was still indeterminate. A. T. Wilson had from the first urged its inclusion in Iraq, but as the question of the new Turkish frontier must be left to the Turkish treaty, it was not possible to make any announcement about Mosul before the Versailles Treaty (with Germany) was signed, on June 28, 1919.

This instrument included the Covenant of the League of Nations, of which Article XXII read as follows:

To these colonies and territories which as a consequence of the late War have ceased to be under the sovereignty of the States which formerly governed them and which are inhabited by peoples not yet able to stand by themselves under the strenuous conditions of the modern world, there should be applied the principle that the well-being and development of such peoples form a sacred trust of civilization and that securities for the performance of this trust should be embodied in this Covenant.

The best method of giving practical effect to this principle is that the tutelage of such peoples should be entrusted to advanced nations who by reason of their resources, their experience or their geographical position, can best undertake this responsibility, and who are willing to accept it, and that this tutelage should be exercised by them as Mandatories on behalf of the League.

Certain communities formerly belonging to the Turkish Empire have reached a stage of development where their existence as independent nations can be provisionally recognized subject to the rendering of administrative advice and assistance by a Mandatory until such time as they are able to stand alone. The wishes of these communities must be a principal consideration in the selection of the Mandatory.

The degree of authority, control, or administration to be exercised by the Mandatory shall, if not previously agreed upon by the Members of the League, be explicitly defined in each case by the Council.

A permanent Commission shall be constituted to receive and examine the annual reports of the Mandatories and to advise the Council on all matters relating to the observance of the mandates.

# Iraq

What did the Arabs think of all this?

When Baghdad was captured (March 11, 1917) it had been declared that Basrah would remain British and Baghdad would become Arab. Woodrow Wilson's Twelfth Point (January 8, 1918) appeared to promise "an absolutely unmolested opportunity of autonomous development." On June 11th, the British Government had promised Faisal's Arabs complete and sovereign Arab independence in the areas freed by their own efforts. Now came this new political idea, the "Mandate," a term chosen by General Smuts. The Covenant itself made it perfectly clear that the idea was one of trusteeship, but the other meaning which the word bears, the power of authority and command, was the meaning taken out of it by English-reading Arabs, although when the proclamation was made in Iraq, Arabic words were chosen which avoided the latter connotation. The chief people interested were the educated minority who hoped for place and power. The Arabs in general, and all the minorities, had little interest except in the maintenance of law and the security of finance and commerce. But in Baghdad there was a good deal of agitation and in July A. T. Wilson was protesting against the notice that was being taken by the British of the Baghdadis around Faisal, who, he suggested, were unrepresentative. About the same time a report was received in London of the existence all over Iraq, of a "secret" society, the object of which was the expulsion of British rule.

As usual at this time, the explanation was to be found in Syria. The Mandates were not actually awarded in the League Covenant and among the preoccupations of the British and French Foreign Offices during that autumn was the question of the Middle East, their object still being to bring European *Realpolitik* into the four corners of American idealism. Long discussions and negotiations took place about the Mandates and although they were not finally and formally decided until April 1920, it was manifest by the autumn of 1919 that the French would go into Syria. About this time the activities of subsidized agents among the Mesopotamian tribes were increasing, and Lawrence was openly advocating Faisal for the throne of an independent Iraq.

On November 1st, the British troops were evacuated from the French sphere and Faisal was advised by the British Government to come to terms with the French. France naturally would not have sanctioned the continuance of his British subsidy, and Faisal pleaded that Britain should not abandon him. His Baghdadi officers now said they regarded the British Civil Administration in Iraq as being like a foreign administration of a people incapable and likely to remain incapable of governing themselves. They contrasted this attitude with the free-and-easy co-operation with Lawrence and the other British officers who regarded themselves as helping the Arabs on the way to self-government. Thus crystallized the difference —temperamental largely, in part born of expediency—between the two schools of political thought, a cleavage that was vitally to affect the history of Iraq.[1] For the cleavage was apparent within the Civil Administration itself; Miss Bell was writing of efforts "to squeeze the Arabs into our mould"; A. T. Wilson saw his own show getting more and more efficient and feared that the better it became the more easy and the more rapid would be the descent to Avernus.

With Lawrence was Young, later for a time to be British Minister in Baghdad, who records how he drew Lord Curzon's attention to the fact that in A. T. Wilson's administration only four officers out of 233 employed were over forty-five years of age—the implication being that in the mass they lacked balance and experience. But Young does not mention the fact that the Arabs who would be likely to get the principal posts in an independent Iraq, and who were already in the saddle in Syria, were of like age, and in general, without the experience and qualifications of Wilson's best men. These, and similar discussions, dragged through the autumn into winter.

Suddenly, before the year ended, a raid was made on Dair-as-Zor, on the Iraqi–Syrian frontier, whose inhabitants had already asked for a British officer to be sent to maintain law and order. This raid, against the British administration in Iraq, was admittedly instigated from Syria, although Faisal himself disclaimed all knowledge of it and gave instructions restraining the prevailing excitement. Young, who is frankly on the side of the Arab Nationalists, says,

---

[1] The delay in awarding the Mandate and in signing the Turkish Treaty was a factor which "had disastrous results in Iraq."—H. W. V. Temperley, *History of the Peace Conference of Paris*, Vol. VI, p. 180.

with delicate meiosis: "This did not of course popularize the Arab Government of Damascus with the British Authorities in Mesopotamia, who suspected Faisal of encouraging the Arab Nationalists to cause trouble to the British as well as to the French. Nor would it have been surprising if he had in fact done so though His Majesty's Government were satisfied that he personally had had no hand in the disturbance. Whether the same can truthfully be said of those who were in charge of the administration at Damascus and Aleppo in his absence (in Europe) is another matter, *into which it would be profitless to enquire*." The italics are mine: Young, who was on the spot, need not have pursued his inquiries very far before coming on the facts.

The Dair-as-Zor raid, in fact, established beyond doubt that the Arab Nationalists in Syria with Faisal recognized that the game was up in Syria and were moving forward on a new line. Faisal himself was in Europe, where with the able and whole-hearted assistance of Lawrence he was doing all he could to retain his position, and the support of Britain. It was clearly of importance to his followers to do their utmost in the meantime to strengthen their claims in Iraq.

Meantime, to the north, the rise of the Nationalist party in Turkey was importing a new factor into the situation. The Allies had been waiting to see if Woodrow Wilson would take a hand in the Ottoman Mandates; before they gave up their vain expectation, the new Turkey had arisen, and the question of Mosul, which it was thought had been settled by conquest, began to arise with it. This tended to complicate affairs, both as regards the Mandate for Iraq and the peace with Turkey. The possibility that the Turks might return to Iraq was still present in the minds of many of the resident Arabs, who, unlike the Nationalists with Faisal, had not burnt all their boats, and so were constrained to be circumspect in the expression of their views.

The situation was summed up by Lloyd George in the House of Commons. On March 25th the Prime Minister, in declaring the probability that the Mandate would be given to Britain, put the case thus:

Our point of view is that they should govern themselves and that we should be responsible as the mandatory for advising, for counselling, for assisting, but that the government must be Arab. . . . We will respect the solemn undertaking which we gave to the Allies in November 1918, upon that subject, but it would be fatal unless some country undertook the responsibility, the supreme responsibility, of constituting this Government and advising it. What other country will undertake that responsibility except Great Britain? To hand it over to anyone else would be contrary to the wishes of the Arab population there. They absolutely agree that they do not want Turkish rule again. They are also agreed that they want the British Government and British supervision. When they come to consider whether they would have a member of the Sharifian family over them, or somebody else, they are hopelessly divided, and that is one of the difficulties. We have no right to talk as if we were the Mandatory of Mesopotamia when the Treaty with Turkey is not yet completed. When that has been finally decided, and the question of who the mandatories are has been settled, we shall certainly claim the right as the Mandatory Power of Mesopotamia, including Mosul.

This followed the meeting of a "Syrian Congress" in Damascus at which Faisal had been proclaimed King of Syria. Another "congress" composed of the Iraqi officers with Faisal, met and proclaimed Abdullah, his brother, Amir of Iraq. This effort to present the Allies with a *fait accompli* was doomed to failure because there was nothing behind it. The Arab Government in Damascus was but a façade, which was bound to collapse as soon as British support was withdrawn. The British troops had gone in the early winter, and in April, as had been shaping for some time, the San Remo agreement awarded the Syrian Mandate to France, and that for Iraq to Britain. With the stopping, within a month or two, of the British supplies of money the Arab masses folded their tents.

The difficulty in Iraq now was that Britain must not appear to have her hand forced in framing the constitution, whereas Faisal's Nationalists, at the end of their run in Syria, were certain to become extremists in Iraq. Britain's policy, as it developed through the years, was to maintain a friendly and strong Iraq on the flank of the land route to India.[1] The Nationalist leaders intensified a thousandfold their subversive propaganda among the Mesopotamian tribes, and this was succeeding the more as the British troops were being withdrawn from the country. As A. T. Wilson was later to point out to London, the successive British evacuations, apparently

---

[1] See chapter on Britain's Imperial Communications.

under pressure from Syria, of Dair-as-Zor and other frontier posts,[1] coupled with the public knowledge that the army was being reduced, was interpreted as weakness, if not of an actual determination entirely to abandon the country. These ideas were skilfully fomented, especially among the Euphrates tribes.

In June the return of Sir Percy Cox, as High Commissioner administering the Mandate, was decided upon. Sir Percy Cox was known and respected as a strong and honourable man. His official record and his personality made him a popular figure among the Arabs, and "Kokus"[2] was a man whose fairness and political sagacity all could, and most did, trust. His part, indeed, in the upbuilding of the modern Iraq has never been sufficiently emphasized or even adequately recognized. He took pains to know everybody and to learn the views of the people who counted. He was patient when patience was needed, and strong when firmness had to be shown. Without his sagacious guidance Iraq could not have progressed towards independence as she has done. As an official he had to work out a policy of conciliation and withdrawal. In this policy he had an enthusiastic supporter in his Oriental Secretary, the late Miss Gertrude Bell, whose sympathies were well known to be entirely with the Arab nationalists. As she herself wrote (September 27, 1920): "What I hope Sir Percy will do is to give a very wide responsibility to natives of this country. It is the only way of teaching them how hard the task of government is. . . . I should stand by and let them do it for a bit and then see if a better adjustment is not possible."[3]

On April 10 she had written to her mother, "What I do feel pretty sure of is that if we leave this country to go to the dogs it will mean that we shall have to reconsider our whole position in Asia. If Mesopotamia goes, Persia goes inevitably and then India.

[1] In May 1920 a Sharifian force had appeared from Syria on the Khabur River, under Jamil Beg Madfai, who has since held high office in Iraqi cabinets. It is not certain whether he was working *with the Turks* or not.

[2] So his name was pronounced. The Arab normally inserts an intrusive vowel between two consonants, or in double consonant like x. The newsboys who shout *The Iraq Times* in the streets of Baghdad pronounce *Times* as a dissyllable.

[3] Bell: *Letters of Gertrude Bell*, II, p. 500. Just before the rebellion began she was asking her father to "do as much propaganda" as he could in favour of the official policy.

THE SHAIKH'S FALCONER. HAWKING IS A FAVOURITE
WINTER SPORT

WATER-SELLER FILLING HIS GOATSKINS AT A WATER-
HOLE OUTSIDE ZUBAIR

# Lawrence and the Arabs of Iraq

And the place which we leave empty will be occupied by seven devils and a good deal worse than any which existed before we came." This appears to imply that if the British were to have left in 1920, Mesopotamia would have gone to the dogs. This from an avowed and enthusiastic pro-Arab is a startling confession of her real views on Arab political and administrative capacity. She saw, too, one of the great difficulties which could confront an independent Iraq—"you can't have a central Government if no one will pay taxes unless they are constrained to do so. Nor will they preserve a sufficient amount of order to permit of trade."[1]

So far as it had been declared, British policy was substantially that outlined by Lloyd George in his Commons speech quoted above. The authorities on the spot were confronted with manifold difficulties in translating this into action. The old incompatibility between the India Office and the Foreign Office, the susceptibilities of France, the delicacy of the general diplomatic situation, the frequent and lengthy absences of responsible Ministers from London —all these factors tended towards delay in issuing instructions to the men on the spot. Furthermore, the suggestion that the "opinion" of the public in Iraq should be taken, was not practicable. There is no public opinion in a country where nine-tenths of the population are scarcely civilized. It is, on the other hand, possible to produce any desired "opinion" by a process of selection among the educated and influential classes. Moreover, the Jews and the Christians, strong minorities possessing in general a higher standard of education and civilization, were certain to hold views not in consonance with Arab views,[2] and yet the assumption from the beginning had been that the new states were to be "Arab" states—the only positive exception being Palestine, in which the Balfour Declaration had placed the national home for the Jews.

The local difficulties, as has been seen, were increased by the subversive agitation directed from Syria by the nationalists around Faisal,[3] and by the fact of the steady reduction in the British forces.

---

[1] Bell, *op. cit.*, II, 497.

[2] The Jews, immediately the Anglo-French Declaration of November 1918 was published, asked to be allowed to become British subjects.

[3] A. T. Wilson, *op. cit.*, p. 260. "Nothing indicated that the popular mind was seriously exercised over the Mandate, or that the Administration had fallen into disfavour except among a small group of politically-minded

# Iraq

Sir Percy Cox, though appointed, would not arrive until the end of the hot weather, and the efforts of the propagandists were directed against the administration of A. T. Wilson. The propagandists knew well that they had the support of Miss Bell. They were also fully aware of the attacks that were being made in the British Parliament and in sections of the London press (which had been turning Lawrence into a figure of glamour and romance) against the continuance of British rule in Mesopotamia, or, alternatively, against the "Indianization" of the administration which in certain quarters had come to be associated with Wilson's name. Among the Baghdad effendis the nationalist propaganda found fertile soil. There were constant meetings in the mosques, where a turbulent nationalism was being preached. In the Holy Cities on the Euphrates, Najaf and Karbala, agitation also began to centre, for the Persian priesthood were anxious to upset any Government that might become strong enough to control them. The weak British garrisons on the lower and middle Euphrates were noted, the rise of Turkey and the possibility of complications in that quarter (perhaps even the return of the Turks!) were in the minds of all. The fast of Ramadhan, with its nervous strain and its nights given to social visits and interminable talk, coincided, and on July 3rd, at Rumaitha, in the Muntafiq area, rebellious for centuries, the rebellion broke out.

No adequate force being available, the trouble spread. The flame was fanned by the priestly caste in the Holy Cities, who having received timely supplies of Turkish gold were preaching the Holy War and the complete ejection of the British from the country. A. T. Wilson had from the first taken a serious view of the situation, a view which was not shared by the military command. In the middle of June he had telegraphed to London: (1) that Britain could not maintain her position as mandatory by a policy of conciliation of extremists; (2) that she must be prepared to furnish alike men and money and to maintain continuity of control for years to come; (3) that "if His Majesty's Government regard such a policy as im-

men whose salaries came from Damascus." *Ibid.*, p. 258. "Letters had been issued by a group of Syrian and ex-Turkish officers now in the Amir Faisal's employ, urging the tribes and people of Najaf . . . to rise against the British."

practicable or beyond our strength (as well they may) I submit that they would do better to face the alternative, formidable, and from the local point of view terrible, as it is, and evacuate Mesopotamia."

This telegram—which Young[1] then at the Foreign Office, says he regarded as tantamount to a resignation—was sent off at a time when British political officers all over the country were reporting unrest and uneasiness, and in many cases the success of the anti-British propaganda that was being financed from Syria. At the same time the British Commander-in-Chief and his staff were in summer quarters at Karind in the Persian Hills. General Haldane did not view the situation in the serious light in which Wilson saw it— "I did not," he has recorded, "place great faith in the reports that came in steadily and voluminously." The Arabs knew all about the British military movements; they may have known that Miss Bell had written privately to Haldane in optimistic terms. Be that as it may, the tribes were out and the railway cut in three places, small British garrisons being besieged. There was sharp fighting on the Euphrates, and many casualties. The disturbances spread and by the end of July the Hillah district had risen and three companies of the Manchesters suffered severely—"an unfortunate affair," as General Haldane described it. It had the effect of reinforcing the propagandist allegations that the British were no longer able to hold the country. The trouble spread to the north of Baghdad, and the belief became general that the British were leaving the country for good.

Individual British officers[2] were murdered. The one bright spot was that the Kurds remained steady. On the middle Euphrates things were going from bad to worse, supply steamers being attacked and their crews murdered. But by the beginning of the cold weather the British High Command had regained control of the situation.[3] On October 11th, Sir Percy Cox arrived.

It is amply established that much of the driving force behind the

---

[1] *Op. cit.*, p. 316.

[2] Including Leachman (see pp. 50–51) who was treacherously killed. He had *single-handed* and without a penny to spend on bribes held the Upper Euphrates tribes steady in this time of full rebellion, all the troops having been withdrawn—an individual achievement greater than any of Lawrence's.

[3] For the rebellion, see Haldane, *The Insurrection in Mesopotamia 1920*, and A. T. Wilson, *op. cit.*

# Iraq

1920 rebellion was provided by the Arab Nationalists in Syria. Their finances, in turn, were provided by the British Government, and the capture, within Mesopotamia, of *British* rifles and ammunition, proved without doubt the source whence the insurgents were drawing at least part of their sinews of war.[1] Yet this rebellion demanded the employment of 65,000 troops to quell it, and the expenditure of £100,000,000 by the Imperial Exchequer.

Things in Syria had been moving fast enough. Just before the rebellion began Jafar Pasha al Askari,[2] who was with Faisal, had offered to leave Syria for Baghdad "to remove misunderstandings regarding the attitude of Faisal's Government (in Syria) towards the Mesopotamian administration."[3] In this connection it is relevant to point out that after the San Remo decision (allocating the Iraqi Mandate to Britain and the Syrian Mandate to France), Faisal as head of the Arab Government and "King of Syria" in Damascus, had announced that he could not acquiesce in any part of Syria being placed under any foreign domination. The Arabs knew very well the strength of the French forces (General Gouraud had 90,000 troops), they knew that Britain must support France, and they knew that all British financial assistance must stop. On July 25th, when the rebellion in Iraq was becoming really serious, the French after a tussle ejected Faisal from Damascus.[4]

Just before the rebellion began, the British, announcing the return of Sir Percy Cox, had declared their intention of setting up in the autumn a provisional Arab Government. This was done in October, and the question of the Amir for the new state then became urgent. Faisal was now without occupation,[5] but the British Foreign Office hesitated under pressure from France, which declared that the "employment" of Faisal in Iraq immediately after his expulsion from Syria would be regarded by French opinion as an unfriendly act.

The winter of 1920–21 passed in scheming and intriguing on the

---

[1] See A. T. Wilson, *op. cit.*, p. 79, for details.

[2] Later Iraqi Minister in London.

[3] A. T. Wilson, *op. cit.*, II, p. 303. In fact Jafar did not arrive in Baghdad until October; he was the first to return from Syria.

[4] His own diary of the events, as handed to Reuter's Cairo correspondent, is given in Appendix B.

[5] In December 1918 the British Authorities in Baghdad had been informed that Faisal was not available for Iraq, Syria having been earmarked for him.

# Lawrence and the Arabs of Iraq

part of the Arabs, and in further reconstruction efforts by the British. The extreme Nationalists, now finished in Syria, had their undivided attention upon Iraq. In Britain a new policy was shaping —to concentrate Middle East affairs in the hands of the Colonial Office, thus ending the division of responsibility between the Foreign Office, the India Office and the War Office. Winston Churchill, the Secretary of State for War and Air, became Colonial Secretary and immediately called a conference at Cairo, which met in March 1921. Lawrence was there and found that by this time the force of circumstances was working in favour of his plan to give Faisal the "throne" of the new Iraqi state. On the military side the Conference, under the economy instructions of the time, decided that the Royal Air Force should take over from the army, effecting an annual reduction from £35,000,000 (which would drop to £10,000,000) to £4,000,000. At Cairo, British policy was seen to be crystallizing in favour of clearing out of Iraq, provided the security of British communications from the Eastern Mediterranean to the head of the Persian Gulf were assured. A democratic decision being out of the question, a nominated King and a cabal, so far as possible subservient, was the called-for expedient. For Faisal it appeared to be Hobson's choice, there being no immediate possibility of any other state coming on the market. His own ability was unquestioned; his views at the time coincided as nearly as was possible with British policy. His immediate followers were also willing to assume posts in the new state, and it says much for their capacity that they have, most of them, remained in the governing oligarchy ever since.[1]

[1] Faisal arrived in Basrah from Mecca; simultaneously Basrah submitted a request for a separate legislature, army and police *plus* fiscal independence. Miss Bell records an opinion expressed by Sir (then Mr.) Kinahan Cornwallis that "the people were standing back," uncertain what or whom the British wanted. She also records (Vol. II, p. 597) her anxiety less Faisal should come in, not by popular acclaim, but by a *coup* of the extremists (which, by implication, seemed to her to be possible), but as soon as the people knew that "Kokus" wanted Faisal, there was no further difficulty. Among the tribes, the 80 per cent vote for Faisal was only made possible because the British political officers told the shaikhs how to vote. Philby's quarrel with the authorities came at this point because he wanted the referendum to be free and uninfluenced. At all events Faisal made good within a few years.

# CHAPTER IV

## ANGLO-IRAQI RELATIONS

WHEN Sir Percy Cox, as the first High Commissioner, arrived in Iraq in October 1920, the British Government's declared policy was not to hold Iraq as a colony or protectorate but to set up the beginnings of an independent Government. Within the country the large British community were insistent that this policy must fail. In so far as such views were dictated by personal motives, careerist or commercial, they were to be discounted; but it certainly at the time seemed a leap in the dark. So far as Sir Percy himself was concerned he appeared to regard this apprenticeship to independence as the only alternative to a complete British evacuation, and, "fortifying myself with the conviction that the project had at least an even chance of success . . . I took heart of grace."[1] Miss Bell and others in his administration he found to be keen supporters of London's policy and we find, within a month, a Provisional Council of State brought into being. This Council of State, under the venerable Naqib of Baghdad,[2] was made responsible for the conduct and control of the government of the country, with the exception of foreign relation and military matters, which remained under the High Commissioner. Thus were taken the first steps to demolish A. T. Wilson's splendid machine.

Up to this time the opposition to the Mandate was evident only among ultra-Nationalists and place-hunters. The immediate question was the form which the new constitution should take. According to the *Progress of Iraq*,[3] from the first "the Ministers seem to have had no doubt as to what they wanted, nor indeed had any of the politically minded public of the country, who were unanimously in favour of a democratic constitutional government." At that time the "politically minded public" probably did not exceed two or three thousand Arabs all told; the Jews, Christians, Kurds and

---

[1] Bell, *op. cit.*, II, p. 528.

[2] The Naqib is a hereditary ecclesiastical dignitary whose duty is to maintain the nominal roll of Sayyids, or descendants of the Prophet.

[3] *Progress of Iraq (1920–1931)*: British Colonial Office (Colonial No. 58).

others held varying views. This was not surprising. Even the British Government (*op. cit.*, p. 13) admits that it could not be said "that any clear idea of the duties and privileges of democratic citizenship had been widely spread among all classes of the people." In part no doubt the new democratic zeal was a healthy reaction against Ottoman autocracy; in part it simply meant that those in possession of money or power knew that the machinery of election in such a country would afford them ample opportunities of pulling wires in their own interests. Moreover, those in influence or authority could not fail to observe the democratic blasts that were blowing about the world; there were in addition the professional and student classes, anxious to carve out lucrative careers for themselves and, in large part honestly, swayed by Western political and economic ideas. The democratic basis was therefore the basis for the new constitution.

We have seen how the early secret inter-Allied pacts had given the lower Mesopotamian plains to Britain. There was then no talk of Mandates; it was the usual carving up, by the conquerors, of an enemy's territory, and there was no *arrière pensée* except to do the best possible between friends. Logically therefore Britain must ensure her position in Iraq[1] after the termination of the Mandate; it was also necessary for Britain to find some centre of stability in the new state, some source of power upon which she could depend.

We have seen how British policy saw in the selection of Faisal the opportunity of combining gratitude with interest. There was a school of thought, of which Philby was an exponent, which had sought to establish a republic of Iraq under a strong leader. The name mentioned (apart from men of straw who might have been put up temporarily) was that of Sayyid Talib Pasha, an extraordinary personage who lived in a mansion at Sibilliyat on the right bank of the Shatt-al-Arab, a few miles below Basrah. Sayyid Talib gave his sons a Western education, but, until he realized that British rule had at last brought order into the country, he remained the typical medieval robber baron. Philby himself refers to him as "the accomplished villain in the drama of Basrah politics before the war." The merchants of Basrah hid their wealth from him, as did those of Mohammerah from Shaikh Sir Khazaal Khan, who

---

[1] See Chapter on British Imperial Communications.

was his opposite number on the Persian side of the river. He was the terror of the countryside. Only a year before the war, fearing for his own life, he had had the Turkish Governor in Basrah, Farid Bey, murdered in an open place near the Artillery Park, and the body lay where it fell for some days, for no one dare remove it until he had given permission to have it taken away.[1] He was a strong man, but was not his influence too local? and could Downing Street depend on him? To some extent he solved the problem himself by his intrigues; his arrest and exile to Ceylon in April 1921 finally removed a factor disturbing to Britain's plans.

The *Progress of Iraq* (p. 14) puts it that Faisal's "position in the Arab world and valuable services to the Allied cause during the war appealed alike to British and Iraqi." This is an exaggeration, for at that time Shiah Iraq could not be said to be in favour of a Sunni Sharifian. The British Government had taken care to ascertain previously (*op. cit.*, p. 14) that Faisal "fully understood the responsibilities of His Majesty's Government towards the League, and that he would, if he became King of Iraq, be prepared to negotiate an Anglo-Iraqi treaty." In other words, it was made clear to Faisal in Cairo that his candidature for the throne of Iraq must be conditional on his support of British policy. His formal accession took place at Baghdad on August 23, 1921, and on September 10th a Royal decree appointed the first Council of Ministers to take over the functions of the existing Council of State.

Trouble at once arose, and in three places. Kurdistan did not want the Sharifian Faisal, and the unrest in the north was accentuated by the fact that peace with Turkey had not yet been concluded. In the Southern Desert, Ibn Rashid of Hayil caused difficulties until his capture, in November 1921, inaugurated a brief period of tranquillity.[2] In Baghdad itself Faisal, no longer quite so anxious to please as he had been in Cairo, began to demand that a treaty should replace the Mandate, whereas the British view was that the proposed treaty could come into being only within and by virtue of the Mandate. Gradually, however, the ground was cleared for the negotiation of a treaty which should define the British position in

---

[1] Yet Lawrence, on reaching Damascus, could not (Chap. XXXVII) "set the Arabs an example of precautionary murder as part of politics."
[2] But see Chapter VII for Iraqi-Najdi Relations.

# Anglo-Iraqi Relations

Iraq, with particular reference to the financial and international interests of Britain, after the termination of the Mandate.

It was already clear—although the League still recognized the Mandate and was to continue to do so until 1932—that Iraq, unlike Syria and Palestine (with Transjordan), would not be administered under the fundamental terms of the instrument known as the Mandate. Instead, the place of a Mandate properly so called was taken by a series of bilateral agreements between Britain and Iraq. Thus it happened that Iraq was the first mandated territory to receive a parliament, a constitution and a settled government. Iraqi Nationalism, in large part sincere, set the pace for the dropping of the Mandate and the treaty progression towards independence. A further impetus came from the experience of the Arab officers who in service with Lawrence and Faisal had learned the sweetness of the fruits of power and longed for the taste again. So far as Britain was concerned, a nominally free Iraq in which the Arab politicians should have within limits a free hand and open access to the spoils of office, would be the best and the cheapest way to attain her imperial objects. Independence doubtless came sooner than Britain originally intended; Iraqi nationalism grew faster and more vociferously than anyone expected.

After the British military occupation ended in 1920, political developments in Iraq may be said to have passed through two phases. From 1920 to 1924 was the period of strenuous fighting against the Mandate idea, with Britain trying to negotiate the treaty which should best suit her policy. The Nationalists thought that with Faisal's accession and treaty demands they had made such excellent progress that they could go on in this way indefinitely. Faisal himself, although (or because) put on the throne by Britain, saw the necessity of creating within the state a party upon which he could depend for support. It was early seen by the acuter Arabs that determined opposition to the Mandate would be the quickest way to end it. Not unnaturally, therefore, the first treaty negotiations proved difficult. The first draft did not explicitly abolish the Mandate and there was an immediate outburst of feeling. When Sir Percy Cox called to congratulate the King on the first anniversary of his accession, on August 23, 1922, he was abused outside the palace by hostile demonstrators. Disturbances were fomented in

F

Kurdistan and on the Euphrates but within two or three weeks things had again quieted down.

The treaty was signed in October, after the British Government had given an assurance that it would do everything in its power "to speed delimitation of the frontiers of Iraq, in order that Iraq may be in a position, when the Treaty and the subsidiary agreements therein provided for have been duly ratified and the Organic Law has been brought into effect, to apply for admission to membership of the League of Nations."[1]

It is important to note the fundamental points of difference between this treaty and the Mandate, and at the same time to realize that the general resemblance between the two instruments further embittered the extreme nationalists, who were also angered by the subsidiary agreements. Two years were to pass before final ratification took place. Instead of the Mandate, a new "basis of alliance" was constituted, and Britain recognized Faisal as constitutional King of Iraq. There was no definite recognition of Iraq as a sovereign state, but British advice and assistance were to be given as required "without prejudice to Iraq's national sovereignty." Further, disputes as to the interpretation of the treaty were to be referred not to Geneva but to the Permanent Court of International Justice at the Hague.

Objection was taken chiefly to the subsidiary agreements. The British Officials Agreement provided that in the case of eighteen specified posts—including Advisers in the Ministry of Interior, Finance, Defence, Justice and Communications and Works; Directors or Inspectors of Irrigation, Public Works, Agriculture, Land Registration, Surveys, Veterinary Service, Police, Post Office, Health, Education, Customs and Excise, Court of Appeal, and Government Audit—the Iraqi Government must appoint British officials as and when requested to do so. Other British officials in other grades were to be appointed, all to be employed by Iraq. The agreement specified for monthly salaries rising to £250 sterling in the case of the highest placed officials; no gazetted official was to draw much less than £60 a month. In addition ample leave with free passage was provided for, as well as a provident fund, to which both state and official would contribute and which would

---

[1] *Iraq: Annual Report, 1922–23*, p. 23.

provide for a lump-sum payment at the end of service, which was to be by contract for a period of years, the longest contracts being for ten. Unfortunately it was the case—and the Iraqis saw it all too clearly—that most of the higher British officials were not more than second-class, although the Junior Grades were well up to the average of other similar services.

The second bone of contention was the Military Agreement, subsidiary to the Treaty. Both contracting parties agreed in principle that the Government of Iraq should at the earliest possible date accept full responsibility for the maintenance of internal order and the defence of the country from foreign aggression; British military assistance was to be progressively reduced "with all possible expedition." This assistance might take the form of an imperial garrison or of locally recruited forces maintained by Britain. So far as the Iraqi Government's forces were concerned, British military missions would be provided when required and the Iraqi Government must devote 25 per cent of its annual revenue to the maintenance of the army and reserve. In practice this was later found to be too burdensome and the British grants-in-aid made up the percentage when necessary.

The agreement further provided that the Iraqi Government would not be entitled to British military assistance if it failed to follow any recommendation of the High Commissioner regarding the movements of the Iraqi army, or if the High Commissioner considered that an external attack or civil disturbance was caused by any action taken by the Iraqi Government against his advice; in the event of joint action the military commander would be British; Iraqi wireless stations would be put at the disposal of the British forces when the High Commissioner so requested. This military programme maintained the nationalist temper for ten years, and in fact still maintains it, the argument being that no country can be independent while foreign troops remain within her frontiers.[1]

The third bone of contention was the financial agreement. During the war the British military authorities, in their own interest and for the more successful prosecution of the war against Turkey, had undertaken on a big scale the construction of docks, railways, roads,

[1] *Vide infra* (Appendix A) the 1930 Treaty.

bridges, telegraphs, telephones and irrigation works. With the end of the war, many of these works could as easily be turned to the ends of peace. They had been constructed at war-time costs, quite out of proportion to subsequent values, and the Iraqi nationalists have never ceased to argue that they should be handed over either free of charge or at a negligible valuation.[1] The 1922 treaty provided that the roads, bridges, telegraphs, telephones and irrigation works should be transferred at a valuation of about £7,000,000 sterling payable in annuities over twenty years. The railways were in the meantime to remain the property of the British Government, but during the treaty period their administration would be transferred to the Iraqi Government the revenues being kept separate. The Port of Basrah was valued at 72 lakhs of rupees, in consideration for which the British Government was willing to hand it over as a going concern for administration by an Iraqi Government department, provided the accounts were kept separate from the general accounts of Iraq and on the understanding that when the debt was finally liquidated Britain would cease to control the Port Trust which was proposed. A further agreement provided that the Iraqi Government should bear all the administrative expenses of the country; and in addition the cost of maintaining the British Residency. This latter provision was later modified and finally done away with. Lastly, Iraq was to meet all payments in respect of her share of the Ottoman Public Debt.

Not until 1924, and then only under strong British pressure, was this 1922 treaty finally ratified by Iraq. For the Shiahs boycotted the 1922 elections. To resolve the deadlock that followed, Britain had to compromise by reducing the term of the treaty from twenty years to "four years after the ratification of peace with Turkey, if Iraq in the meantime had not become a member of the League." There was great excitement in the country. Sir Percy Cox flew to London in January 1923, his object according to Miss Bell being to persuade the British Cabinet that "even if they don't want to shoulder the burden they have got to learn that it is amazingly difficult to let it drop with a bump. It is almost impossible to believe that a few years ago the human race was more or less governed by

[1] For the final settlement and comments made by the Permanent Mandates Commission of the League, see pp. 110 *et seqq.*

reason."[1] A protocol signed in April 1923 provided that before the treaty expired negotiations for its successor should be begun. In the meantime a new High Commissioner[2] assumed office. The elections then went on, this time with Shiah co-operation, the principal recalcitrant divine having been deported.

The Constituent Assembly, duly elected, met in the spring of 1924. At once strong divergences made themselves evident between the British view and the Nationalist view, and for nine months heated discussions continued. The Nationalists resented the proposed control of the army by British officers; they fiercely opposed the control of the administration by British officials, objecting particularly to the proposed scale of salaries; they fought against the powers conferred by the Treaty upon the High Commissioner; they argued that the financial agreement was more than Iraq could bear. Each side accused the other of misrepresentation, and by means of a smoke-screen of calumny and vituperation a violent anti-British sentiment was stirred up by the Nationalist leaders and their satellites. The King being unable to force the Assembly to conform to the British view, Britain finally applied force. The High Commissioner issued an ultimatum that if the treaty were not ratified by June 10, 1924, this would be read as rejection and Britain would at once ask the League Council to confirm the Mandate in its original terms. This threat almost failed. On June 10th the Assembly broke up without deciding anything. Partly the feeling was so strong and the issues so difficult; partly the Eastern love of procrastination led the deputies to decide to try Britain's patience for another day and see what London would do next. But the deputies, who had gone home, were brought back and compelled, though it was now the early hours of the 11th, to accept the Treaty and its subsidiary agreements. The figures of the voting are of interest. Thirty-seven voted for acceptance and twenty-four against. Eight deputies abstained from voting and thirty-one were absent. It is of interest, too, to note the text of the resolution which accepted the Treaty and the agreements:

This Assembly considers that many of the Articles of the Treaty and Agreements are so severe that Iraq would be unable to discharge the responsibilities of the alliance desired by the people of Iraq. But it relies

---

[1] Bell, *op. cit.*, II, p. 642.                    [2] Sir Henry Dobbs.

upon and trusts the honour of the British Government and nobility of the British nation and is confident that they will not agree to burden Iraq, nor to prejudice the aspirations of its people. It is only this confidence and trust on the part of Iraq which has induced the Assembly to accept the statements which have been received from His Excellency the High Commissioner on behalf of the British Government, to the effect that the British Government, after the ratification of the Treaty, will amend with all possible speed the Financial Agreement in the spirit of generosity and sympathy for which the British people are famous. In view of this, the Assembly recommends that His Majesty the King should ratify the Treaty, Protocol and Agreements, provided that immediately after such ratification His Majesty shall enter into negotiations with the British Government for securing the amendments suggested by the Committee of the Assembly. . . .

The League Council in September approved the Treaty and the subsidiary agreements as being an adequate substitute for the Mandate under which it had been proposed to administer Iraq. In November the Treaty and the subsidiary agreements were at last ratified. The general feeling was expressed by Sir Henry Dobbs when he wrote:[1] "The more far-seeing people feared that the reduced period was too short to enable Iraq to stand on her own feet, but the politicians welcomed it with enthusiasm and even King Faisal and his Ministers, while expressing constant gratitude for the support and favours received in the past, were undisguisedly delighted that a near term had been put to authoritative control by Britain of their affairs." All this time the Turkish settlement was dragging on. The Lausanne Treaty in 1923 had left the Turco-Iraqi frontier undetermined. The Turks had been fomenting disturbances in the debatable land but these were ended by firm air action,[2] undertaken by the British Air Force, which in accordance with the Cairo decisions had taken over in October 1922. It was this question of the Mosul frontier which before long led the Iraqis to agree to a twenty-five years' extension of the agreements which at the cost of so much unpleasantness they had just succeeded in reducing to four years. This Mosul frontier problem was a thorny one. The Treaty of Lausanne of 1923 had provided that the boundary should be demarcated by friendly arrangement between Britain and Turkey and failing this should be referred to the League

---

[1] Bell, *op. cit.*, II, p. 543.　　　　[2] See p. 115.

Council. Agreement was found to be impossible and the League sent out a Commission.

Each side appointed assessors who from opposite sides bombarded the League's Commissioners. Much was made of Ottoman and Kurdish excesses against the Christian populations of the area in question, and the humanitarian influence of Geneva led the Council of the League to insist on a new Anglo-Iraqi treaty which should provide that the Mosul *vilayet* be allocated to Iraq on condition that the British treaty relationship should be extended to twenty-five years, unless Iraq were admitted a member of the League before then. The Council expressed the view that if the mandate were not to last for the twenty-five years, then Mosul had best go to Turkey.

Many Iraqis, with their one eye on "independence," were apparently willing to throw away the wealth of Mosul and the northern districts in order to cut out the twenty-five years' provision.[1] But the Iraqi ruling oligarchy, who saw clearly what oil meant, decided that Mosul was worth some sacrifice, hoping the while that a continuance of pressure might compel Britain to push Iraq into the League before the end of the twenty-five years' term. With little loss of time, therefore, a new treaty was negotiated. It was signed on January 13, 1926, and fixed the twenty-five years "from the 16th day of December 1925." But a new clause provided that at four-year intervals Britain should consider Iraq's progress towards the stage at which she might be deemed to be able to stand on her own feet as an independent state.

In the meantime (July 1925) the first Iraqi Parliament under the new constitution had met, and in November of that year the position of the British officials in the country was fundamentally changed. When British military control ended after the rebellion of 1920, the existing Civil Administration was taken over by the new High Commissioner. Numbers of Wilson's young political officers became "advisers" under the Mandate. In November 1920 it was laid down by the High Commissioner that—

The Head of each State Department will be the minister in charge of it and the administration of such department will vest in him subject

---

[1] Some of them of course may have been in Turkish pay.

(*a*) to the control of the Council over the action of Ministers;

(*b*) to the hearing of the views expressed by the British officers selected by me as advisers to the several departments;

(*c*) to the fact that in the last resort supreme control will vest in my own person.

The High Commissioner's instruction made it clear that the functions of these advisers were not to be executive but advisory, and that "it is necessary that attention should be paid (by the Arabs) to their views and that the latter should be taken into careful consideration." The Instruction added that all matters concerning a particular Ministry were to be referred to its Minister through his Adviser, and that in cases where a Minister desired to initiate any action, he must call his Adviser into consultation in the first instance. The Advisers were thus responsible to the High Commissioner. With the accession of the King in August 1921, the position was entirely changed, the constitutional head of the state being now the King and no longer the High Commissioner.

According to the *Progress of Iraq* (p. 24) Britain was anxious "to preserve the foundations of progressive and enlightened government which had been laid by the Civil Administration during the military occupation." It was finally decided that the British advisers should be employed by and be responsible to the Iraqi Government, but that they should keep the High Commissioner fully informed at all stages. Every British adviser then in employment, or employed later, received a copy of the following letter:

LETTER OF APPOINTMENT FOR BRITISH OFFICIALS

THE RESIDENCY, BAGHDAD

, 19

SIR,

By direction of the Secretary of State for the Colonies I have the honour to address you as follows:—

His Britannic Majesty has received a request from His Majesty the King of Iraq for your services as a member of the Iraq Service in the $\frac{\text{Ministry}}{\text{Department}}$ of ................................ and has consented to your appointment.

I enclose a copy of the Treaty and Protocol which regulate the relations between His Britannic Majesty and the Government of Iraq, with copies of the subsidiary agreements arising therefrom. You will see that by

# Anglo-Iraqi Relations

Article IV of the Treaty His Majesty the King of Iraq agrees to be guided by the advice of His Britannic Majesty tendered through the High Commissioner on all important matters affecting the international and financial obligations and interests of His Britannic Majesty for the whole period of this Treaty. His Majesty the King of Iraq will fully consult the High Commissioner on what is conducive to a sound financial and fiscal policy and will ensure the stability and good organization of the finances of the Iraq Government so long as that Government is under financial obligations to the Government of His Britannic Majesty. The agreed procedure by which the High Commissioner is to be kept informed at every stage on the matters referred to in this Article is as follows:—

The members of the High Commissioner's staff will be the servants of His Britannic Majesty, and responsible for placing the High Commissioner in a position to offer his advice on all subjects referred to in the Treaty. You and your colleagues will be responsible to the Iraq Government and not to the High Commissioner, but His Majesty the King of Iraq has agreed that the High Commissioner should at all times be furnished with such information as he may require relating to your official duties in the Iraq Government; he has also agreed that the High Commissioner should be informed in advance of any step which the Government of Iraq proposes to take which may affect the international and financial obligations and interests of His Britannic Majesty's Government. This information will be communicated through the Ministry to which you are responsible to the member of the High Commissioner's staff who is primarily concerned, and the Iraq Government will be informed on each occasion that the information has been supplied.

The basic principle underlying the relations between the two Governments is co-operation towards a common end, namely the establishment of an independent Government of Iraq, friendly to and bound by gratitude and obligation to His Britannic Majesty's Government. There is no question of His Britannic Majesty's Government pursuing a policy with any other object in view and, provided that the Treaty and its subsidiary agreements are duly observed, the High Commissioner has been instructed that His Britannic Majesty's Government do not propose to criticize in detail or to influence in any way the detailed financial or administrative arrangements of the Iraq Government.

The four principles upon which the co-operation of His Britannic Majesty's Government with the Government of Iraq must necessarily be conditional are:—

(1) that the interests of foreigners are adequately protected;
(2) that the financial interests of His Britannic Majesty's Government are safeguarded;
(3) that the best possible use is made of the resources of the country; and

(4) that the administration should conform to the traditions and principles of progressive and enlightened government.

His Britannic Majesty's Government have left the fulfilment of the third and fourth of these principles to the Iraq Administration, since His Majesty King Faisal has agreed to employ a number of British officials which will, in the opinion of His Britannic Majesty's Government, ensure that the administration is not conducted in such a way as to prejudice their observance. The Secretary of State desires me to point out to you that although you and your colleagues will not be officially responsible to His Britannic Majesty's Government your appointment has only been approved in the full confidence that you will use your influence to secure the attainment of these objects. The Secretary of State feels that he may rely upon you to do your utmost to uphold British prestige and traditions, and that no occasion will arise which will lead to the High Commissioner seeking his authority to bring to the notice of His Majesty the King of Iraq any action on your part which he may regard as detrimental thereto.

The terms of service upon which you are engaged have been set forth in a contract which has been given to you by His Majesty the King of Iraq.

His Majesty the King of Iraq, in consultation with whom this letter has been drafted, and who concurs in its terms, has further agreed that in deciding in what localities British women and children can safely reside he will be guided by the advice of the High Commissioner.

I have the honour to be,
Sir,
Your obedient servant,

*His Britannic Majesty's High Commissioner for Iraq.*

The cardinal points are: the emphasis on the advance information to be given by the Advisers through the High Commissioner to the British Government regarding any step proposed by the Iraqi Government which might affect the international and financial obligations of the British Government; the fact that the Advisers were specially selected with a view, not merely to furthering Iraqi interests, but also to see that British interests should not be prejudiced.

This in effect was the system adopted from 1922–23. In practice it worked tolerably well. The senior Arab officials had nearly all been in the Turkish service and the new generation, with genuine Arab training and ideals, had not yet come along. The country was still full of money and Iraq was still a land of promise. There still remained large numbers of British officers and officials and the British community in the country, swollen to meet war-time requirements, was still at its maximum. No one guessed that the boom years would end so soon; trade flourished and big profits were made on all hands. The country had never seen such prosperity, or so much money.

But complaints and criticism soon began to appear in the National and other factious newsprints. People began to point out that it was anomalous to have a double set of officials in each department, paid by the Iraqi Government—the Iraqi executive moreover receiving a salary invariably very much smaller than that of his British adviser, who was in addition on a long contract. People also began to point out that in many cases the British officials were obviously second-rate or even third-rate men, who had been chosen not for their ability or their administrative record elsewhere, but who, in the chances of war, had been thrown up on the spot just at the moment when the occupation authorities were looking for individuals of their particular military rank. Thenceforward these individuals progressed from one job to another. It is true that many of the British officials were of first-class calibre, but there was enough obvious truth in the criticisms made against the rest to make it hard to meet them.[1]

While the administration was proceeding on these lines with a good deal of apparent smoothness, excellent work was also progressing under the various British technical experts, as distinct from the purely administrative advisers. Communications by road and rail were improved beyond all recognition. The hospitals and health services were extended. The police were transformed from the old Turkish *gendarmerie* into as smart a force as might be seen east of Suez. The recruitment and promotion of officials was removed from the field of graft where it had flourished for generations. The integrity of British judges in civil cases led to the appearance of litigants who in other circumstances would have been too poor to think of claiming justice, however clearly it might have been on their side. Irrigation and agriculture were put on a new scientific basis. Educa-

[1] It is however fair to point out that earlier refusals to offer pensionable contracts had the effect of driving many of the best men back to more attractive careers elsewhere.

tion was taken in hand, teachers were trained and schools were opened everywhere. Public finance was raised far above the old Turkish standard, and the minorities, for four hundred years accustomed to the Ottoman, began to get a square deal.

But Britain was still pressing for a satisfactory settlement of the financial and military agreements, which were subsidiary to the existing treaty and on which the Iraqis were holding out with a view to bargaining on the independence issue. As time passed more and more Nationalists were being bred, and criticisms against the British connection continued to come, both from the more efficient of the educated classes, who felt that they could do the work of administration better than the more indifferent British officials were doing it, and even more strongly and in greater volume from the inefficient, who felt that their only chance of obtaining or remaining in official employment was to get rid of British supervision.

In 1927 a further effort was made to revise the Treaty and with the presence of the Iraqi King and some of his Ministers in London the negotiations were completed by winter and a new treaty was signed on December 15th of that year. Like its predecessor it was an effort on the part of the British Government to bring Iraq, before the termination of the Mandate, into a definite treaty relationship with Britain ensuring certain advantages to both parties. For the first time an Anglo-Iraqi Treaty expressly recognized Iraq as an independent state (Article 1). Britain undertook to support Iraq's application for membership to the League in 1932, provided the existing rate of progress was maintained and all went well in Iraq in the interval. The treaty, it was understood, would not be ratified until the financial and military agreements had been revised and approved by the League.

So began a further stormy period in Anglo-Iraqi relations, with the Nationalists more and more anti-British. In the new year both sides tackled the financial questions but completely failed to reach agreement regarding either the Railways or the Basrah Port. Britain insisted that the debts to her must be discharged before these properties could be wholly handed over; Iraq maintained that the price was too high. The military agreement similarly provided a deadlock. From the beginning, in 1921, Faisal's officers and ministers had envisaged conscription; it was part and parcel of their declared policy, on the twofold ground that a conscript army would be cheaper than the existing voluntary army and would provide a bigger reserve. But the Shiahs objected to conscription, the governing oligarchy being Sunni. The tribal shaikhs said they would not hear of it, and the townsmen agreed that it would not be real universal service until every Iraqi, tribal and non-tribal, was liable to be called up. The issue was for the moment settled by the British Government's announcing that in the event of conscript service being introduced, British troops could not be used to quell any resultant disturbances. This, as usual, was turned into an accusation of bad faith against Britain on the grounds that it was a refusal to help the Iraqi Government in its efforts to set the country on its feet.[1]

A further demand by Britain that Iraq should pay that part of the expenses incurred in maintaining the British forces in Iraq over and above what it would have cost to maintain them in Britain, was rejected by Iraq. While the deadlock continued a new High Commissioner arrived, Sir Henry Dobbs's term having expired. Sir Gilbert Clayton, Sir Henry's successor, died within twelve months, leaving the situation to his successor, Sir Francis Humphrys, more or less as it was. The British Report for 1928 referred pointedly to the

increasing intolerance of British guidance and a disposition to feel that Iraq is ringed in by obstacles which at every turn thwart her efforts to be free. The idea is growing that the Treaty of Alliance concluded with Great Britain in 1922 set up a state of affairs which, if continued, will not only impede the realization of the country's political aspirations, but will also prove inimical to the economic and social development of the country. The Iraqi critic argues that the government of a country by two governments, one foreign and the other national, is an abnormality which, although possibly feasible in theory, is not in practice a workable scheme, and during the year under report this state of affairs in Iraq has been freely and openly condemned by many prominent Iraqi politicians, both in Parliament and in the Press. . . . The term "the perplexing predicament" is used to cover the anomaly that Iraq has national sovereignty and is yet under a mandate, to suggest the dilemma of Ministers, constitutionally responsible to Parliament, but subject to the influence of their

---

[1] It may be noted that early in 1934 a conscription measure was introduced, but as a £30 exemption fee was mentioned, it may simply have been a device for the raising of revenue.

British advisers, and to explain why it is that Iraq cannot create an army large enough to defend her frontiers without conscription and cannot apply conscription without having a strong army to enforce it. Iraq Ministers and administrators profess to find "the perplexing predicament" in every department of the administration of the country. The Iraq Government controls and administers the railways and the Basra port, but does not own them, can declare martial law, but, under the Military Agreement, cannot administer it, and has an army but cannot move it except with the concurrence of the British High Commissioner. Foreign Governments (which are members of the League) can discriminate in tariff and other matters against Iraq subjects, but the Iraq Government has no power to retaliate; foreign subjects have special judicial privileges in Iraq while Iraqi subjects have no reciprocal advantages abroad. The Iraq Government pay half the cost of the expenses of the British High Commissioner and his staff in Iraq but have no control over the expenditure incurred on this account, and finally, although under the Military Agreement the Iraq Government should, not later than four years from the date of the conclusion of the Agreement, accept full responsibility for the maintenance of internal order and for the defence of Iraq from external aggression, she had not up to the end of 1928 in practice assumed this responsibility.

Just before Sir Gilbert Clayton died, the Socialist Government then in power in Britain declared that it would unconditionally support Iraq's application for League membership in 1932. The proviso in the 1929 Treaty that British support for such application would depend on whether "the present rate of progress was maintained and all went well in the interval" had caused much trouble and in 1929 the High Commissioner recommended its withdrawal, the official explanation being that it was reasonable to expect a continuance of recent progress and that "in the absence of some really serious and unexpected set-back, Iraq, judged by the criteria of internal security, sound public finance, and stable administration, would be in every way fit for admission to the League of Nations by 1932." The British Government decided to adopt the recommendation and in September of that year informed Iraq and the League accordingly. This did not however involve the immediate termination of Britain's mandatory responsibility nor did it mean that intervention by the High Commissioner would cease. But the extremer elements, always endeavouring to be at least one move ahead, at once adopted this line and a prolonged Cabinet crisis led to the suicide of the Prime Minister, Sir Abdul Muhsin Beg as Sadun, a member of a family whose later history has been tragic to a degree.

But the new understanding implied a more rapid and complete devolution from the British Advisory officials to their Iraqi executives and a second letter (January 1930) to the officials defined the new position. This letter ran as follows:

## SECOND LETTER TO BRITISH OFFICIALS

THE RESIDENCY, BAGHDAD

, 1930

SIR,

By direction of the Secretary of State for the Colonies I have the honour to address you as follows:—

2. You are aware that, by Article III of the Anglo-Iraq Treaty of 1926, His Majesty's Government promised to take into active consideration at successive intervals of four years the question whether it was possible for them to press for the admission of Iraq into the League of Nations. By Article VIII of the unratified Treaty of December 1927, His Majesty's Government undertook to support the candidature of Iraq for admission to the League of Nations in 1932 (one of the quadrennial dates contemplated in the Treaty of 1926) "provided the present rate of progress in Iraq is maintained and all goes well in the interval." On the recommendation of the late Sir Gilbert Clayton, His Majesty's Government withdrew these provisos in an announcement which was made to the Iraq Government on September 14, 1929. They have now pledged themselves, without qualification, to support Iraq's candidature for admission to the League of Nations in 1932. They have done this because they are satisfied that the present treaty arrangements between His Majesty's Government and the Iraq Government are working satisfactorily and that there is a reasonable prospect that they will by 1932 have resulted in the Iraq Government having reached a stage of development which will satisfy the League of Nations that they are qualified for membership.

3. I need hardly say that there is no question of the relations between His Majesty's Government and the Iraq Government, as defined in the original Treaty of 1922, being altered in any way between now and the date when His Majesty's Government have undertaken to support the candidature of Iraq for admission to the League of Nations. At the same time, His Majesty's Government realize that in order to enable the Iraq Government to enter the League on that date, it is desirable to accelerate the assumption of administrative responsibility by the Iraq Government, so far as this is consistent with their treaty obligations. The Secretary of State has authorized me to consider sympathetically any proposals

which the Iraq Government may have to make with the object of ensuring this and it is in order that there may be no misunderstanding that I have invited His Majesty King Faisal to concur in the following general statement of the policy which I have decided to follow in this respect.

4. As you are aware from the terms of your original letter of appointment, His Majesty's Government have handed over to the Iraq Government the responsibility for the administration of the country, on the understanding that there is a sufficient number of British officials to ensure that the best possible use is made of the resources of the country and that the administration should conform to the traditions and principles of progressive and enlightened government. It is the intention and wish of His Majesty's Government, during the intervening period before Iraq is recommended for admission to the League, that a progressively increasing share in the responsibility for the administration of the country should be assumed by Iraqi Ministers and officials. This does not mean that there is to be a wholesale reduction in the number of British officials employed by the Iraq Government. On the contrary, such a reduction would, in the considered opinion of His Majesty's Government, be opposed to the best interest of Iraq and would in any case be unnecessary for the fulfilment of the policy enunciated above. It is, however, the desire of His Majesty's Government that, during the next few years, British officials should, as much as possible, leave the real, as well as the ostensible, control of administration in the hands of their Iraqi colleagues. Only thus can the latter be encouraged to assume an increasing measure of responsibility and to prepare themselves for the day when they will be in a position to carry on without British advice or assistance.

5. I shall of course rely upon the British Advisers to keep me informed of any reductions in the numbers of the British Advisory Staff which the Iraq Government may have in contemplation, and shall consider sympathetically the opinion of those Advisers on the question whether such reductions are likely to militate against the fulfilment of the principles referred to in the preceding paragraph. If the British Advisers concerned feel that this is likely to be the effect of any reductions contemplated by the Iraq Government, they should inform me accordingly in order that I may have an opportunity, should I consider such a course desirable, of discussing the matter with the Iraq Government.

6. In general I do not propose to intervene in any domestic matter where the responsible British Adviser concerned is satisfied that the action which the Iraq Government propose to take will ensure that the best possible use is made of the resources of the country and that the traditions and principles of progressive and enlightened government are upheld.

7. The existing system by which I am kept informed through the

members of my Staff of the inception and progress of any administrative measures which the Iraq Government may have in contemplation will remain unaltered. The object of this system is not to enable me to intervene in domestic matters with which His Majesty's Government have no concern, but merely in order to enable me to let it be known unofficially at the earliest possible stage, what attitude I intend to adopt in the event of the responsible British Adviser concerned being unsuccessful in inducing the Iraq Government to follow his advice. His Majesty's Government rely on the British Advisory Staff to continue in the future, as they have in the past, to give disinterested advice to the Iraq Government with the object of ensuring that Iraq shall be in a position to enter the League in 1932. The fact that His Majesty's Government have promised to further the candidature of Iraq for membership on that date renders it all the more desirable that the official intervention of the High Commissioner during the intervening period should be reduced to a minimum, and that every available opportunity should be seized to encourage the Iraqi Ministers and officials to shoulder an increasing measure of responsibility for the administration of the country.

8. I have shown a draft of this letter to His Majesty King Faisal, who has concurred in its terms and has asked me to express once more the deep gratitude of the Iraq Government for the devoted and disinterested work accomplished in circumstances of some difficulty by all the British officials whose services have been placed at their disposal by His Majesty's Government. His Majesty and myself are in full agreement that the question of the number of British officials to be employed in the Iraq Government remains one of the important matters referred to in Article IV of the Treaty of Alliance, and it will continue to be the subject of the closest co-operation between us.

I have the honour to be,<br>
Sir,<br>
Your obedient servant,

*His Majesty's High Commissioner for Iraq.*

The cardinal points are: the "acceleration of the assumption of administrative responsibility by the Iraq Government so far as consistent with treaty obligations"; British officials were, as much as possible, to leave the real as well as the ostensible control of administration in the hands of their Iraqi colleagues; the Iraqi Government was to have a fairly free hand in dismissing British officials; for the first time documentary reference is made to the possibility of British advice not being accepted. For a long time the Nationalists had been commenting adversely on the control which the High Commissioner continued to exercise. In all questions of importance, they said, the High Commissioner sent to the British officials—some of whom were still holding King George's commission —in the employment of the Iraqi Government, orders which those officials were bound to obey. In effect, therefore, argued the Nationalists, all that the Iraqi Ministers were allowed to deal with was questions of minor importance, and the British attitude was designed to prevent the Iraqi ministers and officials coming to grips with the responsibilities which—if Britain's promises were sincere —they would have to take up in 1932.

Not unnaturally difficulties arose also on personal issues. In cases where the Arab executive and his British adviser were on good terms and got on well together, the new dispensation worked smoothly enough. But where the Arab was obstinate or inefficient much ill-feeling was engendered. A further factor now entered. It became fashionable to express anti-British sentiments,[1] and it was fatal to a young official's chances of promotion if he were found to be pro-British, or too openly friendly with British people; young Arabs employed by British firms had their legs pulled by their friends for their "betrayal" of the Arab cause.

British advice, however much it was valued by the more responsible men within Government circles, was openly ridiculed in the press. Even the Antiquities Department was accused of robbery and fraud. Specimens of gold headgear worn by the ancient queens at Ur of the Chaldees were discovered and sent to the British Museum for restoration. It was at once put about that the originals were retained

[1] The reaction against the employment of British officials became pronounced in 1931. The British Director of Antiquities, who had been loaned by the British Museum, was due to return to his duties in London. The Iraqi Government asked the British authorities to find a successor, but the reply was that no British archaeologist of sufficient eminence could be got for the salary offered. The German authorities, who were then approached, said the same, whereupon the salary offered was raised to a level high enough to attract the best archaeologists in Germany, and an eminent German scholar was appointed, soon to become "Scientific Adviser to the Department," under an Iraqi nominal Director. Just before the mandate terminated, the Iraqi Government invited an American professor, Dr. Paul Monro, to report on the system of education which had been under British control and advice for ten years. After the Mandate terminated, a Dutch and a Danish expert were at once invited to report on what improvements could be effected in the Customs administration.

in London and worthless copies sent back to Baghdad.[1] A violent anti-Mandate demonstration took place in Baghdad in March 1930, and on instructions from the British Residency, British subjects were asked to remain indoors and British firms to close their places of business. A new treaty was clearly indicated. For Iraq and Britain alike time was getting short. For Iraq the new independence was approaching; for Britain the financial and military agreements were not yet on a satisfactory footing. In brief, it was now urgent that the post-Mandate relations of the two Governments should be finally regulated.

April 1930 saw the beginning, and June 1930, the end of the negotiations for the new treaty, which was ratified by a specially elected new Parliament. The text of this treaty will be found in Appendix A. Its salient points are: Provision for an offensive and defensive alliance, Britain to have right-of-way through Iraq for her armed forces; the continuance of British air-bases west of the Euphrates; the complete supersession of the existing agreements; the establishment of Iraq's sovereignty and her assumption of responsibility for her internal affairs. The treaty is for twenty-five years. It is discussed more fully in the next chapter, particularly in its bearing upon the question of the independence of Iraq.

Before closing this section it will be of interest to trace the development of Britain's chief civil representative in Iraq. During the war and until the end of the military occupation in 1920, the Civil Administration was a department, under a Civil Commissioner, whose function it was to re-start the country on a sound basis, with a progressive, enlightened and incorrupt government. When the League Mandate was accepted, the machinery provided for a High Commissioner, to whom the elected, or selected, Council of State was responsible. In those days mandates were new things, the country had just emerged from a serious rebellion, the Nationalists did not quite know what they wanted, there seemed no reason why the Mandate should not survive most of the adults then living in

[1] The Baghdad Press has in general been unable or unwilling to be convinced that the value of "antikas" lies not in their intrinsic worth as *objets d'art* but in the archaeological evidence they afford as they lie *in situ*. Perhaps this misconception is due to the Arabs' inability to understand that anybody should be willing to put up money for any object without the certainty of getting it back.

the country. It was inevitable therefore that the administration should be entirely and absolutely in the hands of the High Commissioner.

The change came gradually but with ever-increasing momentum. From being the constitutional ruler, the High Commissioner, at all times the representative of the League of Nations, became an adviser whose fate it was, as time went on, to have less and less attention paid to his advice. During all this period he was also acting as a British diplomatic representative engaged in negotiating treaties to the mutual benefit of his own country and the country in which his lot was cast. So far as British trading interests were concerned the British High Commissioner did little or nothing to help them. The argument used was that as the Mandate derived from the League, a position of partiality in commercial affairs could not properly be assumed. On the other hand, the High Commissioner from 1921 onwards was almost constantly engaged in treaty negotiations the object of which was to gain political advantages for Britain. Towards the end of the Mandate the High Commissioner was more and more becoming a specially privileged foreign representative, until with the Treaty of 1930 he became an Ambassador and the permanent *doyen* of the Diplomatic Corps in Baghdad. The Germans had already seen their opportunity. They already had on the spot their heaviest-calibre diplomat in the Middle East, and he it was who became the first German Minister.[1] The United States Government, in a sudden reshuffle, moved to Baghdad their most experienced consular representative in this part of the world and appointed him Minister.[2] The French were much less interested—their sphere of influence being on the Mediterranean side—and the Italians had their eyes elsewhere. Egypt, regarding herself as the leader among the Arab countries, did lip-service to Iraq's new independence but treated Iraq's representatives in Egypt with but modest courtesy. The two remaining diplomatic posts in Baghdad were maintained by the Turks and by the Persians. The Turks had forgotten their soreness over the Mosul frontier delimitation. King Faisal visited Ankara in 1931 and the seal was set on a *modus vivendi* which no "incidents" have upset. Persia maintains a Minister in Baghdad,

[1] Dr. F. Grobba, formerly Minister in Kabul.
[2] Mr. Paul Knabenshue, formerly Consul-General in Jerusalem.

and Iraq a Minister in Teheran. Apart from the question of the Persian transit trade through Iraq, which is discussed elsewhere,[1] Iraq holds the holy cities of the Shiahs.[2] In Najaf, Karbala, and Kadhimain the majority of the priesthood are Persians and most of the property-owners are Persians. Until Riza Shah stepped in and discouraged Persian pilgrims from going to Iraq on the ground that Persia had perfectly good shrines of her own, the pilgrimages from Persia were a source of considerable revenue. This fact, with the loss of the transit trade, has had an undoubted effect upon Iraq's Persian policy. The question of the Shatt-al-Arab is also a fruitful source of trouble.[3] All this time the keynote of Iraq's policy has been to obtain as much as possible for the new state consonant with the fact that Britain still holds the whip-hand politically and militarily. Britain's policy has been to hold to essentials and let the rest go.[4]

The attitude of the official Iraqi Opposition is here worthy of attention. For a number of years, up to the admission of Iraq to the League in 1932, this opposition was led by Yassin Pasha al Hashimi, a statesman of personality and great ability. Since then he has held the offices of Minister of Court and Finance Minister. His attitude briefly has been that the 1932 "independence" is not real independence. He has argued that no country can be independent if it has to rely on foreign troops for defence, and must also see foreign military bases established within its boundaries. The opposition has also very well-defined and somewhat extreme views regarding the military and international requirements of Britain, which proved such a stumbling-block in the succession of treaties between 1922 and 1930.

The position of the King also demands some attention. From his accession Faisal was recognized as head of the state. Before he was actually chosen, the British Government had done its best to ensure that he would support the British policy. In return he was guaranteed British support on a throne which to begin with might prove to be an uneasy one. By his charm of manner and his clever diplomacy Faisal within a year or two had put himself into a very strong position and had gained the confidence, good will and support of

---

[1] See p. 214.  [2] Persia is predominantly Shiah. See Chapter IX.
[3] See p. 126.  [4] See chapters on Communications and Oil.

the masses. While it remained true that in the final issue Britain could normally count on his support for her policy, it was clear that by becoming a British tool he would weaken his position among his ministers and subjects. For a decade he manipulated ministries, shelved awkward questions, and balanced issues as between Britain and his own extremists, until Iraq had been successfully steered into independence in 1932. During those years he repeatedly proved his amazing cleverness as a diplomatist—everything that Iraq achieved appeared to be achieved by him—and it was not until 1933 that he found himself, as he thought, in an impossible position. In August of that year, ten months after Iraq had achieved her independence, the Assyrian trouble[1] compelled his early return to Baghdad from Switzerland, whither he had proceeded after visiting London. In the spring he had re-shuffled his cabinet, holding the opinion that during his absence such a re-shuffle would ensure a better balance. The mismanagement of the Assyrian affair he knew would be certain to raise awkward questions in Europe and he determined on a new re-shuffle. But under the constitution, the King can only *accept* a Cabinet's resignation; and it is not incumbent upon a Cabinet to resign unless at least four ministers go out. He found three willing to go out but could not find a fourth. After the Simel massacre on August 11th, he determined to return to Europe in order to recover his health. Many said his intention was to abdicate. The Assyrian affair, and his certainty of the trouble it would cause to Iraq, had thrown him into a state of acute collapse, aggravating his ill-health, and after remaining in Baghdad long enough to discuss the situation with the British Ambassador, who had been recalled from leave for the purpose, he returned to Switzerland at the end of the month. Within a week, on September 8th, he was dead.

Baghdad was stunned. The situation at the moment was electric. Anything, it was recognized, might happen, the King's death was the one thing no one expected. The position changed at once. Faisal had been the only person able to manipulate the factious leaders and bring the intrigues of Iraqi politics into some kind of satisfactory relationship with Britain. Now he was gone and his heir was his young son of twenty-two. Faisal had been the leader of some of his

[1] See pp. 139 *et seqq.*

Ministers since the days when they had served together in the desert with Lawrence. Not surprisingly were they rudderless. It is true to say that Faisal, in the first few months after his death, was more generally popular in Baghdad than he had ever been in his lifetime. His untimely death was a heavy blow to his people and they did not realize his inestimable worth to the country of his adoption until it was too late.

CHAPTER V

# THE LEAGUE OF NATIONS AND IRAQ'S INDEPENDENCE

THE Opposition party in Iraq, as has been shown in the preceding chapter, have consistently argued that the "independence" of Iraq under the 1930 treaty is neither real nor complete. This was clearly the view of many at Geneva when the British Government's decision to postpone full independence for Iraq was officially brought before the League of Nations.

It was the first occasion on which had arisen the involved questions of determining *how* a League Mandate should end; what conditions, if any, should be imposed; and how the territory in question should qualify for League membership. The British proposal was put forward in November 1929, the British Government having already assured King Faisal that it would, without qualification or proviso, support Iraq's candidature for League membership in 1932. Three months after receiving the British proposal the Council of the League asked the Permanent Mandates Commission of the League to draw up general conditions on which a mandate might be terminated. After lengthy discussions of the legal questions involved, the Permanent Mandates Commission at last formulated, in June 1931, the general conditions for which the Council had asked; they were accepted by the Council on September 4, 1931.[1] The Commission declared that whether a people was, in the words of the Covenant, capable of standing alone, was a question of fact and not of principle, and could be settled only by careful observation of its political, social and economic development. The pre-requisites laid down and accepted were five in number. In order to secure release from a mandate, a state must:

(a) have a settled government and an administration capable of maintaining the regular operation of essential government services;
(b) be capable of maintaining its territorial integrity and political independence;

---

[1] *Minutes of the 64th Session of the Council*, p. 2055.

(c) be able to maintain internal peace and order;
(d) have at its disposal adequate financial resources to provide regularly for normal governmental requirements;
(e) possess laws and a judicial organization which will afford equal and regular justice to all.

The Commission at the same time insisted that before release from a mandate a new state should guarantee the protection of minorities, the judicial rights of foreigners, freedom of conscience and worship, and the free exercise of missions. It should also assume all obligations legally acquired during the mandatory regime.

During the next two months the Commission gave its attention to applying these conditions to the case of Iraq, devoting particular study—at the request of the Council—to the 1930 treaty which in the opinion of some was not compatible with Iraq's independence. In acquiring the information which it must have before coming to any decision, the Commission decided that it must rely on the reports of the mandatory Power. The British Colonial Office had issued annual progress reports since 1920, and in addition a special report on the "Progress of Iraq during the period 1920–1931." In the nature of things these reports had been at all stages most carefully edited in accordance with British policy. They contained no errors or mis-statements, except by occasional inadvertence; but clearly it was beyond the ability of most of the League *personnel* in Geneva to make good any omission, to detect any whitewashing, to fill out any understatement or check any exaggeration dictated by policy. The Commission decided at the same time to examine the British officials concerned. Thus the only information officially available to the members of the Commission was British, and some of them argued that the Commission should go no farther than a declaration that it could see no reason "to oppose the statement of the British Government as to the maturity of Iraq" and should not declare its own opinion on this point. In the end the Commission decided to base its judgment on the British presentation of the case. It recalled a statement, a few months earlier, by the British High Commissioner, that should Iraq "prove unworthy of the confidence which has been placed in her, the moral responsibility must rest with His Majesty's Government"; and it concluded[1] "Had it not

[1] Permanent Mandates Commission: *Minutes of the 21st Session*, p. 222.

been for this declaration the Commission would have been unable to contemplate the termination of a regime which appeared some years ago to be necessary in the interests of all sections of the population." The Commission then proceeded to apply the five test points to the case of Iraq, in the light of the information supplied by the British reports and extracted, in personal examination, from the British representatives. From the beginning the British Government took the line that the attainment of an ideal standard of administrative efficiency was not a necessary condition either of the termination of the mandatory regime or of the admission of Iraq to membership of the League of Nations. The Commission accepted this in its application of the five points.

The first point was "a settled government and an administration capable of maintaining the regular operation of essential governmental services." The Commission accepted this assumption in the case of Iraq, adding that it had "no information which would justify a contrary opinion."

The second point was capability "of maintaining territorial integrity and political independence." In fact, the Commission found that Iraq did not have military forces sufficient to maintain its frontiers and independence, but that if released from the mandate it would be protected both by its League membership and its alliance with Britain. On these grounds the Commission found that Iraq met the second condition.

The third point was "ability to maintain internal peace and order." On this the Commission accepted the British assurances in the absence of information to the contrary. It is a strange commentary that within ten months of independence the Assyrian question should have blazed up into rebellion and massacre.

The fourth point was "adequate finance." On this the Commission expressed no opinion, on the ground that Iraq's credit had not yet been tested, although it admitted the soundness of the existing financial position and the "considerable" volume of the country's potential resources. On the whole it found nothing in the information supplied by Britain "to cause it to doubt Iraq's ability to provide regularly for normal governmental requirements."

The fifth point was "laws and a judicial organization which will afford equal and regular justice to all." The Commission agreed, "subject to certain re-adjustment and improvements," that this point was adequately met.

Thus the British assurances of Iraq's maturity were accepted by the Permanent Mandates Commission with marked hesitation. In Iraq itself the general feeling of the European communities (not merely the British) was that the British reports were whitewashing reports and that Britain was scuttling out of the mandate too soon. The official reply was repeated, that Iraq was at least as advanced as some states already independent and members of the League.[1] It was further to be feared that if Geneva had refused to accept the British assurances, the Arabs would at once have assumed that such a refusal could only be the result of Britain's Machiavellian policy and further trouble would have ensued. It is certain that it was now too late to go back. The British policy of hastening the termination of the mandate was decided upon by the Socialist Government in 1929, and from that date the British withdrawal from the control of affairs became more and more complete.

It has been stated that the Permanent Mandates Commission was unwilling to agree to the termination of the Iraq Mandate. Repeatedly in the minutes of the proceedings there are hints and suggestions by various members of the Commission that in their view it was not Iraq's maturity but British policy that was behind the British proposal. Study of the documents proves clearly that within the Commission there was for long considerable opposition to terminating a mandate which only a decade previously had been regarded as necessary in view of Iraq's backward condition. Grudgingly the Commission finally accepted the British proposal, but at the same time it drew up certain guarantees which Iraq had to give. The five test-points affected Iraq herself; the guarantees were on questions of international concern. These guarantees covered the national minorities, the judicial administration, and commercial relations with states members of the League.

As will be seen more fully in the chapter on Minorities, both Kurds and Assyrians had complained to the League that the 1930 Treaty offered them no satisfactory guarantees. While the British Government's case was that such guarantees regarding the treatment of minorities could not properly find a place in a treaty between

[1] But Iraq was not yet a homogeneous nation.

friendly and independent[1] states, the Permanent Mandates Commission, expressing no opinion on that point, was none the less seriously concerned about the omission, which it proceeded to make good. These guarantees, accepted by Iraq in May 1932, were to be recognized as part of the law of Iraq. They provided for no discrimination in elections, in appointments, in religion, in language, in the expression of public opinion,[2] and they were declared to constitute international obligations under the League.

The second guarantee demanded by the League Council was one safeguarding foreign interests in the Iraqi Courts. There was in existence a judicial agreement of March 1931, between Iraq and Britain, due to expire on Iraq's entering the League as an independent state member. This agreement put an end to special treatment for foreigners in the Iraqi Courts and set up what was called "a uniform system of justice" for natives and foreigners alike. At the same time it provided for nine British judges. These judges were all to be on long contracts. The Permanent Mandates Commission finding that some of these judges were still to be appointed, insisted that they should be "selected without distinction of nationality." The British Government found it easy to agree to this, as practically no country but Britain has a cadre of Arabic-speaking European judges.

It will be recalled that in the early days of the war it was generally assumed that in the event of victory Britain would take Mesopotamia. During the peace negotiations this idea disappeared from view and in its place the mandate came into being. The mandate for Iraq was awarded to Britain as the most interested Power, and the preceding chapter shows how the years of the mandatory regime were occupied by Britain in trying to find a suitable basis for Anglo-Iraqi relations after the termination of the mandate. Such a basis was found in the 1930 treaty which, whatever it may have conferred on Iraq, gave to Britain certain political and strategic advantages at a relatively low cost. The world at large had few objections to offer to this political predominance, but the discussions at Geneva showed that there existed a strong feeling that Britain should not be permitted to turn this into economic predominance also. The Commission therefore suggested at first that Iraq, on

---

[1] The Treaty was only to become operative when Iraq attained independence.    [2] But see the provisions of the Press Law, p. 180.

attaining independence and League membership should grant most-favoured-nation treatment to all states members of the League. Italy at once demanded that new states should only establish their economic independence upon the twin base of "reciprocity and the open door." Thereupon the League Council ordered an examination, in this light, of the 1930 Treaty. The Permanent Mandates Commission discovered nothing sinister in it and Britain announced (1931) that no commercial agreement should be negotiated until the mandate had been terminated. Regarding the duration of the most-favoured-nation treatment to states members of the League, a period of ten years was fixed, subject to reciprocity and some minor qualifications. These various guarantees were finally admitted by Iraq to be international, and to be unalterable except by the League Council's consent.

The Permanent Mandates Commission then took up the question whether the treaty was compatible with Iraq's independence. The treaty, to remain in force for a period of twenty-five years, is a treaty of alliance. The maintenance of order is declared to be Iraq's own affair. The maintenance and preservation of British imperial communications is to be Britain's affair, Iraq merely providing on certain terms the military bases necessary for the purpose. During the validity of the treaty Britain is to have air-bases west of the Euphrates, any bases now in existence east of that river to be removed by 1937. The bases will be two in number—a big one near Habbaniyah, about fifty miles west of Baghdad, and a smaller one near Basrah.[1] The treaty expressly provides that these bases and the presence of British armed forces "shall not constitute in any manner an occupation and will in no way prejudice the sovereign rights of Iraq." The treaty further provides for the grant of "all possible facilities" for the movement of British forces of all kinds across the country, and in brief is the instrument of an extremely close military alliance between the two countries.

This was clearly seen at Geneva, where several members of the Permanent Mandates Commission subjected the treaty to intense criticism, on the ground that it proved Iraq's inability either to defend herself or to stand up in independence of the special position which Britain was to enjoy within her frontier, and that if Iraq

[1] See Chapter on British Imperial Communications.

still needed British armed forces in the country for a generation then the mandate should not be terminated. The British Government pointed out in reply that if the alliance were to exist at all is must be fulfilled in the only way in which it could be put into execution; and that in any case the strength of the British Air Force in Iraq would probably not exceed two thousand. It was also pointed out that Britain would in no way be able to control the Legislature in Baghdad. Italy expressed the fear that while Britain could easily watch Iraq's policy, Iraq could not in any way control British policy; the reply was that Britain was anxious to ensure that no future government in Baghdad should embark on a policy likely to involve Britain with other states in the Middle East. The doubts which existed that under the treaty the weaker partner might lose its independence, crystallized in the Commission's final resolution, accepted by the Council. It ran thus:

After having carefully considered the text of these undertakings and having heard the explanations and information on the subject from the accredited representative, the Commission came to the conclusion that, although certain of the provisions of the Treaty of Alliance of June 30, 1930, were somewhat unusual in treaties of this kind, the obligations entered into by Iraq towards Great Britain did not explicitly infringe the independence of the new state.

To the 1930 treaty there was appended a financial agreement setting out Iraq's obligations to Britain, obligations which came under three heads—military works, the Iraq Railways and the Port of Basrah. The property at the air-bases which Britain is to evacuate is to be bought by Iraq at one-third of the cost price—a valuation which is causing much difficulty in view of the fall in prices during the intervening years and the strong feeling that exists in Iraq that a depreciation of two-thirds is not enough. Britain is to continue to pay rent for all retained properties, and the new bases are to be rent free if on waste land, and if on non-government land to be leased by the Iraqi Government at Britain's expense.

The railways settlement has been hanging fire for years. Apart from a comparatively small stretch, the railway system of Iraq was born of the war, being brought into being by Britain. Since then it has laboured under considerable financial difficulties. Iraqis say that the difficulties have been caused by the high salaries of the big

British staff; on the other hand, had it not been for this British staff the railways would not have reached their present state of efficiency. Under the financial agreement legal ownership will be vested in Iraq, with beneficial ownership in a statutory trust, to which the management and control will be transferred from the Government department which has been responsible for the working of the railways in the past. The capital involved is over £4,000,000 (gold). Of this nearly half is to be assigned to Britain in 6 per cent preferred stock, non-cumulative for twenty years and cumulative thereafter. Iraq is to have Rs.45.85 lakhs of preferred stock, the rest of her share being in deferred or common stock. Iraq has the option of buying the British share at any time at par. The Rs.45.85 lakhs represents interest-free loans made by Iraq to the railways. Several members of the Permanent Mandates Commission seemed to feel that the agreement might bear too heavily on Iraq and that it might give Britain too thorough-going a control over the railways. But the Commission finally accepted the arrangement as a fair one, having regard to the fact that the railways cost Britain in all about fourteen and a half million gold pounds and that their valuation in 1930–31 was approximately £3,400,000, whereas Britain under the agreement was to get for them only about £2,000,000.

As with the Railways so with the Port of Basrah. In 1914 the Port of Basrah as such did not exist;[1] to-day it is a flourishing concern. The present administration, which is a department of the Iraqi Ministry of Finance, took over the port equipment from the British Government in 1920 at an agreed price of Rs. 72,11,654–3–0, payable over thirty years at 5 per cent; of this total about 50 lakhs are still unpaid. Under the new financial agreement, the Iraq Government acquires the legal ownership, the beneficial ownership being vested in a statutory Port Trust, the powers of which may not be changed without British consent as long as any of the debt to Britain remains unpaid. This debt is in respect of the purchase of the Port property, wharfage and sheds, etc.; the loan raised by the Port for dredging purposes is in a separate category and is being paid off by special *ad hoc* dues. Under the new agreement Britain agrees to accept as full payment less than 5 per cent of the amount she spent on the Port. This was described, even by members of

[1] See Chapter XIV.

the Commission who had shown themselves to be most critical during the discussion of the termination of Iraq's mandate, as being "extremely generous."

This concluded the examination by the Permanent Mandates Commission, of the questions remitted to them by the Council of the League. The report of the Commission, approving—as has been shown above—the termination of the mandate and recommending the guarantees to be given by the new state, was approved by the Council in January 1932, subject to Iraq's formal acceptance of the guarantees and on condition that the mandate should end "only as from the date on which Iraq has been admitted to the League of Nations." The guarantees were formally accepted by Iraq in May, and the Baghdad Government in July requested that Iraq's application should be placed on the agenda of the September meeting of the Assembly of the League. Owing to some formal error, the question was at first not put on the agenda, and in the late summer of 1932 Baghdad buzzed with rumours that Britain's *mala fides* had once again put the coveted prize beyond Iraq's reach. These fears proved groundless. When the Assembly met, there was no difficulty at all. Iraq was welcomed into the League as a full independent member, and on that day, October 3, 1932, the mandate came to an end and the High Commissioner became the Ambassador at a foreign court.

# CHAPTER VI

## THE R.A.F. AND THE NEW IRAQ

THE new State of Iraq owes to the British Royal Air Force a debt bigger than it can ever repay. For it was the work of the Air Force which more than anything else enabled the League of Nations in 1932 to decide that Iraq was fit for independence.

It has been shown how at the Cairo Conference of 1921, the decision was reached to substitute air control for the existing form of control in Iraq, and the Air Force formally took over responsibility on October 1, 1922. From that date onwards Iraq was under air control. The official definition of air control is as follows:

The political administration of undeveloped countries inhabited by backward and semi-civilized populations, rests in the last resort upon military force in one form or another. The term "air control" implies that control is applied by aircraft as the primary arm, usually supplemented by forces on the ground, which may be armoured vehicles, regular or irregular troops, armed police or tribal forces according to particular requirements.

The late Sir Henry Dobbs, a former High Commissioner for Iraq, framed the following definition. Air control, he said, means

that in the selected region the Royal Air Force shall be considered a predominant arm, and that the general control of all forces in the region shall lie with Air Headquarters, in consultation with responsible representatives of other forces employed, whether naval, military or police. There is, so far at least as land is concerned, no proposal that other forces shall be completely abolished and replaced by air forces. No one pretends that a troublesome tract can be held by Air Forces, without the help of a single soldier, or "irregular," or policeman.

Air control is claimed to be the cheapest, quickest and most effective method of dealing with inaccessible regions peopled by backward and troublesome peoples. Some of these regions are in fact inaccessible to such a degree as to make ground action so costly, that in the past the despatch of a column has invariably been delayed until, the tribesmen getting bolder and bolder, a long score finally has to be paid off. This frequently has involved heavy casualties both in the course of fighting and as the result of sickness and disease. The air-arm, spending its nights comfortably in secure bases, can now be on the spot as soon as trouble breaks; indeed the droning of the aeroplanes overhead often catches the tribesmen while their plans are still incomplete. Air control is thus speedy, as well as being economical (both of life and money). Its powers of penetration are incomparably superior to those of land forces; so too its invulnerability. These claims can scarcely be contested.

Psychologically, the effect of air control upon tribesmen is intensely interesting. The mountain tribesmen of Iraq quite enjoy a scrap provided there is the prospect of loot. The advance of a big military column into their guerrilla country thus affords a first-rate opportunity of replenishing their supplies of arms, ammunition and general stores. Air action, however, offers no such plums, and air tactics see to it that the tribesmen are kept uncomfortable. By bombing and threats of bombing they are kept away from their villages and their food and water supplies. The discomfort of life in caves and other places of refuge soon drives them to contemplate submission, particularly if their flocks and property have not been completely scattered or destroyed. There is indeed no point in destruction of the villages from the air, for that simply turns the harried tribesmen into brigands, thus increasing the general insecurity and unrest in the neighbourhood. A necessary corollary of air control is the provision of intelligence officers and wireless operators at all key points, so that the air-arm is fully and accurately aware of all personalities and policies in the region affected. The result of all this co-operation is that order is kept at much less expense than in any other way, particularly in countries such as Iraq, where the advantage of terrain is all on the side of the recalcitrant tribesmen.

The method generally employed is to drop leaflets warning the recalcitrant villagers to clear out, a time limit being attached to this "ultimatum" within which they may come to terms. The inhabitants then move out of their villages, taking with them their cattle and all they need. They have been told that any showing themselves in the open are liable to be shot or bombed; so they usually hide in caves. The empty villages are not destroyed, an occasional bomb being dropped, partly to keep the villagers from returning, partly to show that the aeroplanes if they liked could reduce the mud huts to ruins in a few minutes. As the days pass, life in the hiding places becomes more and more uncomfortable, for it is dangerous to come out into the open for any purpose whatever, and supplies soon begin to go down. There is prospect neither of retaliation nor loot, and submission is a matter of time. There have been in all likelihood no casualties, but flocks have strayed, houses have to be built up again, and in general the affair has been a nuisance, without the fight which is half the fun to the tribesmen. The political administration of the area can then proceed.

In Iraq the cost of the R.A.F. services to the British Exchequer is now less than £1,500,000 a year.[1] Air Control has been organized on the lines described above. The Iraqi Air Force is as yet only adolescent, and the Iraqi Army for the first few years after 1920 was by no means capable of standing on its own feet. Within that period there was an invasion by the Turks, two "invasions" by the Akhwan of the southern desert, a group of serious rebellions in Kurdistan, and minor troubles on the middle Euphrates and in the marshes of the Hammar Lakes. Under the 1930 treaty Britain is pledged to help Iraqi against external aggression; from 1930 to 1932 Iraq's chief trouble was rebellious Kurdistan, a purely internal issue. Yet nothing is more certain than that Air Force rapidity prevented these small affairs from becoming big.

The Turkish "invasion" took place in 1922. The Turks were just rising to their knees, having been fighting continuously since 1911 in various wars against various enemies and always on the losing side. They were putting up a fight for the Mosul *vilayet*, and, but for the fact that they were hampered by the knowledge that an Italian invasion of Anatolia was contemplated, they might have caused much trouble in the north of Iraq. The new Arab army was of little use, British troops would have had to be brought back, at great cost and doubtless to the accompaniment of a great outcry in England. But the Royal Air Force, cheaply and speedily, bombed the Turkish columns out of Rowanduz and the frontier has been peaceful ever since.

The Akhwan trouble was if anything more serious and more

[1] See p. 77.

long drawn out. In the chapter on Foreign Relations[1] is is shown that the Najd frontier is one that has potentialities of trouble for Iraq. The successive reduction by Ibn Saud of Hayil and Mecca meant that he had no other open frontier save the new delimited one with Iraq. By 1927 raids from Najd territory had become so serious a problem that operations on a comparatively big scale had to be undertaken. The success of these was due primarily to the work of the R.A.F. aeroplanes and armoured cars. The Iraqi authorities set up police posts in the southern desert, the object of these being to try to stop raiding (in which they were ineffectual), to aid intelligence (in which the system proved slower than aeroplanes) and to protect advanced landing grounds (in which they were of some use). The Basrah garrison was reinforced by the Iraqi authorities and blockhouses were constructed to cover the Zubair gap, the Arab army being concentrated at Zubair. Advanced air headquarters were established at Ur, where there were three bombing squadrons, six sections of armoured cars, and the Iraqi army's motor machine-gun section. The raiding from Najd continued into 1928, but the Iraqi shepherds[2] had by then been withdrawn, and Faisal ad-Dawish, the Najdi leader turned his attention to Kuwait, whose shaikh was in close treaty relations with Britain. The relationship between Faisal ad-Dawish and Ibn Saud has never been satisfactorily ascertained. Officially he was leading a rebellion of the Mutair tribesmen against Ibn Saud, but some of the tribal movements were conceived and carried out in such a way as to lead to the assumption that they might be official Najdi movements against Iraq. For instance, the Busaiyah raid of November 5–6, 1927, when a small Iraqi police post was wiped out and the men massacred and mutilated was certainly a deliberate attack on the Iraqi Government and was intended by Ibn Saud to be such. By 1929 it was becoming clear that the British R.A.F. counter-measures must in the long run establish the desert frontier in security and it was brought home to Ibn Saud that he had two alternatives—he must control his tribes or fall out with the British Government. He was not prepared to do the latter, and so Faisal ad-Dawish became officially a rebel against his authority. Having lost Ibn Saud's backing his end did not remain long in doubt, and the

[1] See p. 127.　　　　　　　　　　　[2] See pp. 128–30.

# The R.A.F. and the New Iraq

R.A.F. rounded him up at Jahrah, near Kuwait, at the end of 1929, and since then the southern desert frontier has been quiet.

The rest of the Royal Air Force operations in Iraq since 1922 were undertaken with the object of establishing the Baghdad Government's authority within its frontiers. It may be stated here that the fact that there was no trouble in the north-west mountains was largely due to the fact that the Assyrians, enlisted in the Levies, regarded themselves as *protégés* of the British, whom they did not expect to cease having responsibility for internal order in Iraq as soon as 1932.[1] In the north-east there was trouble with the Kurds almost continuously, rising to a periodical climax with the movements headed by Shaikh Mahmud in 1922-23, in 1927 and again in 1930-31; and by Shaikh Ahmed of Barzan in 1932. These "troubles" were serious ones, and it is no exaggeration to say that but for British air co-operation Kurdistan to-day would not be administered by an Arab Government in Baghdad. The later rebellions, following, that is, the signing of the 1930 treaty between Britain and Iraq, were the most serious. For the Kurds realized that they would have few more chances of upsetting Iraq's entry into the League, and British policy had to ensure that there was no mistake about the Kurdish defeat. Shaikh Mahmud was an insurgent leader moving through territory administered by the Baghdad Government and inhabited by people, numbers of whom were not openly hostile to the Iraqi Government. Shaikh Ahmed, however, was the powerful leader (whose influence was religious as well as political) of a compact, inaccessible territory, which had never been properly administered and was to all intents and purposes an enemy land. The Air Force action was primarily in support of the Iraqi ground troops, but latterly, especially in the Barzan operations of 1932, the British aeroplanes were compelled to take a major part in the actual hostilities.[2] So confident of success was Shaikh Ahmed that on one occasion (April 26, 1932) when a British machine was forced down and its pilot injured, he permitted medical assistance to be brought to the injured man, but soon made it clear that any political messenger coming with the offer of terms would be shot. But the inevitable end came before long and the continued pressure from the air compelled Shaikh Ahmed to

[1] See pp. 139 *et seqq.* for the political aspect.  [2] See p. 138 for further details.

117

disappear across the frontier and surrender to the Turkish authorities.

Two minor internal operations had to be undertaken by the Royal Air Force. Trouble on the middle Euphrates, that perennial source of rebellion, about which the Baghdad Government is probably more seriously concerned than about any other problem that faces it, arose in 1923, when the priesthood of the Holy Cities, ever drawing their inspiration from Persia, fomented a subversive movement among the tribes. It was stopped almost at once by air action, and the police then passed through the district and there was no more trouble. In 1925 a small shaikh in the Hammar Lakes area suddenly become rebellious. The marshes and the 30-foot reeds in the waterways surrounding his village made him completely inaccessible, but air action solved the problem without loss of time.

The most ignorant tribesmen in Iraq now know what the aeroplane means. In the old days, when an insurrectionary movement began, the people in the region affected would sit on the fence until they thought they saw clearly which side was winning. To-day the aeroplane makes them sit on the fence much longer, and that margin of time is just enough to prevent the rapid and dangerous spread of any rebellious movement. There is no doubt at all that the Kurdish troubles since 1930 would have prevented any satisfactory compliance being given at Geneva in 1932 with at least two of the five conditions[1] which, it was decided, every mandated territory as candidate for independence must fulfil. These are: its possession of a settled Government and administration within its territories, and its ability to maintain internal peace and order. As Chapter V shows it was in 1932 hard enough to squeeze Iraq through this needle's eye; with Kurdistan in flames it would have been manifestly impossible. The extremer Iraqi nationalists have of course alleged that Britain is using Iraq for her own ends, and that the crushing burden of taxation necessary to maintain the Iraqi army and police is really in British interests and in effect saves the British tax-payer the cost of maintaining British ground troops to back the work of the R.A.F. This is merely begging the question. British policy demands a strong Iraq; without British air backing Iraq would not

[1] See p. 104.

have come near independence in 1932. At present the Iraqi Air Force is not yet fit to assume the entire responsibility.

The extreme difficulty of the terrain is the final point that must be borne in mind in estimating the value of the work done by the British R.A.F. in Iraq. In the desert the success of operations has depended on the provision of dumps and landing-grounds and the careful air surveys made by the Air Force. For the desert surface is deceptive and what looks solid from the air may merely be a baked crust on top of mud, or the surface may in some other way be entirely unsuitable for landing. So far as the northern operations are concerned, it may be said that in the mountains there are no landing-grounds at all, and on every flight up the precipitous gorges and over the barren peaks and summits of Kurdistan, the pilots took their lives in their hands.

## CHAPTER VII

## DEFENCE AND FOREIGN RELATIONS

IT was early seen that independence, the ultimate goal of the Mandatory policy, would be a vain gift to Iraq unless she had the strength to hold it against all comers. By 1921 at Cairo the British Government had completed its consideration of this aspect of the question, and the decision was reached that until Iraq's own national forces were ready to assume the burden in its entirety, Britain would undertake the defence of the country. At the same time it was decided, as a measure of economy, that the Royal Air Force should take over the responsibility from the Army.[1] This was done as from October 1, 1922. In addition to sending out the Royal Air Force, Britain took over a small force of Levies, mostly Assyrians, organized on Indian Army lines. According to the *Progress of Iraq* it was decided not to embody this force in the new Iraqi army, because there was an insufficient supply of trained Iraqi officers immediately available to fill the higher ranks, and it was not the intention to ask British officers to exercise executive command in the Iraqi army. The decision thus to recruit and maintain the Levies, in addition to meeting these requirements, had the further merit of ensuring the existence within the country of a force loyal to Britain and possessing an efficiency and reliability that could be depended upon absolutely. The Levies—they latterly had become entirely Assyrian—were a splendid body of men and there was no trouble with them until the summer of 1932, when the prospect of Iraq's independence in the autumn led them to make certain political demands, and numbers took advantage of the opportunity to leave the service.[2] Since then the Levies, not now entirely Assyrian, have been reconstituted as aerodrome and other guards. They remain, however, British-officered and British-maintained, in effect a small but sturdy force of British infantry.

The British Royal Air Force maintains a full Command in Iraq, with an Air Vice-Marshal as Air Officer Commanding. At present the Air Headquarters are at Hinaidi, a few miles south of Baghdad,

[1] See p. 77.  [2] See p. 141.

ENTRANCE TO THE MOSQUE AT KADHIMAIN

THE GOLDEN DOMES OF KADHIMAIN

on the east side of the Tigris. Here there are hangars, depots and supply dumps, and all the multitudinous offices of a general headquarters. Alone among the Royal Air Force overseas commands, the term of service in Iraq is two years, as against five in India and Egypt. Thus on the average two-and-a-half times as many pilots per squadron have served in Iraq as anywhere else, thus providing a big reserve of officers who know every foot of the terrain between the Eastern Mediterranean and the Persian and Turkish frontiers of Iraq, and every part of the Arabian coast of the Persian Gulf. In addition the almost constant operations against the Kurdish and other tribes during the past ten years have provided experience under war conditions for a very large number of British pilots. Recently long flights have been carried out from Iraq to the North-West Frontier of India and other places in the East.

The effective troops at Hinaidi comprise a bomber-transport squadron, a bomber squadron, and an Armoured Car Company. At Mosul there is one bomber squadron and at Shaibah, about seventeen miles from Basrah, towards the desert, there is another bomber squadron. Basrah and Mosul also have armoured car detachments and Basrah has a squadron of flying-boats the main duties of which are to link up with the patrolling work of the Royal Navy in the Persian Gulf. This squadron has also carried out flights to and from the Mediterranean, India and Australia.

The Royal Air Force are thus within easy reach of any frontier, whether with planes or armoured cars. They maintain constant air communication with the R.A.F. Command in Egypt, and practically the whole of the desert is now completely surveyed, with landing-places and dumps arranged along all the main flying-routes. The Air Force also maintains a most thoroughgoing and effective intelligence service covering almost the whole of the Middle East. The military operations of the Royal Air Force since 1922 have been chiefly concerned with the establishing of effective Iraqi control over recalcitrant chieftains, rather than with fighting external enemies.[1]

The Iraqi Army is a voluntary service army. Men enlist for two years and may re-engage. The recruits are of a fair to good type and make good material. A conscription law has been passed, partly

[1] For a fuller discussion of the work of the R.A.F. in Iraq, see Chap. VI.

because conscripts are cheaper than voluntary troops, largely because of the feeling that the country cannot be really independent while a foreign military force is based within its frontiers for its defence. But it will be difficult to apply conscription to the tribes, and the townspeople would not tolerate discrimination in favour of the tribes—apart from the effendis' dislike of the prospect of military service, however much it might improve the physique of the younger generation. The youngsters still at school, however, are already taking up scouting and games with zeal, and it may be that national service will be easier to achieve in a few years than it would be at present. It should be noted that conscription was one of the first proposals put forward in 1921 by the Arab officers, now largely Iraqi Ministers, who came from Syria with the new King.

The Army has been trained by a British mission. The senior officers are mostly Turkish-trained, and they often speak Turkish in their messes. But the juniors, many of whom have been at Sandhurst, are all trained on British lines. There are curious differences. When an airman has been lost in the desert, the older tradition has been against the expenditure of money on saving the life, although an expedition to salve the machine would be understood. The British conception of saving the man and if necessary writing off the machine, is a new one. The immediate issue is whether the younger officers can hold on to their training ideals until the older men have disappeared. The events of 1933[1] showed that the army was most violently anti-British, far more so than the Iraqi civil authorities. With the slackening of British control and the possible further reduction of the British mission, it is not certain what will happen. In many respects the behaviour of the Iraqi Army during the Barzan operations left much to be desired.[2]

So far as the Iraqi Air Force is concerned there is no old Turkish tradition to contend with. Iraq is rapidly becoming an air-minded nation, situated as it is on one of the great world-routes and realizing as it does that in certain areas among the northern mountains air action is the only action possible. The principal towns and provinces of Iraq have all been raising funds for the purchase of further aeroplanes, and the production of Iraqi pilots has become one of the major needs of the moment. A suggestion has been made that a

[1] See p. 139.          [2] See p. 117 and p. 138.

training school for pilots and mechanics should be established in Baghdad, in order to save some of the high costs involved in sending young men to England for training.

The 1930 treaty provides for a mutually defensive alliance between Britain and Iraq.[1] The assistance that Iraq could give to Britain in the event of a war in which Britain was engaged would be the provision of a base between Palestine and the Persian Gulf. The assistance which Britain could give to Iraq would be, in the event of a war between Iraq and any of the neighbouring states—Turkey, Persia, Najd. Syria and Palestine (with Transjordan) although neighbouring states, may be ruled out as aggressors. The possibility of the Iraq Government being unable to cope with internal risings is ignored by the Treaty. In such an event Britain would be directly interested if British communications between the Mediterranean and the East were threatened or affected. The question has been asked whether British military aid would be put at the disposal of the Iraqi Government in the event of internal revolts, precipitated by the policy of the Iraqi Government, a policy with which Britain through her Ambassador might even have discountenanced. Most questions of the kind, however, are questions of political opinion rather than of military fact, and in practice what will happen is that each case will be determined on its merits, and Britain will act in furtherance of her interests. It might be that her interests would call for intervention in an internal rising on an issue on which the Iraqi Government was demonstrably in the wrong, but British interests are bound to be the deciding factor. The official British reply has invariably been that Britain would intervene only if British interests were concerned. This does not answer the question, What are British interests? Clearly the Baghdad–Basrah railway is a major British interest, and the railway is the first thing that would be attacked if trouble arose on the Middle Euphrates, the most dangerous district of all. What would be Britain's policy if it were found, on investigation, that such a rising was due to maladministration from Baghdad? Once the rising had been put down by British aeroplanes, would not Britain insist on safeguards to prevent any recurrence?

Turkey and Persia are the two neighbouring states sufficiently

[1] See Appendix A and chapter on British Imperial Communications.

organized to fight Iraq. Najd does not possess such an organization, but she holds perhaps more potentialities for trouble. In the case of Turkey and Persia Iraq has established satisfactory relations, and Ibn Saud, King of the Hidjaz and Najd, with whom friendly agreements have also been made, has found his finances seriously affected by the comparative failure of the great Mecca pilgrimage during the past three or four years. Persia is the principal political danger, as will be seen below.

Iraq's relations with Turkey were strained for some considerable time. The Treaty of Lausanne, which regulated the peace with Turkey, left undecided the question of the Turco-Iraqi frontier. The Mosul question included not merely the possession of the important market town of Mosul, but economically part of an area known to be petroliferous, and strategically a highland region peopled by hardy fighters possessing an inherent contempt for the plainsmen, and commanding the whole of the riverain plain. The people, moreover, were neither Arab nor Turk. Those who were not Kurdish Muslims were chiefly Christians of various communions. The Treaty of Lausanne left the question, with a time limit of nine months, to direct negotiations between the British and Turkish Governments. When these failed the League of Nations sent out a delimitation commission,[1] and even after this further direct negotiations between Britain and Turkey were necessary before the League's decision was accepted.

When the Royal Air Force took over in 1922, the Turks, with their successes against the Greeks fresh in their minds and hoping similarly to settle the frontier question by a *fait accompli*, had sent troops into the northern districts of Iraq, where they remained until the Air Force bombed them out. They then concentrated at Rowanduz, whence they were finally ejected in April 1923 by the Air Force, co-operating with ground troops comprising a column of Imperial forces and Levies. This appeared to quieten the frontier. June 1926 saw the signing of a pact between Britain, Iraq and Turkey, accepting the League's delimitation and providing for co-operation in the maintenance of frontier peace. The diplomatic representation of Turkey in Baghdad and of Iraq in Ankara followed in due course and in 1931 King Faisal paid a state visit to the

[1] See also chapter on Anglo-Iraqi relations.

# Defence and Foreign Relations

Turkish capital where he was cordially greeted by the Ghazi. The present relations of the two countries are cordial.

The case of Persia is rather different. Iraq possesses the principal Holy Cities of the Shiah sect of the Muhammadans. Persia is predominantly Shiah and the Persian pilgrims to the Holy Cities in the past have been a lucrative source of revenue. Conversely the Persian theocracy in the Holy Cities has been an important spearhead of Persian influence.[1] Moreover, until Persia under Riza Shah developed her recent ultra-national characteristics and policy, a large part of Iraq's commercial revenue was derived from the transit trade through Baghdad and Basrah into and out of Persia. For some years, too, the Persian Government resented the exclusion of Persian nationals from the privileges of the judicial agreement subsidiary to the Anglo-Iraqi treaty of 1922, but there were other questions that were causing anxiety to Persia. When he seized power, Riza Shah had to reduce one after the other local rulers whose sway in their own districts menaced his centralizing policy. Numbers of these, or their relatives, took refuge in Iraq, or used Iraq as a jumping-off ground for subversive attempts. The Persians suspected Iraq, and Britain too, of double-dealing, but things steadily improved and by 1929 the way was clear for the new Anglo-Iraqi judicial agreement of 1930, which created a uniform standard of justice in the Iraqi courts for Iraqis and foreigners alike. Persian resentment was appeased by this, and by Britain's simultaneous suggestion that Persia should state her views on the Shatt-al-Arab question.[2] Persia then officially recognized Iraq. Diplomatic representatives were then exchanged, and King Faisal paid a state visit to the Shah in Teheran in the early summer of 1932, making a tour throughout Persia. But it is known that King Faisal's one fear was Persia, either as a direct menace, or as an indirect menace among the Euphrates tribes.

The direct menace from Persia began to make itself felt in 1934 and at the end of the year Iraq was moved to protest to the League of Nations. Persia had for long expressed dissatisfaction over the question of the Transferred Territories, which as the result of a pre-war boundary agreement had been assigned to the Ottoman

---

[1] See chapter on the Holy Cities.     [2] See p. 126.

Empire and since the war had been regarded as Iraqi. The area in question includes the oilfield operated by the Rafidain Oil Company, a subsidiary company, incorporated in Iraq, of the Anglo-Persian. Since the accession of Riza Shah in Persia, there have been clear indications that only fear of possible consequences has deterred Persia from trying to gain possession of the Transferred Territories by force. The town of Khanaqin itself has been mentioned as Persia's objective and there have been innumerable frontier incidents. In large part Persia's forward policy has been encouraged by Britain's policy of conciliation, which Riza Shah appears consistently to have regarded as an indication of weakness.[1]

One other major issue that arose in 1935 between Iraq and Persia is the question of the Shatt-al-Arab. Britain is closely interested in this question. By the Treaty of Erzerum of 1854, the river frontier between Iraq (the Ottoman Empire in those days) and Persia is the low-water mark on the Persian side. The anchorage at Moham-merah is specifically excluded, but northwards from a point six miles above Mohammerah, and from Mohammerah southwards to the mouth of the river, the whole of this fine waterway is in Iraq. It is maintained by the Basrah Port Directorate[2] and thanks to the fact that all the Anglo-Persian Oil Company's shipments of oil and refined spirit are made from Abadan, all the harbour and dredging dues from the Persian tankers go to the Iraqi and not to the Persian Government. Basrah's trade alone would not suffice to maintain the Basrah Port Directorate on its present basis. Persia sees this clearly. The alternatives open to her are to press for a revision of the treaty so as to provide for a change of frontier to the usual *thalweg* principle, or to create a new port in Persian waters and then compel the Oil Company to run their pipe-lines from the Abadan refineries to it. The Persians have found such a port at Bandar Shahpour, behind Abadan island. The fairway here gives a depth of thirty fathoms at low water and no dredging would be necessary and therefore no dredging dues. The difficulty is the nature of the land, which is low and swampy, so that wharves and warehouses are difficult to build and railways require special foundations.

[1] The list of the humiliations which the Persians have inflicted on British subjects and British interests is a lengthening one. There have been too many insults to the British flag for them all to have been accidental.

[2] See p. 198.

# Defence and Foreign Relations

Whether the cost would justify the results commercially is one question; the question of Persian national pride is another.

Britain is closely interested in this matter of the Shatt-al-Arab. The Basrah Port wharfage and equipment were taken over from the British Government, which had built them for military purposes, and the purchase has not yet been completed. Further, Basrah is within thirty miles of Abadan, the seat of the offices, the refineries and the huge tank-farm of the Anglo-Persian Oil Company. The British Government is a major shareholder in this great concern, and the British Navy depends in large part upon Abadan for its oil supply. The British sloops of the Persian Gulf Division pay frequent and regular visits to Basrah showing the flag as they pass Abadan, at which they frequently call. The Royal Air Force base at Basrah (flying-boats, bombers, armoured cars, and a small hospital), is closely associated with the Navy's activities; Basrah, or rather Shaibah, seventeen miles distant, is one of the stopping-places on the civil air-routes to the East. The sixty odd miles of the Shatt-al-Arab from the head of the Gulf to Basrah are thus of peculiar importance to Britain.[1]

The essence of the difficulties that have arisen and may again arise in the southern desert, is that the Baduin for thousands of years have been wont to traverse the desert as they liked. They do not understand that a line on a map is a frontier; the only frontier they understand is one that they cannot pass, except by force. The southern desert covers hundreds of thousands of square miles of steppe-land, sand patches and gravel and gypsum stretches, with waterholes and villages dotted here and there. All the tracks in the desert lead to and from these waterholes, and most of the tracks are as clearly defined and can be mapped almost as easily as the streets of a town. Until 1914 the whole of the Arabian peninsula was nominally Turkish; when the new states were set up, none of the frontiers was so shadowy as that between the new kingdom of Iraq and the territories of Ibn Saud.

Ibn Saud is a remarkable figure in a land famous for the remarkable men it has produced. At one stage early in the war it was just possible that he, and not Hussain and his sons, would have carried Britain's

---

[1] See chapter on British Imperial Communications. The Basrah air base adjoins the Basrah Port, still under British supervision. The local power station, owned by the Port, is within this enclave.

money.[1] But, as has been shown in another chapter, the fortunes of war in 1915 upset his plans, and his activities were confined to central Arabia, around his capital Riyadh. He had long been at enmity with the Sharifians, and during the war he was being subsidized by the British Government to refrain from attacking the territories of Hussain. For all the amirs of Arabia were more or less at enmity with each other; raids and counter-raids had been carried out since time immemorial. The event of the war imported a new factor into Arabia—the drawing of political frontiers, which had never before been known.

The existence of such frontiers put a new complexion upon the secular raiding of the Baduin, and by his defeat in 1921 of Ibn Rashid, who had checked him in 1915, Ibn Saud's territories marched with those of the new Iraq. His Baduin were of course camel-breeders from the high desert, rearing such flocks of smaller cattle as the desert water-holes could provide in the summer when water is scarce. In the summer, however, the Euphrates tribes, now Iraqi subjects, move down to the river and its swamps so that they get good grazing; in winter, they move out into the desert. The Baduin need camels, and must therefore breed them, to ensure their mobility in the arid desert; the Euphrates tribes are mainly shepherds, with no camels but with large flocks that are walked from pasture to pasture as the seasons dictate. In the old days these Euphrates shepherds bought immunity from raids by paying tribute to the tribes that were for the moment in the ascendancy in their area. This was necessary for their safety, as the desert south-west of the Euphrates had for generations been the

[1] See chapter on Lawrence and the Arabs of Iraq. While Lawrence was working with his Sharifian Allies, Britain found it necessary to pay a subsidy to Ibn Saud to refrain from attacking them in the south. At a later stage this subsidy rose to the figure of £5,000 a month. But Ibn Saud had a hearty contempt for Hussain, and moreover wished to get the control of the Hidjaz and the Holy Places into his own hands. The inevitable happened. Hussain put the finishing touch to his career of vainglory by assuming the title of Khalif which the new Dictator in Turkey had just abolished, and he was deposed by his people in face of open hostilities begun by Ibn Saud in August 1924, by which time the £5,000 subsidy had ceased. Hussain's son Ali succeeded, but before long was forced out of Mecca to Jiddah and in a year's time he too abdicated, leaving Ibn Saud King of the Hidjaz, as well as ruler of Najd, and controller of Mecca and Medina.

MANDAEAN SILVERSMITHS. NOTE THE NON-ARAB TYPE

ARAB COPPERSMITHS, BAGHDAD

# Defence and Foreign Relations

fighting-grounds of the great Baduin tribes, much more warlike than the shepherds. When the political frontiers were finally drawn, two results began to follow. The Euphrates shepherds becoming Iraqi subjects, found themselves increasingly under the control of the revenue authorities. In the past they had paid blackmail to the Baduin tribes; now they began to argue that as they were paying taxes to Baghdad, it was Baghdad's duty to ensure their safety when engaged on their lawful occasions within the frontiers of Iraq. This was an unassailable argument but the difficulty was that Ibn Saud was now the southern neighbour and his Akhwan had introduced new methods into desert-raiding.

The Akhwan, or Brotherhood, are a fighting force of Baduin pledged to puritanize Islam. Instead of the old raids which were the equivalent of the old Border cattle-raiding, the Akhwan introduced massacre as a principle, and when they raided a shepherd encampment they left not a man alive, in addition to driving off the stock. Ibn Saud was to an enormous extent dependent upon the Akhwan for the furtherance of his policy and the maintenance of his power. Iraq itself, after its 1920 rebellion, had passed from the British occupation to the Mandatory administration and the establishment of a kingdom, the King being the son of Hussain, Ibn Saud's hated rival. The Akhwan had been making brutal raids into Iraq, but the frontier idea was too new and feelings were not calm enough to permit of an immediate satisfactory settlement. There was a "treaty" in 1922 but apart from a clear delimitation of the frontier, it settled little, although both states agreed that neither would raid the other. This was a farcical provision. The Akhwan continued their raids into Iraq, and while the shepherds were not and never had been raiders, there were on the Iraqi side of the frontier northern Baduin and also Baduin from Najd; both raided freely on their enemies in Najd. Heavy losses were thus suffered by the Iraqi shepherd tribesmen, and although the raiding from Najd all but ceased about 1924-25, this was because Ibn Saud and his followers were then engaged in ejecting the Sharifians from the Hidjaz. By 1926 the Iraqi Government had established two small desert police-posts to check Iraqi raids into Najd and to give the alarm in case of raids from the south. One of these posts was massacred by raiders from Najd and Ibn Saud's explanations proved that he himself had to some extent lost control of his tribes. His old tribesmen were jealous of the new adherents—the results of the conquests of Hayil and Mecca—to whom naturally Ibn Saud had to show certain favours. This did not please his old Akhwan stalwarts, who began to find that they had rivals at Court. Ibn Saud clearly could not permit them to loot their "fellow-subjects" in his new kingdom of Hidjaz. His only alternative was to see that they had an outlet to raid into Iraq. This was the crux of the desert-frontier problem between him and the Anglo-Iraqi authorities. His Baduin did not like the Iraqi police-posts, knowing that their establishment was the prelude to a regular and complete control of the desert. To this they had strenuous objections, as such control would mean the end of the raiding and looting by which they lived. Under their pressure therefore Ibn Saud continued to protest against Iraqi police-posts on his frontier. On the other side King Faisal could not forget that Ibn Saud had just ejected his father Hussain and his brother Ali from their seat of power; the other brother Abdullah, from Trans-jordan, maintained a hatred which was to persist in more or less active form for several years.

The trouble came to a head in 1929 when a chief of the Mutair (south and west of Kuwait) began to rebel against Ibn Saud. His operations brought him northwards towards Iraq and for a time there was great excitement in Basrah, Zubair and Nasiriyah. The rebel was finally broken by the help of British aircraft and armoured cars,[1] and early in 1930 a conference between the two Kings, Faisal and Ibn Saud, was arranged. It took place on board the British sloop-of-war *Lupin* in the Persian Gulf, and a broad agreement was reached providing in the ultimate resort for arbitration on the out-standing frontier questions. Diplomatic representatives have since been exchanged but they have only been intermittently maintained. During the summer of 1932, subversive movements against Ibn Saud, on the western side of the peninsula, were in many quarters thought to have the support of King Faisal's brother, the Amir Abdullah of Transjordan, and this caused a certain coldness. British policy, however, demands that the Arabian rulers should not be at logger-heads and the entire peninsula is rapidly becoming a comprehensive and thoroughgoing sphere of British influence.

[1] He was finally defeated at Jahrah, near Kuwait. See also p. 116.

# Defence and Foreign Relations

On the west Iraq marches with the French mandated territory of Syria and the British mandated territories of Palestine and Transjordan. Anglo-French co-operation has been cordial and tolerably complete. In the autumn of 1932 a League of Nations commission defined the one doubtful sector of frontier—near the Jebel Sinjar, where the Yezidis[1] live and the French thought there might be mineral deposits. On the basis of nationality, the whole of the area was apportioned to Iraq and the French line was drawn back.

Transjordan is ruled by the Amir Abdullah, another of the Hashimite family for whom a throne was found by Britain. The political position in Palestine is discussed elsewhere.[2] During 1932 it became clear that it was British policy to divert all the communications between Baghdad and the Mediterranean through Palestine.

In 1921 officers of the Royal Air Force ran a furrow across the Syrian desert from Ramadi to Amman. The intention then was to blaze a trail from Baghdad to Egypt largely for service purposes. About the same time two brothers named Nairn, who had served with the British troops in the Middle East, conceived the idea of linking up Baghdad and Damascus by a regular passenger and mail motor-service. This service was soon in operation and after a few vicissitudes during the Druse rebellion in 1925, the westward route from Baghdad was established via Damascus to the sea.

But British interest in the Iraq Petroleum Company and in the development of Haifa as a great port which should ultimately make good the loss of Egypt, led to the elaboration of a definite line of policy. The Iraq Petroleum Company's 1931 agreement provided for the completion of the pipe-line to the Mediterranean by 1935; actually oil was sent through in 1934, although the formal opening did not take place until January 1935. British interests ensured that the line should terminate at Haifa, French interests were strong enough to secure a bifurcation to Tripoli in French-controlled territory. A trans-desert telephone was simultaneously constructed along the pipe-line under the supervision of British engineers. The summer of 1932 saw much discussion over the projected Baghdad-Haifa railway and about the same time the British authorities in Palestine began sending mails direct to Baghdad via Amman, instead of as formerly via Damascus. Negotiations are on foot to have the

[1] See p. 29.     [2] See chapter on British Imperial Communications.

west-bound mails from Iraq (except those for Syria) sent via Amman and Jerusalem instead of by Damascus. There is thus little likelihood of Iraq's meeting trouble on this particular frontier.

It is, however, in the interior where military operations may be likely involving the employment of British forces. There are two danger zones—the northern and eastern mountains and the middle Euphrates. In each of these areas there live tribes—Kurds and Assyrians in the one case, in the other Arabs—impatient of all political control, raiders and looters by inclination and by tradition, and determined opponents of any regime of law and order if they feel strong enough to resist it. The Kurd is anti-Arab by national predilection; like the highlander everywhere he thinks himself a better man and a better fighter than the lowlander, whom he despises. There are few cultural affinities between Kurd and Arab, except the Koran, and unless the Iraqi Government can maintain its effective control of Kurdistan, taxes will come in with greater and greater reluctance. The Kurds and the Assyrians are more fully discussed in Chapter VIII. On the middle Euphrates the feeling is the old hostility between tribesman and townsman, between the Shiah and the Sunni. The Ottoman control never extended to this area and it was here that the 1920 rebellion against the British administration in Baghdad broke out and was chiefly maintained.

In each of these areas the years of the Mandate saw the extension of good roads and bridges making rapid military and police movement possible for immediate needs, and on the longer view making it easier for traders and travellers to pass on their way. Since 1921 the British Air Force and Iraqi Army operations have been in various Kurdish areas; the middle Euphrates except for the air "warning" which was necessary in 1923, has been quiet, possibly because it is more accessible than the mountains are. The maintenance of order in the middle Euphrates is regarded by the Arabs as a barometer of the strength of the central government.

CHAPTER VIII

THE MINORITIES

THE world has heard much and will hear more of the racial minorities in Iraq. The various minority races are briefly described in another chapter;[1] of them only the Kurds and the Assyrians merit lengthy attention here. The other Christians, the Jews and the minor sects are minorities without being "problems."

## I. THE KURDS

Among the racial minorities to whom the allied Powers at first promised autonomy were the Kurds. These brave and hardy high-landers live in the great mountain *massifs* on the Turco-Iraqi-Persian frontiers to the south-west of the Caspian sea. Racially and linguistically they form a distinct entity,[2] Muslim by faith. They are pastoralists, but as always the owners of the fleeter mountain sheep look jealously upon the fatter valley sheep, and the Kurds' main occupation has ever been raiding and banditry. The Kurds are said to be treacherous but the British officers who have served with them speak most highly of their qualities as fighters and as men. Physically they are one of the finest races in the world.

The League of Nations Commission which in 1923 settled the Mosul frontier question, put the total Kurdish population at about 3,000,000, half of whom were unquestionably in Turkey and 700,000 equally unquestionably in Persia. There were about half a million in the area then under dispute, in effect the old Mosul *vilayet* of the Ottomans. The Kurdish population in Iraq to-day may thus be put at approximately 500,000.

The abortive Treaty of Sèvres signed in 1920, provided for an

---

[1] See Chapter I.
[2] This perhaps should be qualified somewhat. The Kurds have never been politically united, and never in history have they formed a nation, and during their more recent risings there has been no co-ordination what-ever. Nor have they thrown up many big personalities (Saladin being an exception). Shaikh in Kurdish, it should be noted, is a religious title, which is not the case among the Arabs.

autonomous Kurdish state comprising, (*a*) the Kurds in Turkey (if they proved to the League Council's satisfaction that a majority desired independence, and the League Council thought they were capable of maintaining such independence), and also (*b*) the Kurds in the old Mosul *vilayat* (provided they wished to join their compatriots in such independence). The Allied Powers, in such an event, pledged themselves to raise no objection to such adhesion. The principle, though accepted, was afterwards repudiated by the Turkish Government.

For three years this principle of Kurdish autonomy formally held the field, but the 1923 Treaty of Lausanne, which finally took the place of the Treaty of Sèvres, contained no such provision. In other words Britain and the Allied Powers had abandoned this policy. By that time the Mandate for Iraq was already three years old, and there was in addition a native Iraqi Government in existence which had very definite ideas both about the integrity of the Iraqi state and also about the Kurds. The Kurds naturally made the most of the autonomy articles in the Sèvres instrument, claiming that if the Allies with no *arrière pensée* on the part of Britain, had then agreed on an independent Kurdish state, the new partition policy was ethically unjustifiable, however politically expedient it might have become.

Turkey, however, as she recovered her strength and stimulated by her spectacular rout of the Greeks, had rejected the idea of detaching her Kurds, preferring to have them where she could manage them rather than have the potential menace of an independent Kurdistan in her rear. The Kurds of the Mosul *vilayat* by the Lausanne settlement and its corollaries, then found themselves on the Iraqi and not on the Turkish side of the new frontier. Conditions and circumstances had clearly changed from those of the Sèvres settlement, but the Kurds of Iraq maintained their claim to autonomy as a state of some half-million inhabitants. While linguistically and racially Iraqi Kurdistan was Kurdish, it would have contained only a minority of the Kurdish people, and both Turkey and Persia might have had good reason to fear it as a potential source of irredentist trouble. In such circumstances these independent Kurds of Iraq would have constituted a standing menace to peace in the Middle East.

# The Minorities

Moreover, Iraqi Kurdistan, however racially pure, is not economically independent. It might have maintained a self-contained existence, but the trade connections of this region are mainly with the plains *via* the Tigris and its tributaries and one or two ancient caravan roads. Nor was a real nationalist spirit evident everywhere although one or two localities were, and were to remain, centres of anti-Arab agitation. These centres were in the region around Sulaimani. When the referendum on the choice of the Amir Faisal as first King of the new Iraq was held,[1] Sulaimani declined to vote, Mosul and Arbil voted (with minor reservations) for the election of the Amir, a Kurdish section in Kirkuk asked for a Kurdish government but refused to be included with Sulaimani.

In 1922 serious trouble broke out in the Sulaimani district. The British official reports emphasize the activities of external agents, but this area needs little external encouragement to go up in flames; the "rebellion" was a natural reaction on the part of brigand shaikhs who did not wish any central government, Kurd or Arab, unless they themselves were running it. This manifestly was impossible. The Kurds for a time proved themselves to be masters of the situation and Sulaimani was evacuated in September of the same year.

The principal character in the drama was Shaikh Mahmud, a born rebel, a strong man and a member of an influential family. This was his second "rebellion." His first had been in 1919, against the British administration in Baghdad and he had then been deported. He was foolishly permitted to return and, more foolishly, installed as Governor or Sulaimani.

Nothing could have suited him better. By November 1922 he was "King of Kurdistan" and had set up a "cabinet." At this time the Treaty of Lausanne had not yet been signed although it was taking shape. It was, therefore, necessary to take stern measures against this comic-opera "king" otherwise it would be impossible to administer the area as an integral part of the Iraqi state, and who knew how the negotiations might go if the Iraqi Government were visibly unable to control it? Force was then employed and the Shaikh was driven out of Sulaimani into the hills. When the treaty had been signed the troops were withdrawn from Sulaimani, and

[1] See p. 77.

Mahmud at once re-entered it in triumph. This was the middle of the summer of 1923. The general feeling among the mountaineers was that he was too strong to be ejected by the British and Iraqi Governments.

The Kurds were then promised certain concessions. The Iraqi Government undertook that all officials in the Kurdish areas should be Kurds and not Arabs (except in technical posts), and that the Kurdish language was to be used in official correspondence. Shaikh Mahmud was left to his own devices for nearly a year, but in the early summer of 1924 his headquarters at Sulaimani were bombed from the air and Iraqi troops reoccupied the town.

A few months later, in February 1925, the League Commission arrived to draw the frontier upon which Britain and Turkey (in their negotiations as provided by the Treaty of Lausanne) had failed to agree. By that time an effective Iraqi administration was working in Sulaimani and the rest of the Kurdish area was similarly under Baghdad's control. The League Commission[1] emphasized the safeguards regarding the use of the Kurdish language and the appointment of Kurdish officials, and the Iraqi Government accepted this principle.[2] Shaikh Mahmud then disappeared across the frontier into Persia, but negotiations went steadily on until in the summer of 1927 his estates were restored to him on his giving certain undertakings. He took up his abode permanently in Persia and for a time it appeared that he intended to keep his word.

During the next year or two even the most responsible among the Kurdish leaders began to complain that the Iraqi Government were not fulfilling their promises regarding the use of the Kurdish language and the appointment of Kurdish officials. At the beginning of 1929 a number of Kurdish deputies put forward a scheme for a special Kurdish administrative unit within Iraq, with special privileges outside the normal administrative structure of the country. They also asked for the allocation of more money for public services in their area. The demand was rejected as being separatist in principle.

The end of the Mandate was now in sight; the negotiations for the Treaty of 1930 alarmed the Kurds and their alarm was increased when it was found that the Treaty contained no articles safeguarding

[1] See chapter on Anglo-Iraqi Relations.　　[2] *Progress of Iraq*, p. 259.

SHAIKH MAHMUD

their national position in the Iraqi state or guaranteeing the promises already made to them by Iraqi statesmen. The British official explanation was that a Treaty between two friendly and independent[1] states could not contain provisions binding one of the parties to the line of action it must adopt towards its minorities. This explanation did not satisfy the minorities who continued to demand a British guarantee. Britain and Iraq thereupon, at the League's request, drew up certain safeguards and guarantees regarding the use of the Kurdish language and the employment of Kurdish officials, and the Iraqi Government reaffirmed its pledges.

When the text of the Treaty was published (June 1930) the Kurds sent petition after petition to the League of Nations. A further complication arose in the allegation, made in the more extreme anti-British circles among the Arabs, that Britain was fomenting the Kurdish unrest with a view to delaying the termination of the Mandate. This allegation went too far for its purpose, for it was a virtual admission that the Kurdish protests (whether genuine or artificial) were in essence such as to justify a refusal by the League to grant immediate independence to Iraq. It was, however, found necessary to send the Acting High Commissioner and the Acting Prime Minister by air to the Kurdish districts to repeat formally the Iraqi Government's undertaking regarding the use of the Kurdish language and the employment of Kurdish officials. In September 1930 there were serious riots at Sulaimani on the occasion of the elections. Accounts vary as to the first act of aggression, but a collision occurred between a large mob and the police. Military assistance was summoned and the crowd was fired on. Several on both sides were killed and wounded.

In October Shaikh Mahmud, breaking the undertakings he had given, suddenly appeared on the scene with an armed force which he brought from Persia and which swelled as he advanced into Iraq. He made formal demands, including a Mandate to be exercised by Britain, for Kurdistan. He proved stronger than had been imagined and only the most determined operations by Iraqi troops and police, aided by the British Air Force[2] reduced him after months of fighting. He was forced to come to terms and was sent to live at Nasiriyah on

---

[1] The Treaty was to be operative only after Iraq's independence.
[2] Important enough for the award of decorations and medals.

the lower Euphrates. His last rebellion, begun in October 1930, had lasted till May 1931.

Within a year there was a further rebellion, this time led by Shaikh Ahmed of Barzan, whose father had defeated the Turks in 1909. Whereas Shaikh Mahmud had led his insurgent bands through administered territory, the population of which was not wholly on his side unless he happened to be in the immediate neighbourhood, Shaikh Ahmed was the unquestioned leader of a compact territory, to all intents and purposes a hostile country, and moreover was extremely difficult terrain for operations with regular troops. High mountains and deep valleys, rough tracks and stony peaks gave every advantage to the Barzan hillmen. At the beginning of Spring (March 1932) an Iraqi column moved into the mountains against them, supported by R.A.F. machines for reconnaissance purposes. These operations proved a debacle. The Iraqi troops were caught in a narrow defile and as the attack developed on both sides the transport mule-drivers (civilians, not troops) fled. The disorder spread and the troops broke, certain of the officers preferring to fight another day. The British liaison officers helped to stem the rout, but what saved the Iraqi troops from annihilation was the attack on the rebels by the R.A.F. planes, which at great risk flew low and engaged them heavily, while the British officers were extricating the column from its inglorious position. The column finally got out, badly shaken and with the loss of all its food-supplies, tents and blankets and most of its ammunition. As the base was some distance away, the position of the troops in those inhospitable mountains was unenviable in the extreme. But the British again came to the rescue, R.A.F. aeroplanes dropping supplies from the air.

It was then recognized that the only way in which the Iraqis could recover their lost face was by means of determined air action. As the Iraqi air force was too inexperienced this work fell to the British. Aeroplanes dropped warning leaflets and one, with a loud-speaker installed, flew round the villages booming its admonition in the local dialect from the skies. Within a few weeks the discomfort and insecurity which the bombing tactics caused to the Barzan tribesmen compelled Shaikh Ahmed to retire across the Turkish frontier, where he surrendered to the Turkish authorities.

# The Minorities

The future of Kurdistan is not too clear. The Kurds still complain of the policy, which they say is deliberately carried out with anti-Kurdish intent, of appointing Kurdish officials to other parts of Iraq and Arab officials to Kurdistan. The Iraqi reply is that any other policy must tend towards separatism, that the policy of moving officials with reference only to their ability and not to their race or religion is in the best interest of the Iraqi state, and that officials and citizens alike should first regard themselves as Iraqis. In general it may be said that provided the Arabs do not overdo the Arab idea there should not be very much trouble. If the security of life and communications is maintained, a period of tranquillity should be assured. The essential difficulty is that Kurdistan is so inaccessible should it become necessary again to use force.

## II. THE ASSYRIANS

The question of the Assyrians[1] which within a year of Iraq's independence, became a major question, is perhaps even more complicated than that of the Kurds. They are a Christian race, formerly subject to the Ottoman Empire, who rose against the Turks in the war on the side of the Russians. Their homeland is the Hakkiari country—still depopulated—in which they lived between and among Kurdish and Armenian settlements and which the Mosul frontier commission of 1925 gave to Turkey—perhaps because they had given the other controversial territory to Iraq. Had they given the Hakkiari country to Iraq the Assyrian problem would not have arisen, for the Assyrians would have been settled there long since. But the Turks refused to have them on the reasonable ground that they had previous experience of being stabbed in the back by these same Assyrians.

After the Russian debacle following the two revolutions of 1917, the Assyrians fought their way into Iraq, where with all the other refugees from Russia they were maintained in 1918 and 1919 by the British. During the rebellion in Iraq in 1920 the Assyrians gave valuable assistance to the British and it was decided to enrol them as a force of Levies—especially as the British Army in Iraq was

[1] For *all* the facts see Col. R. S. Stafford's *The Tragedy of the Assyrians*, the only complete, accurate and unbiassed account that has been published.

about to be reduced—and as such they did well in minor operations against Turkey.[1] They thus came to regard themselves as to all intents and purposes British. The Arab Nationalists resented this, particularly as the Assyrians were alien both by race and by religion. There was a disturbance at Mosul in August 1923, and another in May 1924 at Kirkuk, where an insignificant incident led to two companies of Levies going round the town systematically "cleaning it up" and murdering fifty-nine Arabs in the process.

Apart from the serving Levies, there was the question of the rest of the Assyrians. They numbered in all some 37,000, and the time-expired men, in addition to their term of discipline under British officers, had returned to their families each with a modern service rifle given to him on discharge, as a means of defence against the Kurds. In all there were ten thousand Assyrians not only capable of bearing arms but actually possessing them, and accustomed to the full discipline and tactical methods of the British Army. Not only so, but for fifteen years they were even aggressively anti-Arab in sentiment and politics, their attitude of superiority being most galling to the Muslims.

It was hoped that the 1925 Frontier Commission would solve the problem but it did not. The Assyrians therefore had to be settled in Iraq. The Turks in 1925 had ruthlessly ejected a number who had returned, and in another case they met with machine-guns some who were trying to return, across the frontier to their Hakkiari homeland. The Assyrians wished to be settled in a compact body but the Iraqis did not wish to see a compact body of armed and drilled men, of semi-hostile views, settled in their midst. In addition the Iraqis pointed out, truly, that there was no available land unless either Arabs or Kurds were dispossessed, and that to show discrimination in favour of Christians by dispossessing Muslims would be certain to cause trouble, even if it could be done legally.

The publication of the 1930 treaty caused anxiety to the Assyrians (as it had to the Kurds) by its omission of any article safeguarding their position in the new Iraqi state, and in June 1932 the issue suddenly came to a head. The Iraqis had long been pressing un-officially for a reconstruction of the Levies so that they should be mixed and not purely Assyrian. In the summer of 1932 Iraq in

[1] See chapter on Foreign Relations and Defence.

general, and Baghdad in particular, was full of rumours about Iraq's entry into the League, and the Assyrians became difficult. Not only did they declare their intention of leaving the British service, but they announced privately that they were about to seize certain areas of land in the Mosul district with a view to settling there. They also made it clear that they would be prepared to defend their position there by force of arms. Britain was in a dilemma. If she did not support the Iraqi Government the Arabs could with some reason say that she had been playing a double game. If she used force against the Assyrians, the nonconformist conscience in Britain, those Liberals surviving in Europe and those that flourish in the United States would immediately criticize the use of force against "the smallest ex-Ally," Christians at that, and the "victims of Muslim intolerance." For some days the situation was grave in the extreme, and a battalion of British infantry were hurriedly flown from Egypt to take the place of those Levies who wished to leave the British service at once.

Meantime the Assyrian Patriarch, His Beatitude the Mar Shimun, was prevailed upon to exercise his influence in favour of a settlement. This prelate, the national and religious head of the Assyrians, a young man of about twenty-five, then proceeded to Geneva to put before the League the case of his people. He is the nephew of a remarkable woman, the Lady Surma, who in person pleaded the case of her people in Europe and who has been regarded as the power behind the throne. For the Patriarchate is a family affair. The office descends normally from uncle to nephew, the Patriarch always being celibate. The Patriarch Benjamin was murdered in 1918, his successor died of consumption in 1920, and their nephew, the present Patriarch, who succeeded as a mere youth, only recently began to emerge from dependence on his aunt. The family's chief preoccupation has been to maintain their own political and financial power.

The trouble in July–August 1932 was averted by British diplomacy at Geneva, where it was agreed, as will be shown later, that if the grant of independence to Iraq were justified the Assyrians need have no anxiety about their future; and that if Iraq proved unworthy of the trust the League was about to repose in her, then the moral responsibility must be Britain's, as the Mandatory Power on whose testimony independence would be granted.[1] By a stroke of ill-luck for the Assyrians, Iraq became an independent state in October 1932, whereas the League's machinery did not permit until the following December the meeting of the Council at which, there seems no doubt, an important qualifying condition would have been imposed concerning the settlement of the Assyrians in a compact body within the new state. It was then too late.

In the prolonged and voluminous exchange of communications prior to the termination of the Mandate, petitions and letters from the Assyrians to the League Council were prominent, and in September the Council asked for a report from the Permanent Mandates Commission.

In the various petitions which reached the Permanent Mandates Commission prior to the termination of the mandatory regime in the country the Assyrians had made the following demands:

1. Mass transfer to a country under the rule of any of the Western nations, or, if this were not possible, to Syria;
2. Recognition as a *millet* (nation) domiciled in Iraq.
3. Restoration of their former homes in the regions from which they came, now in Turkish territory, or, failing that, the constitution of a "national home" open to all Assyrians.
4. Attribution to the Assyrian community of various political and educational rights.

The Commission, endorsing the conclusions of its *rapporteur*, first noted the feelings of insecurity inspired in the Assyrians by the climate of the country in which they lived, by the sterility of the land which had been assigned to them, by the precariousness of their rights to cultivate the soil and, especially, by the scattering of their community among populations of other races. It pointed out that the root causes of the state of unrest revealed by the petitions resided in the fact that it had not yet been possible to collect the Assyrians of Iraq into a homogeneous group in a region suitable to their needs. In the opinion of the Commission the absence of lands combining the requisite conditions for a settlement of this kind had not yet been proved, but on this point the Commission was not fully informed; there actually were no such lands in Iraq.

[1] See chapter on Anglo-Iraqi Relations.

Further, there was nothing to show, said the Commission, that the possibility of resettling the Assyrians in their country of origin must be definitely ruled out.

The Commission thought that the Assyrians would be more likely to remain loyal subjects if they were placed in conditions more closely approaching to those which they had been led to expect. On the other hand, it considered that the desire for autonomy shown by the Assyrians could not be encouraged as their autonomy, if conceded, would imperil the unity of the Iraqi State. The Commission in view of these considerations, after having noted the observations of the United Kingdom Government, drew the Council's attention to the great importance, both for Iraq and for the Assyrians, of "providing the Assyrians with opportunities for settlement in a homogeneous group which would be in keeping with their traditions and would satisfy their economic needs."

The Council did not receive this opinion from the Mandates Commission until December 5, 1932. The *rapporteur*[1] recalled to the Council the special circumstances in which the Mandates Commission had examined the petitions from the Assyrians, the British Mandate for Iraq having been terminated before the meeting of the Commission.

The representative of Iraq[2] observed that the Commission's report had been inspired solely by a desire to help in reaching a solution of the question. There were two possibilities; either the Assyrians should be settled on acceptable terms in Iraq or they should be resettled in their country of origin. With reference to the first of these alternatives, the representative of Iraq pointed out that an agreement would be feasible if the Assyrians were willing to settle in other districts than the mountainous country of the *vilayet* of Mosul and if they renounced their desire to live in a compact body. The Iraqi Government had attempted, in so far as it was possible, to settle the Assyrians on such land as was available and had appointed for that purpose a Commission on which a representative of the Assyrian community was sitting. As a result of that Commission's work, steps had been taken to settle a large number of Assyrians, with care to avoid the dispersal of families. The Iraqi

[1] Dr. Beneš, Czechoslovakia.
[2] The Foreign Minister, Nuri Pasha as-Said.

# Iraq

Government was anxious to do everything in its power to assure to the members of the Assyrian community the fullest enjoyment of their rights. The representative of Iraq added that his Government had no objection whatever to the second alternative, namely, the resettlement of the Assyrians in their country of origin, and was prepared to facilitate the carrying out of such a proposal. He observed, in conclusion, that it would be a mistake to suppose that the petitioners whose requests had been considered by the Mandates Commission represented the whole or even a majority of the Assyrians resident in Iraq.

The Council finally, after noting the opinion of the Commission, entrusted the study of its recommendations to a special Committee composed of the representatives of Czechoslovakia, France, Italy, Norway and the United Kingdom. This Committee submitted the following draft resolution to the Council on December 15th:

The Council,
Adopts the view of the Permanent Mandates Commission that the demand of the Assyrians for administrative autonomy within Iraq cannot be accepted;
Notes with satisfaction the declaration by the representative of Iraq of the intention of the Iraqi Government to select from outside Iraq a foreign expert to assist it for a limited period in the settlement of all landless inhabitants of Iraq, including Assyrians, and in the carrying out of its scheme for the settlement of the Assyrians of Iraq under suitable conditions and, so far as may be possible, in homogeneous units, it being understood that the existing rights of the present population shall not be prejudiced;
Feels confident that, if these measures do not provide a complete solution of the problem and there remain Assyrians unwilling or unable to settle in Iraq, the Iraqi Government will take all such measures as may be possible to facilitate the settlement of the said Assyrians elsewhere;
Requests the Iraqi Government to be so good as to keep it informed in due course of the result of the foregoing measures.

Dr. Beneš stated that in the opinion of the Special Committee the draft resolution "would permit of a solution of the question and allow the Assyrian community to be settled in such a way as to obviate its being scattered among populations of other races." The Iraqi representative accepted the draft resolution, and assured the Council that the Iraqi Government would do its utmost to discharge

A KURDISH YOUNG MAN

KURDISH COOLIE. A TYPICAL LOAD

its obligations. The representative of the United Kingdom expressed his satisfaction with the proposed solution. In his opinion there was no reason why the Assyrians should not find in Iraq the prosperity, security, and contentment which everyone wished for them. He felt however that their future lay largely in their own hands. He was sure that the Iraqi Government would treat the Assyrians generously and would by so doing gain a new and valuable source of strength for its country and establish its good faith before the nations of the world. The Council then adopted the draft resolution submitted by the Special Committee.

In spite of the satisfaction thus expressed, the Iraqi Army carried out within eight months a massacre of unarmed Assyrians, and in face of the world imported totally new factors into the Assyrian problem.

The Iraqi Government not only imposed a cable (and many said a mail) censorship but also withheld all news of this massacre. Not a word, save of denials of statements published abroad, appeared in the Iraqi press; the utmost endeavours were made both by the Iraqi Government and by the British Embassy to prevent publication of the facts, but the facts were of such a nature that they could not long be kept from the light of day. The result of this policy was that the presentation of the Assyrian case got a good start in Europe; and not only was Iraq's case—a good arguable case, it may be said —put later and haltingly, but Iraq was made to appear morally in the wrong as the result of the efforts at secrecy which a franker and cleverer policy would have eschewed.[1]

It is necessary in order to understand fully the Assyrian situation in the summer of 1933, to emphasize again the position of the Assyrian Levies—a body of troops maintained by the British Government, officered by British officers, trained and armed on British lines. It is undeniable that the Assyrian Levies were a splendid force. Keen soldiers, of martial spirit and bearing as might be expected of free-minded highlanders, they developed an *esprit de corps* which almost made them more British than the British. They

---

[1] Not the least stupid act of a stupid censorship was the stopping of cables sent off by the resident correspondent of *The Times* and by myself as special correspondent of the *Daily Mail* describing Baghdad's reaction to the unexpected news of King Faisal's death.

despised the Arabs in general and the Arab Army in particular. In this, it must be said, they were largely encouraged by their officers, who were reasonably and justifiably proud of the men they commanded; by the British Royal Air Force, with whom for a decade they were in close touch, either when serving as aerodrome guards, or, when time-expired, as mess-waiters and batmen; and by the general British community in Iraq who appreciated their smart soldierly bearing, their fine spirit of independence, and their British sense of training and discipline. The Assyrians thus became arrogant and swelled-headed. The pay received by the Levies and sent home by them to their families in the north raised to an unheard-of extent the general standard of living to which they were accustomed. Until they emerged into the foreground of the international picture, they were rude, simple tribesmen, living a hard life in the mountains, from which they wrested with difficulty a frugal existence. Suddenly they found themselves the pets of the British, most of whom, in the early days, thought they were going to exercise the right of the conqueror and remain in a conquered country. It was a great opportunity for the Assyrian Patriarchal family to consolidate its power, and with the support of religious and Radical circles in Great Britain the Assyrians were the more encouraged to press their demands.

All this the Arabs and Kurds found most galling. The Arabs in particular took grave exception to the swaggering conceit of the Assyrians, but as they were the *protégés* of the Mandatory Power nothing could be done but grin and bear it. Thus as time went on the feeling between the two races became more and more acute. The Kurds for centuries had known the Assyrians as cut-throat mountaineers, made on their own amiable pattern. The Arab, being a plainsman and lowlander, disliked both, the Assyrians rather the more as being Christians.

We have seen that the Assyrians demanded national autonomy within Iraq under the Mar Shimun, and settlement in a homogeneous body. Most fair-minded people would agree with the Iraqi case that the former demand could not be granted; if the Assyrians were settled *en bloc*, including ten thousand highly trained armed men and a spiritual leader claiming temporal power, the step to complete Assyrian independence would be a short one. Such an *imperium in imperio* was clearly out of the question, even with its proviso *"so far as may be possible*, in homogeneous units." The Iraqi Government decided, therefore, that the Assyrians should be settled as and where possible in scattered villages, pointing out that even if the Assyrians were thus planted in the middle of Kurds, this was what they had always been accustomed to, and indeed it was for this very purpose that they had been given their arms. An experienced British officer from the Sudan was brought to Iraq for the purpose. The difficulty seemed insoluble. While the late King Faisal was in England in June 1933 the trouble began. The Iraqi Government took a firm stand and insisted that the Mar Shimun should sign an undertaking, *inter alia* renouncing any claim to temporal power. About the same time one of his emissaries approached two diplomats in Baghdad, urging that pressure might be brought to bear on the Turkish Government to permit the transfer of the Assyrians to the Hakkiari country. When it was once again made clear that this was impossible, the emissary declared, and made no secret of it, that the Assyrians were determined to do something which would focus world opinion upon them.

The Mar Shimun being in Baghdad, a prominent part in the discussions on the spot was taken by one of his henchmen, a good soldier and a respected if hot-headed man named Yaku Ismail, hailing from the village of Simel, which is a police post about twenty minutes by car from Dohuk, where there is a qaimmaqam of the Arab Government. It was with Yaku, therefore, that the local authorities in Mosul had attempted to enter into discussion. After a good deal of persuasion by British officials of the Iraqi Government, Yaku, who had never ceased to express his distrust of the Arabs and of the Baghdad Government, finally consented to come in to Mosul on a safe-conduct. When he arrived the Iraqi mutasarrif, or governor, asked for a bond for Yaku's good behaviour. This bond was entered into by a Church of England missionary (an American citizen) who had worked in the district for some ten years and to whom Yaku was well known as a man of integrity. Yaku undertook to go to Baghdad to put the Iraqi case, as learned by him in Mosul, before the Mar Shimun but he never went to Baghdad; instead, he led a party of armed men across the flooded Tigris into Syria. Assyrian spokesmen say that Yaku took this action on being told by Iraqi officials that if the Assyrians did not like the settlement plans that were being arranged for them they need not remain in Iraq. The Iraqi officials say that the Assyrians misconstrued, deliberately or otherwise, what they were told, which was that if they did not like the settlement plans that were being prepared for them and refused to accept them, it would be difficult to see how they could remain in Iraq.

Other bands followed the first band and in all about eight hundred men got across. The Iraqi authorities, when the French authorities protested that the migration of these armed men into Syria was embarrassing, gave orders that no more were to be allowed to leave Iraq. At this point it may be stated that some weeks later about sixty of these eight hundred men were interrogated on their return to Iraq by a British officer. Being mostly men of limited intelligence, their evidence is all the more valuable. They were to all intents and purposes unanimous in declaring that the reason why they went to Syria was that their leaders, including Yaku, had told them that the French were willing to settle them on the most favourable terms, and that they went across with a view to seeing the country for themselves before moving their women and children and belongings. The fact remains that within about a fortnight they apparently decided to return—according to the testimony of the sixty interrogated men the decision to return was taken when they discovered that the promises of favourable settlement were false.

This brings us to the 4th–5th August, 1933. By the time they decided to return, the Tigris, which they had had to cross in rafts, had gone down and was fordable. The Iraqi army had posts about a mile apart along the frontier, with a considerable concentration in rear. Accounts vary as to what happened, and the exact truth will probably never be known. But it does appear that near the Christian village of Faish Khabur an Iraqi post was hailed by a small party of Assyrians who said that they wished to re-enter Iraq and give up their arms. When requested to advance they attacked the post and wiped it out. On this a larger body of Assyrians waded across, and through the gap created by the destruction of the Iraqi post moved against the concentration of troops behind. This was an overt act of rebellion. Some comment has been made upon the fact that the Iraqi Government had previously declined to accede to British requests for the removal from the Northern Command of Bekir Sidky Beg, the General Officer Commanding, on the ground that he was a notorious anti-Assyrian and that his presence at the head of the Iraqi Army in that area was a standing provocation. There is much in this argument.

On the other hand the Iraqi Government's refusal to remove him was perhaps not unreasonable. The only danger threatening the state was in the north, and as Bekir Sidky was one of the best Iraqi serving generals, why should he be removed? The question was a particularly pertinent one, having regard to the situation at the moment. Here were the rebel Assyrians—for the Mar Shimun's movement had by now taken a definite military form. It was the first occasion on which Arab troops had come in conflict with the much-vaunted Assyrians. The Arabs themselves were doubtful, having for fifteen years been hypnotized into an inferiority complex *vis-à-vis* the Assyrians, and for fifteen years they had been accustomed to see Britain backing the Assyrians. Moreover, they knew well that the Kurds were watching closely, and if a signal initial success had been gained by the Assyrians the whole of Kurdistan might have gone up as well. It is known that during the periods in which the Kurds have been quiet in the past, what very largely has kept them quiet has been the uncertainty whether or not they would be bombed by British aeroplanes. The 1930 Treaty provides for British military co-operation against Iraq's external enemies, and according to an official reply in the House of Commons, the British Government would discuss on its merits any question of intervention in any internal trouble that might arise within Iraq. If the returning Assyrians had been successful, it is fairly certain that British co-operation with the Iraqi troops against them would at least have been discussed. As things turned out, however, this question never arose, and the Kurds still remain in doubt as to British action in the future. But in the early days of August all that the Arabs could see was that they were now arrayed in open warfare against the famous Assyrians. For them it seemed absolutely essential, the Yaku rebellion having begun, to strike down the Assyrians once and for all. The Assyrians on their part never anticipated that the Arab Army would beat them in a straight fight.

Yet that is what happened. When the returning Assyrians met the

Arab Army concentrated behind Faish Kabur they got as good as they gave. It may be that no one was more suprised than the Arabs themselves, but at all events a pursuit of the retreating rebels began, and there were a good many savage encounters in the hills, quarter neither given nor asked on either side, as is the genial Central Asian custom.

In the meantime, while the pursuit was going on, a number of Assyrian "friendlies"—that is, Assyrians who like many of their nation were unwilling to follow the Mar Shimun in all his wild ideas—thought it advisable to seek the protection of the Iraqi police. In the area affected there was a police post at Simel with the Iraqi flag flying above it, as it had been flown daily for years. To the protection of this flag there came nearly a hundred men of the Baz tribe, voluntarily and of their own free will, to ensure that they should not be slaughtered as the result of becoming involved in the pursuit which was going on in the mountains around. It was also put about in the surrounding villages, notably by the police sergeant in charge of the Simel post, that any Assyrians wishing to make sure of their lives should come in. By August 10th about four hundred male Assyrians had arrived at Simel, and on that day all those who had arms were disarmed.

Next day the Army arrived at Simel. It is clear by now that the Army had taken the bit between its teeth. According to Assyrian propagandists the events now to be described were premeditated. It is argued that, by collusion between certain civil and police authorities on the one hand and the Army Command on the other, the stage was set for a thoroughgoing massacre. It is pointed out that the British inspecting officer of police was suddenly transferred to Baghdad and that two British officers serving with the Iraqi Army were suddenly sent to Mosul and ordered to remain there, the alleged object being to get these Englishmen removed from the possibility of seeing what was going to happen. These suppositions are more than probably justified. On August 11th the Iraqi Army Command found themselves, after several days' savage but victorious fighting against the feared Assyrians, in a position where they had about four hundred of these enemies at their mercy. The chance was too good to be missed. The slaughter began in the morning and went on till afternoon. The unarmed Assyrians were segregated by the police sergeant referred to, and were then murdered by the Iraqi Army, some being shot with revolvers, some clubbed with rifle butts, and the rest machine-gunned within their houses or as they tried to escape from them. While this was going on several Assyrians tried to change into women's clothes, but the same police sergeant busied himself going round the huts and forcing these men out into the open, where the troops dealt with them. A few women and children were killed accidentally.

Following the old Turkish custom, the authorities had brought in tribesmen, Kurds and Shammar Arabs, to loot and destroy. They did their work so well that twenty villages were completely and utterly destroyed, little being left standing, while twenty more were partially destroyed. The looting got so bad that the police finally took it upon themselves to intervene, and they attacked the marauders so heartily that the great Shaikh of the Shammar, Ajil al-Jawer, came in personally to complain to the police authorities that they were "pressing" his people unduly.

To show how completely the Army Command took control of things, it may be pointed out that on August 11th there were two thousand armed police within easy telephone call had there been any disturbance at Simel calling for police action. Moreover, a veil of silence was drawn across the north for five days. It is said, and also denied, that British aeroplanes were forbidden to fly north to Mosul. At all events during these days the British R.A.F. rest camp, which for a number of years had been established in the mountains of Ser Amadiya, was not once flown over and the troops there, who had heard vague reports of trouble, began to wonder how serious things were. What is certain is that the qaimmaqam of Dohuk, the chief local government officer in the area and only a few miles distant from Simel, did not learn of the massacre until the 16th, on which date the Minister of Interior who was then in the north, also got the first news of what had happened. He at once gave instructions for medical and every other kind of assistance to be sent up. He was also able to stop further massacres which were about to take place in two other villages. The bodies were buried within a day or two, one officer being known to have buried those of three hundred and five men, one woman and four children. Six weeks later a British officer found a few bodies of men still unburied in the houses, the whole place being completely uninhabitable.

In two other districts, Kirkuk and Rowanduz, trouble was narrowly averted. The Muslim bazaar in Kirkuk, where it is still remembered that in 1925 the Assyrian Levies ran amok and murdered about fifty or sixty Arabs, was extremely excited by a rumour that a young Muslim girl, who had been reported missing, had been murdered by the Assyrians. The timely discovery by the police that she had in fact been murdered by her aunt prevented the outbreak of an anti-Assyrian movement. The Iraqi authorities kept a firm hand on the situation and Kirkuk remained quiet. In the Rowanduz area it is known that a high Iraqi police officer had for some little time previously been going round the Kurdish tribes, endeavouring to incite them against the Assyrians. It is believed that when he learned that a small party of Assyrians decided one night to leave their village, he arranged for an "incident" to take place between them and the police. Fortunately a certain person in the neighbour-hood, whose identity I have been specially asked not to reveal, heard of the departure of these Assyrians and sent out messengers with instructions at all costs to bring them back. The messengers succeeded in intercepting them and bringing them back before any such incident could take place. Thus nothing happened at Rowanduz. At Baiji however, while there was no actual killing of Assyrians, there was a disturbance sufficient to hold up work on the Iraq Petroleum Company's pipe-line for a week. The Assyrian workmen employed by the Company became very nervous; a sub-section of the Shammar came in on motor-lorries and attempted looting and incendiarism. The Iraq Railways, a Government department, also had trouble with their Assyrians, who declined for a time to work except in a body and insisted on sending their women and children to Baghdad—where possible to the R.A.F. camp at Hinaidi.

The Muslim reaction to these events, in so far as the news was known, was extremely interesting. What every Muslim realized was that, Simel or no Simel, the Assyrian bubble was finally burst. The first days of August proved conclusively that in open fight the Arab troops were as good as the Assyrians. Moreover, whatever one's views about the Simel incident may be, there is no doubt that it clinched the matter—to use a grisly pun, the Assyrians were "settled." Opinion among the more intelligent Muslims was distinctly relieved. Among the lower classes there was evidence of great exaltation. All the Arabs were anti-British, having at once assumed that Britain would stand by the Assyrians.

While everyone who stops to think for a moment realizes that the Assyrian question is a complicated problem, containing racial, political, and religious factors, it remains true that the moment the issue comes to arms, everything is forgotten except the religious factor. This explains the state into which the Christian minorities in general were thrown. In Baghdad they were extremely nervous; in Mosul and the north I found them in a state of acute terror. When I left Baghdad I saw Hikmet Beg Sulaiman, the Minister of Interior, who gave me full permission to visit any part of the north I liked, including Simel which I had specially mentioned. When, however, I reached Mosul, I found that the Mosul taxi-drivers who are nearly all Christians, had been informed by the Army Command that any of them taking "an enquirer" around or giving any information to such a person would be killed. It was thus impossible for me to go further north than Mosul. Even in Mosul I came upon one taxi-driver who refused to overtake and pass a body of troops marching along the street, obviously afraid that the "insult" would later be visited upon him. In Mosul I found the general feeling very strongly anti-Christian and in great part anti-British. When I left the country in September, the anti-British feeling was beginning to subside, the reason being that Britain was supporting the Arabs against the Assyrians and the Arabs had begun to see that they must depend on British support at Geneva in any League inquiry into Assyrian affairs.

The Assyrians argue that the massacre was premeditated. But it is clear that when Yaku Ismail left for Syria in July he and his eight hundred followers must have been satisfied that their women-folk and property left behind in the villages would be quite safe—as in fact they were. But between August 4th when the Assyrians began to return from Syria and attacked the frontier post, and the killing at Simel, there was a week in which a massacre could have been organized. Was the killing at Simel organized? On the one hand there is ample evidence of the rounding-up and disarming of Assyrians in the village where they were almost immediately to become targets for machine-guns. There was also the removal of British officers. There are also the efforts made to provoke an "incident" in the Rowanduz area; the fact too that the Shammar were active both at Simel and Baiji needs some explaining. It seems impossible, however, to find any direct evidence bearing on these points. What is absolutely certain is that from the Army Command downwards, every individual who took anti-Assyrian action or measures, must have felt satisfied, if he was not actually assured, that he would be supported. The Government of the day in Baghdad was strongly anti-British in sentiment; indeed King Faisal had hurried home from Europe to replace it by another but found it too strong for him.[1] A blow at the Assyrians was regarded by the Cabinet as a blow at Britain as well and as such to be commended. The state of Muslim opinion was such that the Government dared not, if it would, punish any individual for his share in the massacres. The general in command was given the rank of Pasha. The troops on their return to the garrison towns had hysterical receptions and at a great parade at Mosul the Crown Prince, a few days before he was to become King, pinned decorations to the colours of the regiments which had distinguished themselves in the fighting against the Assyrians; in fairness I must, as an eye-witness, say that the motor machine-gunners, who were responsible for the actual massacres, were not picked out for any special mark of favour by the populace or distinction by the authorities. But the identification of the Assyrians with Britain was most obvious from the demeanour and shouts of the crowd. There were many shouts for the Crown Prince, not one for the King.

The women and children from Simel and refugees from the other destroyed villages were brought in to Mosul where the Iraqi Government maintained a relief camp, run by the British officer who had come from the Sudan to deal with the Assyrian settlement.[2] Later he was able to turn his attention to the question which he had come to Iraq to handle. Of the 37,000 Assyrians in Iraq, about

---

[1] This explains his desire to return at once to Europe, if not actually to abdicate. Under pressure from London he delayed his departure until the British Ambassador arrived. He left as soon thereafter as he could and in a week he was dead.

[2] The British R.A.F. looked after the dependents of men actually serving in the Levies.

a fourth were still prepared to remain—some because they had been living there since before the war and thus were not refugees from the Ottoman Empire, others because they did not support the Mar Shimun in his plans of self-aggrandizement, others again because they were simply willing to take whatever risk might attach to remaining. In the case of the rest numbering some thirty thousand souls it was clear that whatever shred of confidence had existed between them and the Arabs had gone and the only course was to emigrate them. Most of them are likely to go to British Guiana, where land on the Rupununi plateau is available for them.

### III. CHRISTIANS, JEWS AND OTHERS

The question of the other minorities is not a "problem." They comprise about 80,000 Christians of various sects, about 90,000 Jews, about 60,000 Turcoman or Turkish-speaking Muslims, about 40,000 Yezidis (Devil-worshippers), and about 4,000 Sabaeans (Mandaeans). Of these the Christians and the Jews, who for generations have maintained their own schools, are in the mass much better educated than either Arab or Kurd, and they occupy most of the middle-class positions and perform most of the middle-class functions in the towns. In government offices and business houses the Christian or Jewish effendi is ubiquitous although Muslim effendis are increasing in number. The provisions of the debt-recovery laws moreover play into their hands, chiefly the Jews. Practically every subordinate government official is in debt to moneylenders. The law provides that when a decree against a debtor is obtained, if he is an official, not more than one-third of his pay may be attached monthly. As under Scots law, this must on order from the Court be deducted by the employer, upon whom is the responsibility of paying it into court. The moneylender is thus, in all human likelihood, certain of recovering both principal and interest (the legal maximum is 9 per cent) in the case of all money loaned to young officials. All he has to do is to register the promissory agreement with a Notary Public and if the loan is not cleared at the appointed date, he merely produces this document to the judge, who must give decree; no other legal process is necessary. The moneylender then recovers his debt from the court at the rate of one-third of the debtor's salary per month, and as soon as he is finished the next one on the list begins. Thanks to this system the young debtor finds no difficulty in borrowing more, even when paying off earlier loans through the courts.

In this way the bulk of the junior civil service may be said to be in the hands of Jewish (and Christian) moneylenders. If the law were altered and the "one-third" principle done away with, leaving cases to be judged on their merits and permitting private bankruptcy, the moneylenders would not be so ready to advance money to young officials and their stranglehold on the civil service would be broken. Politically the system puts a great deal of undesirable power in the hands of the non-Muslim moneylending communities. One result of this is that the Jews and the Christians, though small minorities, are really in a strong position within the state. Apart from moneylending they control in great part the mercantile and financial business of Iraq and exercise powerful influence.

The Yezidis are a compact body living mostly on the Syrian frontier. They always maintained their independence against the Turk; during the Syrian frontier negotiations in 1932 their influence was mostly exerted in favour of incorporation within Iraq and against incorporation in Syria. The Sabaeans are a gentle race. Their men do not intermarry with the Arab women and all they ask is to be left alone. There is no sign of anything else happening to them, particularly as the silver-engraving work which is their sole calling, is an "invisible export" of some value, being bought chiefly by visitors to the country as souvenirs.

The laws provide for civil and religious freedom for these minorities. While Islam is the official religion of the state, complete freedom of conscience is allowed, both by law and in practice. Within the general provisions of the education laws, these communities may, and do, maintain their own schools. Politically they have equal status as Iraqis and they are represented in Parliament. At present they are under-represented, having regard to the varying standards of education among the Muslims on the one hand and the Christians and Jews on the other. But this must be regarded as a transition stage and in a generation or two the balance in this respect will largely be redressed. In law there are certain religious courts, within the minority communities, established under the Turks and accepted by the Iraqis. These courts deal[1] with "matters relating to marriage, dowry, divorce, separation, alimony, attestations of wills other than those attested by a Notary Public." Under Article 112 the minority non-Muslim communities may have councils to administer religious foundations and charitable bequests. These councils are administered under the supervision of the local representative of the Government. So too with various Christian and Jewish societies. These must be approved by the Ministry of Interior, but this is in accordance with the operation of a law providing for the Government regulation and control of all societies and associations, and has nothing to do with religion *qua* religion. It must, finally, be confessed that there is a good deal of discrimination against non-Muslims in the matter of appointments, particularly the more lucrative. Pressure of varying kinds and degrees is brought to bear by Government departments on non-Muslim traders; at the time of the Assyrian massacres the Iraqi Government opened a relief fund to which comparatively few Muslims contributed but to which the Christian and Jewish communities were compelled to contribute on pain of being regarded as pro-Assyrian and anti-Arab. This kind of discrimination is inevitable in a country like Iraq at its present state of evolution.

[1] Article 79 of the Constitution of Iraq.

# CHAPTER IX

## SUNNI AND SHIAH; THE HOLY CITIES

EVERY year the Shiah Muslims mourn the tragedy of Karbala in the great Passion Play which reaches its climax on the tenth day of the month of Moharram,[1] the anniversary of the battle. The mourning begins on the first day of the month and in the Shiah towns men and boys appear in black, instead of the usual white or coloured garments. There are special prayers in the mosques and the historic account of the battle is read or recited by boys chosen for their clear voices. Their hearers are intensely moved by this recounting of the great Shiah tragedy[2] and work themselves up into an ecstasy of grief. Night after night this is repeated until the eve of the Tenth of Moharram, the actual anniversary, when the Passion Play is performed. The day begins at sunset and the men go to the principal mosque, where the prayers and recitations reach a height of emotion which they have not yet reached. The women meanwhile are assembling along the route of the great procession which moves off from the mosque when the prayers and lamentations are over.

A small band of religious leaders head the procession and then come groups of breast-beaters. The beating of the breasts is a manifestation of mourning in the East. In a cholera epidemic I have seen small children of four or five running about beating their skinny chests with the open palm while dead bodies were being removed from their huts. The Moharram breast-beaters are in groups of twenty or thirty, stripped to the waist and forming a circle surrounding their leader. He acts as conductor and inciter, leading the chant of grief, "Ali! Hussain!" with his arms stretched above his head, and at rhythmic intervals he brings his flat palms down on his chest. His group follow the rhythm, each man has his left arm round the waist or shoulders of the man on his left. They bend forward as they chant, and at the appropriate intervals they strike their left breast as hard as they can with their open right hand. This is repeated a dozen or twenty times, when the group breaks up and moves forward to another station a few yards farther along,

---

[1] The first month of the Muslim year.　　　　[2] See p. 165.

when the circle is reformed and the chanting and the breast-beating are resumed. Many groups of breast-beaters thus pass in procession and then the flagellants, or chain-men, make their appearance. They walk in slow march, serried rows of them, in long black garments like executioners', which are cut away on the back, leaving the shoulder blades exposed. Each man carries a kind of cat-o'-nine-tails, consisting of chains a foot long attached to a wooden haft. They move along to their continued, ever-recurrent hoarse chant "Ali! Ali! Hussain! Hussain!" and, following a rhythm like the breast-beaters, they throw the chains over their shoulders, letting them strike on the bare flesh. They hold the haft of their scourge in both hands and bring the chains over each shoulder alternately. So the grim procession goes on, at a pace compared with which a British funeral is a brisk affair. The women along the streets ululate to show their grief, and the mourning chant comes from time to time from the watchers in the windows of the houses.

Then follows the symbolic part of this Passion Play. Men come past carrying great swinging lamps, numbers of them hung on a huge pole carried horizontally and representing the lights in the camp of the host at Karbala. Riderless camels[1] are led along, the crowd shouting in grief over the loss of their riders, Ali and Hussain. Then comes a small child on a led horse, the young son of Hussain, who was one of the last survivors of the ill-fated expedition. A strange figure now appears on horseback, wearing a travesty of European dress. Tradition says that a Christian was present at the battle and fought on the side of the defeated army. The grisliest part of the procession is to come. The head-cutters now begin to appear. They are dressed all in white, and look like men risen from the grave. Their heads are shaved and they carry in their hands huge swords. Like the breast-beaters they form themselves in circles, chanting hoarsely and fanatically, and at the same beat in the rhythm they wave their swords and bring them down, with a sharp downward movement, so that if they did touch the skin, a long incision would be made on the front part of the head, above the brow. Like the breast-beaters they repeat this a dozen or a score of times before moving along to their next station. Each circle of head-cutters has its leader, who stands in the middle shouting and

[1] Represented by horses with a "hump" on the saddle-cloth.

inciting them. Thus the procession moves along and as the night passes the emotion that grips the participants increases visibly. It is best for non-Muslims to keep out of the streets on this night of the Tenth of Moharram.

As dawn approaches the procession will have arrived at the mosque where the final prayers and recitations are repeated. By this time the celebrants are completely fanatical, in the sense that they are beside themselves with a frenzy of grief which defies analysis and baffles description. It must be remembered that the mourning has been going on for ten days, that the tragedy of Karbala is a real thing to the Shiah, who is as devout as he is ignorant, and that the whole celebration is an emotional purge. The emotion grows through the last dark hour, and when the watcher on the minaret announces the dawn the head-cutters reach their ghastly climax. All night long they have been chanting their grief-refrain and bringing their swords down in front of their heads. Their frenzy has been steadily growing and at dawn their chanting, hoarser now and quicker, works them up to the final pitch, and at a signal from their leaders, as dawn breaks, there is no longer any pretence. The sword's edge is brought down on the head with a savage cut, the blood gushes forth, and their white shrouds become crimson. They rush out into the open, their emotion over, and many are known to faint in the reaction. Now and again one of them will tear off a piece of blood-stained rag, and as he throws it away the waiting women make a dash for it, in the belief that some kind of virtue resides in it. Most of the head-cutters, whose loss of blood is in many instances serious, go to their homes, where their women-folk restore them with herbs and ointments. The morning is quiet. In the afternoon some towns repeat the nocturnal procession in a form very much modified, everyone being now sunk in the anti-climax; other towns perform a representation of the actual battle. The part of Hussain is keenly coveted and it is thought to be a great merit if the actor in this part is actually killed, as has frequently happened.

With nightfall the Tenth of Moharram ends and the Passion Play is over for another year. Cynics say that the whole representation is artificial, that it is carefully financed and organized and not spontaneous, and that the celebrants feel no emotion. It is true that in the larger towns the processions must of necessity be organized,

PRIMITIVE MERRY-GO-ROUND AT A DESERT TOWN'S CELEBRATION OF THE
FEAST THAT FOLLOWS THE FAST OF RAMADHAN

MUHARRAM PROCESSION, ASHAR CREEK, BASRAH. THE MEN WITH RIGHT ARMS
OUTSTRETCHED ARE THE CHAINMEN, HOLDING THE SCOURGE WITH WHICH
THEY FLAGELLATE THEIR BACKS

but this applies only to a nucleus of the participants and it is open to all who care to form or join groups of breast-beaters, chainmen, or head-cutters, provided they fall into their place in the programme. The financing is largely done through charitable bequests left by the pious, and of course the mullahs and mosque attendants draw certain fees and emoluments. It is also said that the breast-beating and the scourging with chains is more symbolic than real. But the dull sound of this beating of hundreds of chests can be heard from great distances on a still night, and bruised and bleeding chests and backs are a common sight. No doubt some of the celebrants are less ascetic than others in their self-imposed agony, but in general the emotional pitch is such that there is small thought of restraint in this martyrdom. But there is no more artificial stimulus than in the case of the more important celebrations of the Christian churches, and if ignorance and illiteracy is a fair test of religious fervour, then there can be no question of the Shiah's emotional purge in Moharram. In the more fanatical towns, such as the Holy Cities of Iraq, or the more out-of-the-way parts of Persia, the Passion Play retains its former purity and intensity. In the more modernized towns it is controlled by the police and has undergone certain modifications in the interests of public order. In the larger cities police are interspersed among various groups in the procession, the swords of the head-cutters are of wood, and the actual incision on the head is made by the police with razors. Thus the fanatical frenzy of the ecstatics is curbed and controlled in the interest of the law. It remains to be said that only the Shiahs hold the first days of Moharram as days of universal mourning. The Sunnis have no interest in the Passion Play.

The Shiah-Sunni schism goes back to the early days of Islam. In Iraq to-day it is strongly in evidence and is indeed a political factor of which the most serious account must be taken. Yet how many people in Britain know anything about it at all! In the former Turkish territories in Asia it was the Sunnis that ruled; in every part of those territories except Lower Mesopotamia, the Sunni population was in the majority. But in the new Iraq, while the oligarchic control is still in the hands of the Sunnis, the Shiahs numerically are in the majority. There are approximately a million and a half Shiah Arabs in Iraq, while the Sunnis total less than a million and a quarter, of whom half a million are Kurds and not Arabs at all. The four Shiah Holy Cities—Najaf, Karbala, Kadhimain and Samarra—are in Iraq and are dominated entirely by the priesthood, which is largely Persian by origin and in sympathy. The percentage of literacy is very low among the Shiahs, and except for the highly organized and wealthy priesthood they have no traditions or experience of ruling. The Holy Cities are enormously wealthy. Pilgrims from Shiah countries, notably Persia and India, come in large numbers and thus spend a good deal of money in the country. There is too a considerable corpse-traffic. Shiahs who are buried in the Holy Cities acquire much religious merit, the result being that these cities are great cities of the dead. The cemeteries contain thousands upon thousands of graves, near to or distant from the principal shrines according to the fees paid—either from money saved up for the purpose by the individual against the day of his burial, or contributed by pious relatives. This corpse-traffic is officially organized, the Customs and the Health Department both being interested. The former collects a small duty and examines the corpse to prevent smuggling; the Health Department must keep a wary eye on epidemics. Most of the corpses thus sent to Iraq for burial are classified as "dry," that is, desiccated as the result of previous burial; the number of "wet" corpses is not so considerable. The "dry" corpses are extremely light; a dozen or so can be tied lengthwise on a donkey, and on the roads to the Holy Cities one can see dozens of donkeys stepping out with their *macabre* loads.

The organization of the pilgrimages is in its way as complete as the organization at Mecca. In its essence it is the same. The pilgrim, having saved up for years, at length makes his pious journey. He gets to the Holy City and remains there till his money is done, after which the Holy City has no further interest in him—even the beggar-classes will see to it that he does not remain. Every inhabitant of these towns lives on religion. The townspeople cater for the pilgrim's material wants. The Shiah pilgrim is even provided with a temporary wife, to whom he is *legally* married during his pilgrimage and whose children, if any, are reared and "educated" by the religious foundations. Much of the pilgrim's money, however, goes in fees to the priesthood and in gifts to the shrines. Members of the principal religious leaders in the Holy Cities of Iraq have annual incomes running into five figures *sterling*. There are monthly distributions of charity doles to the religious, the usual method of election to the approved lists being nepotism. Vice is rampant. Najaf and Karbala are full of colleges where young boys and youths are trained for the priesthood. These colleges are sinks of iniquity. The houses in both towns have tier upon tier of deep cellars, used for coolness during the hot summer days. These cellars, some containing tombs, are a usual feature of Arab houses, but in the Holy Cities the cellars interconnect between house and house. In the past this presented opportunities for crime compared with which the palaces of the Sultans or of Renaissance Italy were Sunday-schools. The increasing power and reach of the Iraqi police has, however, altered this.

Politically, the Shiah Holy Cities were the centres of intrigue during the early days of the British occupation. The object of the priesthood was to resist and prevent any civil control over their activities; they objected to a settled government by whomsoever exercised. The 1920 rebellion, fomented largely as we have seen from Syria, drew much of its inspiration from the Shiah divines who, however troubled the waters, know all the tricks of the weather-wise fisherman. It is by no means certain that the danger is over. The middle and lower Euphrates was always a thorn in the side of the Turks, and the Sunni oligarchy now governing in Baghdad are by no means certain what the future may hold in store for them in this turbulent region. There was trouble in the summer of 1933, but fortunately for the Baghdad Government the trouble was swept on one side by the Assyrian massacres, which caught the attention of all Muslims and the lesser difficulty was swallowed up by the greater. In the early months of that year there was a battle of books in Iraq. A young Sunni of a politico-religious turn of mind published an Eatanswill pamphlet attacking the Shiahs. The Shiah priesthood at once objected and the Government taking proceedings against the youth had him sent to prison for six months. But his pamphlet had raised the ire of a Shiah youth, who retorted in kind and fled from Baghdad to one of the Holy Cities. The Iraqi Government found it impossible to bring him to justice, and the situation became so strained that an elder relative of the boy, a Shiah holding high political office on the side of the Government, found it necessary to "take a holiday" abroad. One of the early difficulties that faced the late King Faisal was to hold even the scales as between Shiah and Sunni; he succeeded by his clever methods of temporizing. But the Shiah problem remains, and Britain is vitally interested in it, for the Shiahs of the Euphrates straddle the communications between the British air-bases and the head of the Persian Gulf.[1]

What then are Shiahs and Sunnis? For Iraq the problem has travelled far from the original schism, which in this sense becomes only of academic interest, but its consequences have become of great political importance. The Laws of Islam are based on the Koran. From the first there were four schools of jurisprudence and the Sunnis still follow the interpretations of the law as laid down by the original founders of those schools. But the Shiahs[2] broke away on a point of interpretation. It is recorded that the Prophet, sending a man out to collect alms for the poor, asked him by what rule he would act in unusual circumstances. The man replied that failing direct guidance from the Koran itself or from the recognized "Traditions of the Prophet," he would himself make a "logical deduction" and act on it. The Shiahs maintain that the Prophet then sanctioned this method of interpreting the law. Thus while the Sunni must still follow the original interpretations, the Shiah priesthood can, and emphatically does, interpret the law to meet circumstances as they arise. That is the arid theological basis for the schism. To this was soon to be added an emotional impetus that has turned an ancient scholastic disputation into a living political issue to-day.

When Muhammad the Prophet died, Ali his cousin and son-in-law, was left as the most saintly of the Muslim leaders. In his old age, as Khalif, noted for his holiness, he was praying in the mosque at Kufa, near Baghdad, when he was mortally wounded by an assassin. In the confusion he escaped on a camel, having left instructions with his followers that they were to follow him and bury him where they found him. Neither camel nor body was found, however,

[1] There is moreover the Oudh Bequest in which Britain is interested. In the 1825 Burmese war the King of Oudh loaned 100 lakhs of rupees to the British authorities. The principal was never to be repaid, but the interest was to be devoted to certain charitable objects, including a distribution among British-Indian Shiahs in Najaf and Karbala.

[2] Britain for reasons of policy does not regard the Shiah as schismatic, holding both Shiah and Sunni as equal.

and there immediately sprang up a cult of Ali. He became the centre of miraculous legend and frenzied devotion, and when, in due time the great Caliph Harun-ar-Rashid, while on a hunting trip from Baghdad, found in a thicket the bones of a man and a camel, everyone knew that God had led him to the sacred spot. A great shrine was built, and what is now the Holy City of Najaf grew around it. Now after the death of Ali, his opponent, who had seized the power, wished to ensure the succession of his own son. But this youth turned out to be a profligate, and the scandalized people of Kufa sent to Mecca for Ali's son Hussain, pledging their support if he would come and seize the Khalifate again for his family. He set out from Mecca with about a hundred foot soldiers and forty horsemen. His enemies mustered three thousand and when the two forces met, on the plains of Karbala, the people of Kufa failed to appear. The little force was reduced by slaughter and by thirst, and after three days only Hussain and his young son were left. A chance missile killed the child. The enemy till then had refrained from harming any of Ali's blood, but now that the child was gone there was no more need for scruples. So Hussain was overborne and killed, his head being cut off and carried away. This is the Battle of Karbala which is annually commemorated in the Moharram Passion Play, which I have described. The small cult of Ali has grown into a great emotional cult of Ali and Hussain. The Sunnis take no part in this Moharram mourning and when the Turks held Iraq they allowed no procession, except in places where they were not in a position to stop them. Thus the Sunni-Shiah differences have come to mean more than a doctrinal schism. The two communities are now deeply coloured by the results of the split—educationally, emotionally and politically. The Shiah question is of the utmost moment in any discussion of the future of this part of the world.

# CHAPTER X

# INTERNAL ADMINISTRATION

## THE CONSTITUTION AND THE CIVIL SERVICE

IRAQ is a constitutional monarchy. When the negotiations were taking place in 1921 for the accession of King Faisal he insisted that, in view of Arab conceptions of monarchy and his own personal position, the "monarchy" in the new state must be made the *legal* property of himself and his direct heirs. He himself had great powers although of necessity he had to do lip-service to the democratic principle which was nominally adopted in 1920–21 to bring the realities of the local situation into line with American idealism. He controlled the ruling junta, and was in effect one of the *media* between British policy and the Arab executive.

But the democratic façade is maintained. The Organic Law provides for the vesting of legislative power in Parliament (an upper and a lower house) with the King. In practice there is no democratic basis for this constitution, for there is no democracy. Of a total population which is estimated at about three millions, the literate and politically conscious do not exceed 500,000, if indeed they reach that figure. The Jews and Christians are literate up to a point, but the tribal Arabs and the labouring classes are almost entirely illiterate. Those Arabs who are educated or literate are, firstly the aristocracy and their sons, and secondly the rapidly increasing number of effendis who are forming a new middle-class and numbers of whom are mercantile by origin. But not even all of these may vote in elections.

Parliament consists of a Senate and a Chamber. The membership of the Senate may not exceed twenty. Members are appointed by the King "from among those who have gained the confidence and trust of the people and who have an honourable past in the service of the Government and the country."[1] The Senate is thus largely composed of the King's Party. In the Chamber there is one deputy for every twenty thousand male Iraqi subjects, and the minorities must be represented. The voting is on the old Turkish system of

[1] *Progress of Iraq.*

primary and secondary elections. In practice the elections are arranged, if not indeed manipulated, by the authorities, who work through the provincial governors and their subordinates. At election times it is vain to expect any urgent work to go through a government department, the reason given being that the high civil servants "are busy with the elections." The letter of the law is by no means adhered to, and most of the election regulations are not observed. The system is not democracy as the Western world has known it. In effect the government is oligarchic, with the King as benevolent autocrat. Until the end of the Mandate the King was in more or less close touch with the High Commissioner, Britain having to be satisfied that no election complications should arise that were likely to compromise British Mandatory responsibilities. The King and his Party now have a freer hand, but Britain's views are always well known to the authorities.

One of the difficulties that face Iraq, and one which will continue for a generation, is the lack of first-class men, or men of what in the West we call "Cabinet rank." At the most there are not more than half a dozen in the country; it is possible, if not probable, that six is an over-estimate. Many members of Parliament are far below Western Parliamentary standards.[1] There are men who have held office in Iraqi Cabinets who if in Britain, would be members of the Second Division of the Civil Service, and no more.[2]

But all this will be remedied as soon as the new generation comes along. The Turks in the old days controlled all the major appointments, and in many cases the Arabs have been thrust too soon into positions rather beyond their grasp. But as the present juniors are promoted and the youngsters graduate from the schools, a new tradition of public service should arise.

There are two dangers. One is the objection to transfer which is frequently made by officials. The other is the possibility of underpayment leading to corruption. It is unfair to submit a judge, on a meagre salary, to the temptation of having to take in the civil

[1] This is not an argument that Iraq should be judged by Western standards: it is a way of illustrating for the enlightenment of Western readers the calibre of the men on whom Iraq can at present call.

[2] Many of them are heavily indebted to an important unofficial moneylender, a once-charming but now middle-aged woman of considerable wealth and great business acumen, who largely controls the Baghdad brothels.

courts commercial cases involving thousands of pounds. The inside police administration, through similar under-payment, is also subjected to undesirable pressure. The ethical position is complicated by the fact that the Turkish tradition, to which the country was accustomed for four hundred years, regarded it as perfectly natural and justifiable that a man should use his official or Parliamentary position to extort what he could from those having official dealings with him. This was true in the old days from the highest to the lowest, and it will take some time to eradicate these ideas. It is probably fair to say that corruption exists in every country in the world and that each country has its own limits to what it will stand in the way of graft by public men. Some countries reach the limit early and mete out drastic punishment to the offenders. It takes longer to stir the public conscience of others. Every country ultimately fixes its own code of honour in official and public life.

The Iraqi Civil Service, as such, suffers from the abnormal haste with which it was called into existence. The Civil Administration, during the British occupation, laid the foundations well, and continuity was ensured by the transference to the new Iraqi departments of many of the British officials and numbers of the Iraqi personnel. The senior Iraqis, tarred with the Turkish brush, and in many cases depending on political and other influence to obtain or retain their jobs, were not of uniform capability, and efforts to clear out the inefficients did not entirely succeed, although the Government still retains ample powers of dismissal. Americans are not surprised, although some Europeans are, at the form of general post in high offices that occasionally follows a change of government; another instance of the maxim that a state will develop its institutions, not on any absolute standard of merit or efficiency, but in accordance with the opinions and predilections of its people. But the civil service in Iraq is definitely underpaid; therein lies this danger of corruption. Not only are they underpaid basically, but they have had their salaries cut and their complement reduced, while British and Indian officials, on contracts, have seen their rates of pay maintained if not increased.[1] It is true that the rate of pay is higher

---

[1] The rupee was currency during the whole of the British period until 1932, and when the new currency was introduced (see p. 188), it did not, as had been hoped, lower the cost of living.

THE KINGDOM OF IRAQ

than in Turkey or Persia, for instance, where the officials are not even regularly paid, but Iraq is a costly country to live in and the rupee is a costly unit of currency. One real trouble that leads to corruption in Iraq is that thanks to British example, Iraqis of the official class have adopted far too high a standard of living. This explains in large measure why nine-tenths of the Government officials are in debt. Yet, especially among the younger officials, there are discernible the beginnings of a tradition, the feeling that the service is a career of honour primarily and not of self-advancement. The trouble is that the average citizen, when he approaches a Government office, remembers the old Ottoman maxim and goes prepared with his bribe. This habit of mind will persist until such time as the civil service pay and conditions of service (chiefly as regards security) improve and the new tradition strengthens. One marked sign of progress is already evident; while the old officials thought it the natural thing to take a bribe, the younger generation, though perhaps accepting bribes, knows that it is wrong to do so.

### THE MINISTRY OF INTERIOR

The Ministry of Interior is the principal department of state. It controls the whole of the administration of the country through the mutasarrifs, or governors, of the provinces into which the country is divided and who are responsible for the administration of all departments in their areas. It also controls the entire machinery of the elections and does not fail to exercise this power. The country is divided into *liwas*, or provinces, each under a mutasarrif. The liwas are subdivided into *qadhas* (under qaimmaqams), which are again subdivided into *nahiyas* (under mudirs).

The senior officials are nearly all men who held official posts under the Ottoman regime. The more incompetent of these were either not employed or were removed at an early date from employment, and there is now a system of selection in operation which on the whole has worked satisfactorily. Until Iraq entered the League as an independent state, each mutasarrif had a British adviser, called the Administrative Inspector for the liwa. As is shown in the chapter on Anglo-Iraqi Relations[1] the functions of the

---

[1] See pp. 78 *et seqq.*

# Iraq

Administrative Inspectors were gradually modified from a position of quasi-executive control to one of advice pure and simple. The reports of these British officials have had in some cases a good deal to do with the subsequent careers of their mutasarrifs. The few remaining British advisers will not be replaced.

The mutasarrif is the representative of the King and the Government and is the chief executive officer in his liwa, being the agent and representative not merely of the Ministry of Interior, which appoints him, but of every Ministry. The qaimmaqams report to their mutasarrif, from whom they receive their orders, and the mudirs in their turn carry out the orders of their qaimmaqam and also any that the mutasarrif may transmit to them direct. In some liwas the British Administrative Inspector has been replaced by an Iraqi official who has the functions of an inspector. This system has yet to prove itself.

Baghdad, Basrah and Mosul are the principal municipalities, with a round dozen of townships of secondary rank. These municipalities are administered by local councils[1] but the Ministry of Interior retains a close control of all their activities by virtue of the fact that each mayor derives his appointment and authority from the Ministry. The Ministry also lays down the general lines which the municipal budgets must follow and thus not only controls but directs the local government in most of its activities. On the whole, municipal administration is not good. In the elections the Ministry, through its district officials, is most active. The electors in the local primary and secondary elections are as carefully "seeded" as lawn-tennis players at Wimbledon; the democratic façade is maintained but the oligarchic principle is maintained. So far as the officials are concerned they are political almost as much as administrative; at the elections not one-tenth of the regulations are carried out.

A strong mutasarrif exercises great moral sway in his area. He can compel support for any object in which he may be interested, simply by letting it be known that he expects the leading merchants and others to give it. This no doubt is an inheritance from the old Ottoman days when it frankly paid the leading people to curry favour

---

[1] Baghdad is administered by a "Lord Mayor" (Amin-al-Asimah) with a City Council; the other municipalities by a Rais-al-Baladiyah, with a Baladiyah Council.

with the Turkish governor. No doubt in the past this influence was exercised in undesirable ways, but the Arab officials have had experience, since the days of the British Civil Administration, of the rigid line which, in the British practice is drawn between a man's official life and his private interests, and between what is constitutional and what is not. A curious inheritance from the Turkish times is that some of the higher officials, and in particular the holders of certain hereditary offices, still think they should enjoy public services, such as the supply of water or electricity, free of charge, or should have a call upon public employees, such as police, soldiers or firemen, to perform private services (as night-watchmen, car-cleaners, and the like) without payment. Apart from the petty corruption, the practice means that other people are kept out of employment.

The maintenance of public order is one of the principal functions of the Ministry of Interior. Police in the modern sense were non-existent when the British entered the country. There was a kind of local gendarmerie, under slack Turkish control, organized municipally and not nationally. There was also a semi-official and ill-organized force of armed night-watchmen maintained by private individuals at their own cost. These night watchmen remain but are less loosely organized now. Most business firms and the bigger private householders employ them, paying their wages and in addition a small tax to the Municipality, which keeps a register with the object of excluding undesirables from this force. The value of the night-watchman, even if he does go to sleep, is that he remains at his post, whereas the night-police are on beat which the criminal soon learns. The night-police, even in the bigger towns, are armed and normally patrol in pairs.

When the British entered the country, they first maintained order by means of military police. Experienced officers were brought from India and the raw Turkish gendarmerie were taken in hand. From this material, an excellent police force was evolved, within a period of half a dozen years. British police officers were in charge in each area as well as at headquarters, controlling both the outdoor work and the department of criminal investigation, which under the Ottoman regime had not existed at all. British non-commissioned officers, too, did excellent work; in some respects their influence was even more marked than that of the British gazetted officers. At the time of the rebellion in 1920 there were regular police only in a few districts and towns. Elsewhere local levies operated under the orders of the Political Officers on the spot; where British control was not yet effective, as in the wilder districts of the north and west, there was then no police at all. But police penetration and organization went ahead rapidly and within eight or ten years the police star[1] was to be seen everywhere, in the desert where the camel and motor patrols work along the principal tracks as far as the frontiers, and in the mountains of the north and north-east, where the police have frequently co-operated in military operations, their training in these operations comparing favourably with that of the army.

The total strength of the police force is about nine thousand. It is now entirely under Iraqi direction. There are about 4,000 foot and 4,000 mounted police (camel and horse). They are predominantly Arabs and in the more northerly districts Kurds. The policy is to maintain a large striking force based on Baghdad, so that order may be maintained in the capital in the event of disturbances. One danger arising out of this policy is that other districts may be dangerously denuded of police in order to maintain this force in Baghdad. In 1931, for instance, when strikes took place in various towns, there were only about fifty police left in Basrah and when trouble broke out there aeroplanes and special trains were required in order to take down reinforcements.

It has been said that with the removal of British control, even of British inspection, the efficiency of the police has suffered. This does not seem to be true as regards the external appearance of the force. It may be true as regards the keeping of station-house records and other details "behind the scenes." It is probably true on the C.I.D. side, for under the Iraqi law the police, in the event of an arrest on certain criminal charges, may decide without reference to the courts that there is no case. But this is a question not so much of professional inefficiency, as of varying standards of professional morality among officers all of whom are underpaid and most of whom are old enough to remember the Ottoman regime, when justice by tradition and practice went to the highest bidder and in an official appointment the salary was normally regarded

[1] Worn on the hat.

as a side-line. There is danger too of political influence in appointments.

The moral effect of having police now in practically every village in the country has had important results. The outlying populations who in the old days never saw the representative of the Government and to whom law and order meant nothing, now realize that the Government can reach them. The statistics of the past ten or fifteen years show a regular annual increase in crimes and in convictions. These increases do not mean that there is more crime, although the slump of the last four years has certainly increased petty crime; it means that the number of detected and reported crimes has gone up. This clearly implies a growing confidence in the police. Indeed it has frequently happened that old crimes that had never been heard of have been reported to the police in outlying districts once confidence in the force was established. The recruiting of the police is easier now than it was, and a good type of man is coming forward. The percentage of literates too is rising. There is a police training school, the object of which is to ensure a uniform system of training, particularly among the higher ranks, members of which return from time to time for refresher courses. The Criminal Investigation Department covers also political enquiries and keeps careful record of the movements of all foreigners—passports, nationality and naturalization are under its control. On the purely criminal side they have some excellent *coups* to their credit.

Why are so many murders committed in Iraq? Most of them follow upon some insult to the family honour and by custom are therefore justifiable.[1] In most cases the persons murdered are women. The family name dishonoured remains the cardinal reason for these murders and the explanation is to be found in the Muslim custom of the seclusion of women. Most of these women are murdered by their male relatives, namely, fathers, brothers or sons. Here is a typical instance taken from police records. A. B. came to the police-station with a blood-stained dagger in his hand and then informed the Police Inspector that he had just killed his sister called C. D. When the Police Inspector asked him why, he replied that one of his fingers was dishonourable and nothing could be done to cure it except to cut it off. This is the traditional metaphor

[1] See p. 20 and also Chapter XII.

used in these cases; the finger is the offending person and the cutting off is death. In this particular case it appeared that the woman's first husband had divorced her some considerable time previously. She then married a second time, but her new husband discovered within a fortnight that she was an expectant mother. He intimated this to her family who then deputed A. B. to kill her. It is to be noted that the husband's "duty" ends when he reports the matter to the wife's family.

Here is another case from police records; E. F. was divorced by her husband and suddenly disappeared, nothing being heard of her except that she had become a prostitute. She was searched out by her brother and her mother, and she told them that she wished to repent of her way of living. As they were walking along past a Kurdish encampment near Baghdad, the son whispered in his mother's ear that his sister had deprived him of his honour and that he would kill her. To this the mother made no answer. The son drew from his pocket a knife, stabbed his sister on the spot, and then gave himself up to a passing policeman. In another case an advocate succeeded in getting a sentence of ten years' imprisonment that had been passed on two men reduced to imprisonment for one year, for murdering their niece because they had found her in a Baduin tent with a police-tracker. They murdered the girl because the discovery was a disgrace to them. The advocate proved to the satisfaction of the court that in such cases only a minimum punishment is inflicted. These are examples taken absolutely at random and typical of the manners and morals which exist. It is of course impossible to pass death-sentence in these cases; the circumstances of the murder are such that the murderer becomes an honoured and respected man for having in this way cleared the family's name.

A further complication arises from the two systems of law that have to be adjusted. The tribesman is subject to tribal custom and very wisely the constitution of Iraq provides for the incorporation of tribal custom within the four corners of the Westernized law which runs in the cities. A tribesman charged with murder of this sort has the right to demand trial by a tribal court, consisting of two or three shaikhs, as opposed to trial in a court of law. The old scriptural maxim of "an eye for an eye and tooth for a tooth" still holds in the desert, but the authority of the Central Government and the police, largely due to the wide adoption of modern methods of transport, is extending and the continuance of a blood-feud by a steadily increasing series of murders is becoming less and less common. As a rule, even before the shaikhs' tribunal, the blood-feud is now patched up by a marriage or by the payment of a certain sum as blood-money. These tribal judgments have the full sanction of the law, and no doubt in time the two systems will fuse into one; it will, however, take some generations before this can be achieved. The town politicians are trying to hasten the process; the desert code however has in practice proved its merits as a code.

The gaols are under separate administration. As in many Eastern countries a European gaol administration is in a dilemma. If humane standards are to be maintained, then gaol-life for the ordinary criminal from the lower classes is more attractive (apart from the lack of liberty) than his "home" life, particularly in bad weather. On the other hand, the comforts of a prison in the East need not necessarily be judged by Western standards. In the Iraqi gaols the prisoners are all engaged on task-work of various sorts. The blankets and socks of the army and police are nearly all made in the gaols by short-term men who quickly learn to work the machines. The long-term men are usually put on carpet-weaving. The designs are Persian, the overseer is always a man of Persian experience, and the carpets turned out are excellent products. Female prisoners are employed on washing and repairing prisoners' clothes. Boys are dealt with in a reformatory school in Baghdad, where elementary schooling is given. As such boys are invariably illiterate this gives them a big advantage on their discharge. The reformatory has been operated on the most enlightened Western lines and has done excellent work.

The remaining major department of the Ministry of Interior is the department of health. When the British Army entered the country they found that whatever rudiments of a health service the Turks had had was destroyed, and there remained only a few medical officers and a handful of French nuns who were nursing the sick in Baghdad. There was thus nothing on which to build and a health service had to be constructed *ab initio*. Numbers of Royal Army Medical Corps personnel were taken over and given civil contracts and a first-class service was thus inaugurated, employing the latest practice and with the most up-to-date equipment and apparatus. British nursing sisters were also given contracts and British medical officers were established in all the urban centres. In Baghdad, Basrah and Mosul higher medical treatment can be given. In Baghdad the standard of proficiency and equipment in the Royal Hospital is as high as any east of Suez.

The transition to Iraqi control though gradual, had an adverse effect upon the standard of efficiency. British doctors, if they were to be attracted to the services, had to receive terms at least as good as they could command at home. The Syrian and Iraqi doctors, numbers of them graduates of British universities, found themselves on very much smaller salaries, and they could not help seeing that many of the British medical officers, in addition to their by no means meagre salaries, were enjoying highly lucrative private practices as consultants. As the long contracts went on, a number of the British doctors allowed themselves to get out of date, the enervating climate making it difficult for them to keep up their reading and maintain touch with the most modern practice. None the less their removal led to a loss to efficiency, as also did the dismissal of British nursing sisters. The difference was to be seen in the general cleanliness, particularly in notions of asepsis. The Iraqi doctors will not leave the big towns, the Syrians are out to make as much as they can and to return to Syria.

There are hospitals and dispensaries scattered throughout the country and the steadily increasing number of out-patients dealt with (increasing from about 700,000 in 1921 to nearly 4,000,000 in 1932) shows the public appreciation of the health service. The in-patients do not show much change because of the limited number of beds. The Royal College of Medicine in Baghdad produced its first crop of graduates in 1932, and lectures and examinations in the Medical College are on the British standard. Tuition is free, but graduates must enter Government service for the five years following their qualification. Training is also given to medical personnel of the lower grades.

Apart from maintaining the day-to-day health of the community, the health service must ever be prepared to cope with epidemics. There is an efficient Pathological Department, under a British

POINT-DUTY POLICEMAN IN BAGHDAD

THE DESERT POLICE-PATROL

specialist, which prepares vaccines to meet the emergencies of epidemics and to cope with the endemic smallpox and rabies. The conditions under which masses of the people live, their ignorance, and their small powers of resistance (due in large part to malnutrition), make them particularly susceptible to the ravages of epidemics. Plague is endemic in Baghdad, and small outbreaks are to be expected in the spring of the year, when the floods come down and the rising Tigris drives the rats up from the cellars and basements. Europeans are seldom affected, although a young Englishman died in Baghdad of plague (a mysteriously isolated case) in the summer of 1932. Cholera appears to sweep through Southern Iraq every four years. The pre-war epidemics were allowed by the Turks to run their course from their outbreak in late summer until the cold weather killed the disease. In post-war years the big epidemics have been in 1923, 1927 and 1931 and Basrah has been the centre of them. There is now a definite anti-cholera plan of operations which is at once put into force whenever the first cases appear. Police guards are put on all the routes into and out of the infected areas and a complete system of inoculation certificates and travel-permits is set up. There is a petty form of graft in connection with the sale of inoculation certificates but this is inevitable when the bulk of the people inoculated are illiterate and the minor officials are poorly paid. One awkward complication of the Basrah cholera epidemics is that when they happen they coincide with the date-season, at a time when it is necessary to bring into the area thousands of packing women, whose low standard of existence makes the type which goes down easily and who are too superstitious and ignorant to take proper precautions against the disease.[1] The medical authorities can only organize this great invasion of labour as best they can, and they do this with the co-operation of the great date-packing firms and the contractors who supply the labour. All they can do is to maintain a reasonably just balance between the claims of the epidemiological purist and the commercial claims of the date trade, which is the life-blood of Southern Iraq and the stoppage of

---

[1] Cholera is water-borne, but these women insist on drinking from creek-water, however filthy; they refuse to drink the municipal tap-water which is of necessity chlorinated, as they think that chlorinated water induces barrenness.

or undue interference with which would mean big losses to the firms engaged in the trade, and plunge into destitution thousands directly and indirectly dependent on it. It should be noted here that even in a cholera season there is no danger in eating these exported dates. The date is the only kind of fruit which when it ripens does not rot but undergoes a chemical change into a sugar compound which kills the germs of diseases of man such as cholera. This has been established by bacteriological tests.[1] Among other minor epidemics which may occur from time to time is typhus, which is present to a greater or less degree every winter. The health authorities can normally control it unless it breaks out in some isolated tribe. In such a case the epidemic may run its course before medical attention can reach it. Moreover the Baduin of the high, clean desert are normally not immune to these diseases, which once they start are apt to sweep unchecked right through a tribe. Smallpox is endemic in Iraq: vaccination is becoming more general and the disease is seldom fatal. One sees fewer pock-marked children in the streets than pock-marked adults, just as there are fewer blind children or children with diseased eyes—an indication of the excellent preventive work that the health department has done during past years.

Syphilis is almost universal. Minor but common diseases are malaria fever, sandfly fever, bilharzia and ankylostomiasis. The Arab is too prone to regard these as normal, or at least not abnormal, conditions and the proportion of the affected is high. Treatment is seldom asked for except in the case of fever, when quinine is in request from the dispensaries or from the employer, and in cases where the treatment is inoculation, for the jab with the needle appears to be regarded as a sure specific. A more general knowledge of the principles of hygiene, partly through observation of the life of the European residents (very much more numerous than before the war), partly through increased facilities for foreign travel, partly through the steady propaganda work done in the schools, in the army and in the police, is evident. The older generation are of course too old to be caught in the change, but the younger generation without doubt are possessed of the new ideas.

Mortality in child-birth is still very high, although not so high

---

[1] For description of date growing, see p. 209.

as it appears to have been in pre-war times, though the absence of Turkish statistics always makes such comparisons difficult. The old-fashioned midwife was the ignorant harpy whose stock-in-trade was filthy habits and superstitious methods. The midwives of to-day are all properly trained, registered and controlled on the same lines as in Britain. The lying-in hospitals are popular among the richer Jewish and Christian women, but the seclusion of Muslim women and the veil prevent their use at present by any save a tiny minority of Arabs. A good deal of welfare work among women is done, but so far there is little grasp of the idea that this is properly a public service and not one that should mainly be left to charity.

One of the major difficulties confronting the Health Service is the primitive standard of life among large sections of the population. Ideas of hygiene are elementary in the extreme. The Koranic injunction of cleanliness is obeyed by washing in water that is running, however dirty it may be. The creeks and streams are used for the supply of drinking water, for ablutions, as wash-tubs, as informal lavatories, sewers—all indiscriminately. It follows that when a water-borne epidemic breaks out, it is liable to sweep through a district, causing heavy mortality. Ancient superstitions too are among the bugbears with which the doctors have to contend. Charms and amulets, usually of turquoise blue, are as popular as quack remedies; all of them are based upon ignorance and it is doubly unfortunate if a cure happens to coincide with the use of such nostrums. In 1931 a man in Baghdad was imprisoned for the manslaughter of a boy from whom he was "exorcising a devil." The wretched boy was beaten to death, but all the neighbours and even his relatives thought the treatment correct.

General sanitation systems are non-existent. In the towns each house has its own cess-pit; in the large towns there is a municipally organized removal of household refuse daily. Baghdad, Basrah and Mosul have adequate systems of chlorinated water supply. But, through ignorance or meanness, a certain number of people are unwilling to instal taps, thus depriving the water authority of revenue. It is only the spread of education that will put this right; the process is helped by good local officials, where such exist.

Among the other varied duties of the Ministry of Interior is the administration of the Law of Association. This is an old law, inherited

Iraq

from the Turkish time, designed to control the activities of organizations which might become secret or subversive. In practice it gives the Government the right to control or interfere with *any* society or club, whether Muslim, Jewish or Christian, whether sporting or dramatic or social.

The Press Bureau is part of the Ministry. Its function is to issue statements and news to the press. The Ministry also administers the extremely rigorous Press Law, which provides that no periodical may be published without a permit, which is not granted until a heavy deposit is paid. The power of suspension, which is unlimited, is freely used by the Government with the result that there is no real expression of whatever public opinion may exist. Baghdad is the centre of political life and all the intriguing and wire-pulling takes place there. Basrah and Mosul have their own problems and are anti-Baghdad in sentiment, largely because of the prevalent, though not quite correct, view that the capital takes from them in taxation more than it returns to them in services. The smaller towns and the villages, while appreciating the new security of life and communications, have no political views except of the parish-pump variety. Moreover as the great mass of people are illiterate there is no popular basis for the press, which also finds distribution through the country so difficult that they have scarcely begun to think about it. Apart, therefore, from one or two purely local papers in Basrah and Mosul[1] the press of Iraq is centred in Baghdad. It is possible for any politician to start a paper to make attacks on his enemies, and if it is suppressed he has by then attained his object. It will have circulated, during its brief life, among the politically minded effendis, and through the coffee-shops, where someone able to read goes through all the papers for the benefit of his illiterate hearers. Many of the political papers have therefore a short or at most intermittent life. Apart from the Arabic press there is one English daily, the *Iraq Times* (formerly the *Baghdad Times*), a commercial concern owned by an Iraqi Company, though it is British-controlled and most of the shareholders are British.[2] It is printed in English and

[1] There is a small paper at Rowanduz, whose editor sets his own type and makes his own woodcuts.
[2] This paper is the survivor of two papers started during the occupation for the benefit of the British troops.

Arabic and gives the news of the day without political bias. Its policy has been to avoid internal politics, except to support the Government of the day, and its editorial influence has been small. Arabic papers come into the country from Syria and Egypt. There is a growing class greedy to read all that they can. The future of journalism in Iraq should be promising provided the standard of qualifications and the code of honour among the Arab journalists can be raised. The Press Law provides that the man responsible for the running of a newspaper shall be a man of certain standards of education. Education of course has nothing to do with journalistic capacity or with professional ethics. At present it is the case that the staffs of two papers of opposing political views carry this opposition to the point of personal enmity. Much of the political argument in the Baghdad papers is of the Eatanswill sort.

CHAPTER XI

FINANCE

ALTHOUGH Iraq is potentially rich and though she has no public debt burden there is chronic difficulty in balancing the budget. The root of the difficulty is that the huge war-expenditure by Britain in Iraq and the boom that followed the peace treaties put Iraq's outgoings and revenues upon a swollen basis. The country had small purchasing power in the days before the war. The *fellahin* and coolie classes live on less than a penny a day per head. The rent of the average reed-hut if set up on private lands varies between a shilling and eighteenpence per month. It is only on festivals and such occasions that new clothes are bought, and then only of the cheapest sort. There are probably two million people in the country living on such standards, and it can be imagined what purchasing power they possess and what revenue they can raise. Clerks skilled neither as accountants nor stenographers make at the most the equivalent of £5 a month. They must buy neat clothes of the European style, shoes, collars and so on. Skilled artisans may possibly make £2 a week, but under £1 is much nearer the average. The merchant-class, many of whom retain the simple Arab garb, are all worth more than they will admit, especially to the income-tax authorities, but they hoard rather than spend and their purchasing-power is only a fraction of what it might be.

This applies similarly to the land-owning aristocracy. A few of the more enlightened merchants pay lengthy or frequent visits to Europe and Iraq does not get the benefit of the money thus spent. The Europeans in the country find it expensive to enjoy the amenities to which the European in the East has accustomed himself, and they are a dwindling band. On the basis of the years of the war and the years immediately following it, exaggerated ideas prevailed of the richness of Iraq. When it was discovered that the country was no El Dorado for the European, a shrinkage took place, and the financial worries of the Iraqi Government are due to the necessity to work down quickly on to a smaller basis.

The British Royal Air Force brings a good deal of money into

# Finance

the country, both by way of contracts for supply and transport and the like, and of the private expenditures of individuals on taxi-fares, entertainments, purchases, and so on. Since the rise in the sterling value of gold, large quantities of hoarded gold have left the country and the sterling value obtained for it has been mostly put into circulation. On the other hand, the money spent in the country by visitors, tourists, the archaeological expeditions, pilgrims, etc., has visibly shrunk since 1929, and trade in general has shrunk with it. Yet the state's commitments largely remain. There are still a number of highly paid British officials in the country and they must either be carried until their contracts expire or paid a lump sum as compensation for earlier dismissal. Foreign representation must now be maintained as part of the price of independence. There is also a small sum still due on Iraq's share of the Ottoman Public Debt. With the dismemberment of the old Ottoman Empire and the division of its public debt among the detached territories, Iraq's share was put at £T7,000,000, plus about £T2,500,000 for the accumulated interest and amortization charges. In 1927 the then Minister of Finance made arrangements to buy, at current market prices and through agents, Ottoman Debt securities, handing over the bonds and securities in settlement of Iraq's liability to the amount of a million and a quarter sterling. This left outstanding a sum of £383,000 sterling, which is being paid off in seven annual instalments.

The oil revenues[1] amounting to a minimum at present of eight hundred thousand pounds (gold), by way of advance royalties, are very considerable for a country of Iraq's financial weight. The original idea was that as oil was properly to be regarded as part of the capital value of the country, the oil revenues should be devoted solely to capital expenditure. During the past three years, however, most if not all of these revenues have been used to balance the budget.

The ten years' average, to 1930, showed the annual revenue to be about 500 lakhs of rupees, say £3,750,000, and the annual expenditure about 475 lakhs, say £3,500,000. The difficult years have been from 1921 to 1923 and from 1929 onwards. In the former case the necessary economies were effected by means of savage cuts

[1] See chapter on Trade and Industry.

in the civil service estimates. This is an economy of doubtful value, as with a poorly paid civil service, or one with a substantial financial grievance, it is not surprising to find petty corruption arising. British financial missions—Sir E. Hilton Young and Mr. R. H. Vernon in 1925 and Sir E. Hilton Young in 1930—investigated and reported but for various reasons their calculations proved useless and it is doubtful what benefit Iraq derived from these enquiries. In 1930–31 further cuts in expenditure were made and taxation was increased, notably customs and income-tax. In some cases the customs duties were increased so much that they affected consumption and it became a question whether the country was not losing more—in loss of port dues, railway freights, wages, due to the fact that smaller quantities were being handled, and profits of wholesalers and retailers—than the higher duties brought in.

The income-tax is extremely fortuitous in its operation; it is quite certain that this tax is not a suitable one for a country like Iraq where civilization has few complications. Income-tax demands a reasonable standard of literacy from the bulk of the people, it demands a reasonable amount of accurate book-keeping, and it demands reasonably honest returns. If these three conditions are not fulfilled, the tax can neither be fairly assessed nor completely collected. In Iraq, while the bulk of the illiterates are below the taxable limit, there are many illiterates who are above it. These men, mostly merchants, keep all their business transactions in their heads, their marvellous memories being seldom at fault; or the records they keep are either incomplete or flagrantly dishonest.[1] In addition, large numbers of these merchants have no place of business. They transact all their affairs in coffee-shops, each man having a favourite coffee-shop where he can always be found at stated times. The only individuals who are fairly assessed are the Government officials and the employees of big firms; the only firms that can be assessed at all are the big ones; the only firms that are fairly assessed are those whose accounts are properly audited by the one firm of British chartered accountants practising in the country. In practice therefore the income-tax is a tax on Government

---

[1] One merchant of my acquaintance keeps three sets of books—one for the income-tax authorities, one for his partners' inspection, and his own private set.

# Finance

officials and on foreigners. Recent as it is—it was established only in 1927—the income-tax in Iraq was increased between 200 and 300 per cent as from April 1931. The present rates are: the first £150 *per annum* free of tax; the next £150 6 per cent; the excess over £300, 9 per cent.[1] The increase resulted in a big jump in revenue in the year 1931–32, but this rate of increase cannot be maintained and the Iraqis are already beginning to see that heavy increases in taxation, of any sort, place an undue strain on the administration of the law.

The Customs department is efficiently run and the principal British officials still maintain executive control as experts; the Inland Revenue Department is Iraqi-administered. The trade slump, coupled with Iraq's higher tariffs, has affected collections adversely. The higher tariffs, having encouraged smuggling, have had the further effect of increasing the Department's preventive expenditure. The long land frontier with Persia makes smuggling, either way, easy; and the Arabian principalities (particularly Kuwait, the nearest), with their small *ad valorem* duties, maintain a flourishing illicit export trade into Iraq. Along these frontiers regular smuggling services by camel-caravan and by motor-car are maintained and the odds are against the Iraqi Customs. The principle on which the department works has been, whenever possible, to put imports on a fixed duty. Protection is ostensibly aimed at in some cases, but in general Iraqi produce cannot yet compete either in quantity, quality or finish with imported goods. The duty on imported spirits does not greatly encourage the distilling of the native arrack, because it appeals to a different taste. Similarly the duty on foreign cloth does not greatly help the Iraqi factories, because of the difference in quality; so with boots and shoes. In effect the tax on these imported goods is paid by the Europeans resident in Iraq.

The Inland Revenue department inherited from the Ottoman regime a complicated system of local taxation. Almost its only merit was that it was familiar and drastic changes would have been

[1] The huge increase represented by these figures is said to have been advised by the British Residency, which, when the Iraqis found they could not owing to the terms of the contracts cut the pay of their British officials, advised an increase of income-tax, still considerably below the British level, as an alternative method of docking pay. The increase has almost certainly resulted in more unemployment and less money spent in the shops.

undesirable if not impossible to put into effect. This department is responsible for the various taxes on agricultural produce and fish, collected at the centres of marketing and evaded by all those who in their business transactions avoid these centres; for the taxes on animals—sheep, goats, camels, cattle, buffaloes: for the property-tax on urban sites, which is akin to the "rating" principle in Britain but is collected locally and then treated as national revenue. In some cases the taxes are farmed out (also a familiar survival from pre-war days), but under safeguards. The property-tax has caused some difficulty owing to frequent collusion between landlord and tenant in making the rent-return low, and the consequent difficulty of assessing the annual rental value on which the tax is based. The agricultural taxes are of great importance, agriculture being the chief industry in Iraq. But much of the country is unsurveyed, or only partially surveyed. The lack of records of business transactions and different customs and trading traditions in different places and among different communities; the ignorance of the people, and the inadequate standard of education and professional independence among the minor officials, have always operated against the collection of revenue. These difficulties have existed since time immemorial and the Ottomans overcame them by farming the taxes out for lump-sum payments by the contractors. This made for simplicity in the Treasury if not for a square deal to the agricultural population. In some parts of the country, notably the Middle Euphrates, it was impossible to collect the taxes at all.

The present method is the rather rough-and-ready, and in practice extremely unsatisfactory, method of assessing average production, based on records so far as they exist, and on observation by officials. In some cases the assessment is made at the place of export, in other cases at a Government headquarters, in other cases at the place of consumption, which has now superseded the "tithe" assessment and collection. But this place of consumption tax is open to almost every possible criticism, and is worse than the "tithe" in that there is greater opportunity for evasion by influential people. Sometimes the basis of assessment is measurement of area, sometimes by counting the producing units. Sometimes the number of ploughs is the basis, sometimes the number and power of pumps. The conservative Arabs would like to see Turkish custom maintained on the ground that it is easier to remain in a rut than to get out of it. The Government is interested in changes largely because of the chance that a change may mean an increased yield; when the cultivators think that this is the object or likely result of change, their objections to change are doubled. On their merits, many changes are doubtless desirable, but drastic alterations are impossible with a slow-moving population, and there are inherent difficulties which prevent the universal application of any one system. Each system has its merits in its own area, where it has been sanctioned by generations of familiarity. Moreover immediate financial requirements, especially in a time of falling agricultural prices, are such that that flow of revenue must be maintained although it may be clear that to stop the flow temporarily here and there would lead to subsequent increase. These taxes produce about 30 per cent of the total revenue of the state.

The root of the difficulty has been the lack of maps and surveys. This is particularly so in the case of the State-owned lands, which amount to about 60 per cent of the cultivated land, and probably all the ultimately cultivatable land. The state owns all land not registered as private property. Except along the rivers, or where an occasional hill breaks the level it is impossible to define boundaries in the desert plain. Further, as in the case of agricultural taxation, there are numberless systems of land-tenure, all sanctioned by custom. It is a common thing, for example, when the Irrigation Department opens up a canal, for a tribe to appear over the horizon with records, usually verbal but sometimes documentary, of their grandfathers or great-grandfathers having lived there when an earlier waterway existed, and thus claiming at least squatters' rights. Real difficulty has been the unwillingness of many Iraqis to see any merit in purely scientific work, and the Ministry of Finance is so hard pressed that almost invariably it demands an immediate return on any expenditure, while the Ministry of Interior is too much interested in maintaining peace and local administration to be much interested in map-making and the compilation of land records. But if any progress is to be made from the land-anarchy of the Ottoman regime this work must ultimately be taken in hand, and sooner rather than later if land revenues are to be increased. The British officials who are now in the Land Settlement department are doing excellent work under a law based on the report made by Sir E. Dowson.

Iraq's own currency came into use in April 1932. In pre-war days the currency was Turkish and the Turkish lira, or gold pound, is still current on the value of its gold content. The smaller Turkish coins have disappeared. The British Army in 1914 brought the rupee and the anna with them from India. The rupee was already a familiar token of exchange throughout Arabia and in what is now Southern Iraq, where the Basrah merchants had long maintained a large and lucrative trade with India. The silver of the rupee, like the gold of the lira, had much to do with its ready acceptance by the people of Basrah and Baghdad. By 1930 it was estimated that the Indian currency in circulation, in notes and coin, represented a total of four crores of rupees. The Iraqis had long desired a currency of their own, realizing that it was the Indian Government that was profiting by the circulation of the Indian money in Iraq.

A good deal of opposition, some of it political in origin, made itself evident against a proposal to introduce the new currency in 1931. An appeal was made to the ignorance of the people in the emphasis that was laid on the fact that the new currency would have no gold backing. For, following the modern principle, the new currency is backed by trustee securities, all the operations being controlled by an independent Currency Board with its seat in London. Not unnaturally the ignorant Arab did not understand this kind of backing; nor did he appreciate the fact that, unlike a gold reserve, which it was suggested should be kept in Baghdad, a security reserve would draw to itself accretions of interest. A further demand made was that a National Bank should be established, to do the business now done by the commercial banks and private financiers and to handle the new currency. This has not yet been found practicable.

After a year's delay the new currency came in on April 1, 1932. The scheme was to pay out new currency in exchange for rupees at the market rate which should prevail in Bombay on the appointed day. All debts and business obligations were, by law, converted into the new currency at that rate, but the actual exchange of money after that date would fluctuate with the market. Actually there has been no fluctuation. The rupees thus collected were shipped back

# Finance

to India by the official bankers and with the credits thus opened the necessary securities were purchased by the Currency Board. The unit of the Iraq currency is the dinar, a note not a coin, which is convertible into one pound sterling. The dinar is divided into one thousand fils, one fils thus being the approximate equivalent of a farthing. One of the drawbacks of the Indian currency in Iraq was that the smallest coin in circulation was the anna, roughly a penny, and the anna was too big a unit for the daily needs of the poorest classes, whose counterpart in India had the pie, or one-twelfth of an anna. The new fils thus met the needs of large sections of the population. The usual media, except among the poorest people, are the four-fils piece, the ten-fils piece, the fifty-fils piece, which is equivalent to the British shilling, and the two-hundred-fils piece, or Riyal. There was considerable excitement the day the currency came in, the banks being besieged by those anxious to see it; the Arab, like the Greek, always likes to see and talk about something new. But the change was effected easily in the towns. In the villages however unscrupulous brokers and others made for a time profits by changing rupees at a discount. This was quite unjustifiable and the cases that came to light were dealt with by the authorities. The rupee still exists, and will continue to exist for years, in the outlying districts and among the tribes.[1] The new currency is perfectly sound and it will remain close to the pound sterling as long as the Currency Board remains functioning in London. The Currency Law, however, provides that if and when a National Bank is established in Iraq, the Currency Board will cease to exist and its functions and responsibilities be transferred to the new Bank in Baghdad. Fears have been expressed that such a step would mean early inflation and a consequent fall of the dinar. But there seems no reason why this should be so, for the Bank would have the accumulated experience of the Currency Board to guide it, and, short of corruption, there is no apparent object in depreciating the country's currency. In any event the end of the Currency Board must, it would seem, be delayed until such time as Baghdad can offer similar facilities to those offered by London for the quick buying and selling of the securities on which the currency is based.

[1] The Maria Theresa dollar of 1780 is still current in Arabia.

# CHAPTER XII

## JUSTICE

THE Ministry of Justice controls the courts—civil, criminal and religious. Two systems of law exist in Iraq. In the towns the old Ottoman code is the basis of the law. There are at the same time religious courts which administer the Koranic law in certain matters and in addition there are Jewish or Christian tribunals which settle cases within these communities. The British occupation during the war brought in a stratum of Indian law, to cover fields that the Ottoman law did not touch. All these to-day form a law system which is administered by the National Courts and to which the average citizen is subject. Outside the towns, however, and outside this system of law, comes the tribesman. Hundreds of thousands of tribespeople, either settled as cultivators in various parts of the country or as nomadic wanderers, recognize only the law of the tribes. Over the centuries life in the desert has developed its own way of law-making and its own way of dealing with disputes and difficulties. In the nature of things desert customs differ from town customs, and when both appear side by side in a modern state the essential difficulty is that for countless generations the law of the tribes has had no sanction other than that enforced by tribal custom itself. Iraq has solved the problem, not unsatisfactorily, by giving tribal law a recognized place. If a tribesman is accused of a criminal offence he may claim trial by tribal law. This normally applies to the average unlettered tribesman, but tribal law was successfully pleaded in a *cause célèbre* in Baghdad in 1931 when a member of a great tribal aristocracy, a former deputy and an educated man, was accused of murder. The murder was a deliberate one but the plea raised was tribal custom. Instead of the death penalty the murderer was given a term of penal servitude which was later shortened, by Royal clemency, and finally washed out.[1] Normally the penalty of murder is death by hanging, but murders committed to avenge the tribal notion of family honour are in practice never punished in this way.[2]

[1] See Appendix C.  [2] See pp. 173 *et seqq*.

# Justice

The Anglo-Iraqi judicial agreement of 1930 provides for a number of foreign judges—in practice these are British—sufficient to ensure that all cases in which foreigners are concerned will be tried by them or under their supervision. There are now no capitulations and the law is the same, and is administered in the same way, to all, Iraqi and foreigner alike. There is no question that the British judges have brought justice into courts that had not known it for centuries. Whether the Arabs appreciate the possibly bleak ideals of British justice is another matter. The Arab judges are not well enough paid to ensure their independence, especially in commercial cases where much money is at stake. Social influence, too, is unduly strong, as might be expected in a country where a semi-feudalism still persists. This influence is frequently exercised; most of the aristocracy seem to take it for granted that they are above the law. Actual bribery would possibly be hard to prove. Corruption is not usually directed to swaying the verdict of the court. But the strong man with a weak case can always buy adjournments, until his weaker opponent with the stronger case is forced, by the continued post-ponements, to come to terms. These adjournments, which in a big case, invariably mean financial benefit for someone, are open to the further objection that they clog up the business of the courts. Nor is the standard of advocacy high. The actual presentation of the case before the judge is usually done competently and at times brilliantly. But there is no Bar as distinct from the profession of solicitor, and the average quality is not high. Some advocates, appearing for one side, are not above making surreptitious approaches to the other suggesting that for a fee a settlement could be arranged. Two such cases[1] came within my knowledge within a period of a few months. Moreover, as in most countries, the lawyer in Iraq makes a good politician, and the elective methods of the country ensure that the good lawyer with political leanings will go for politics rather than for the bench; while the eager politician may take up law because he is interested in politics.

The religious courts must in time be merged in the ordinary courts. As early as 1923 Shiah *qadhis*[2] were appointed, breaking the age-old practice that *qadhis* must be Sunni. So far as non-

---

[1] In both cases the lawyers were Christians, not Arabs.
[2] In English usually *cadi*, a judge of a Muslim religious court.

Muslims are concerned the old Koranic rule of evidence, which in effect permitted Muslims to perjure themselves against non-Muslims, was abrogated in 1929, when any party could demand the transfer of such a mixed suit to the civil courts.

There is a steady and at times voluminous output of legislation, and much remains to be done. The present law is a conglomerate, but steady progress is being made towards unification. The official language of the courts is Arabic, and from time to time extraordinary discrepancies in translation make their appearance. A big insurance case in 1930, which began in Basrah and ended in the Court of Appeal, disclosed the fact that the official Arabic translation of the Indian Companies' Act, which had been transplanted to Iraq with the British occupation, had translated the English word "or" by the Arabic for "and," making the penal section read fine *and* imprisonment instead of fine *or* imprisonment. Translating the other way, the very rhetorical Arabic when rendered literally into English often appears tautological or even obscure. As in all Middle East countries, the bureaucracy is very powerful and exercises great influence on legislation as it is passed.

# CHAPTER XIII

## AWQAF

Of all the departments of state, that of Awqaf was the first to become fully emancipated from British control and advice. This was inevitable, for the maintenance of the pious foundations is a function that is best left to Muslims, in a Muslim country. It has been claimed that the British, when they occupied the country, did much to make good the neglect that was evident in mosque and garden, but this Turkish neglect was general and not confined to Awqaf. One real difficulty was that the retreating Turks took away or destroyed most of the official records, but in the case of Awqaf these were replaced more easily than was the case in some other departments of state. The British occupied Baghdad in 1917 and in the first year the Awqaf revenues were Rs. 3,000,000. Within three years the figure was nearly Rs. 17,000,000. The Iraqis thus took over a more efficient Awqaf service than had been known for generations. By 1921 the British executive had become merely advisory and from 1929 there was no British official at all in the Department.

# CHAPTER XIV

## RAILWAY, ROAD AND RIVER

TRANSPORT within Iraq is very much easier to-day than it was before the war. In pre-war days only a short mileage of railway existed, to-day the Iraq Railways cover most of the country. The railway lines centre upon Baghdad. One line runs down to Basrah *via* the Euphrates. The journey takes approximately twenty-two hours, but comfortable cars for dining and sleeping are provided, with bedding for those who carry none of their own. In the summer months it is advisable to carry a supply of ice, as by the afternoon the temperature within the coaches becomes very high. Another line runs north to Qaraghan where it branches, the main line continuing to Kirkuk and the other to Khanaqin on the Persian frontier. The Kirkuk line is the main line for the north, for it is at Kirkuk where the motor connection waits to take passengers to Nisibin, the terminus of the direct railway line from the Bosporus. At the Khanaqin terminus an efficient system of motor transport connects with the road service to Teheran. All these lines are metre-gauge.

The other line, from Baghdad to Baiji, is standard gauge, being the remnant of the old Baghdad railway which the Germans planned before the war. On all trains the first- and second-class accommodation is roomy and comfortable. On many trains there are restaurant cars with good food and excellent service. Another of the activities of the Railways' administration is the provision of comfortable and clean rest-houses for travellers in places where there are no hotels. These rest-houses exist at Margil, the Basrah Railways terminus, Hillah, Ur Junction and one or two smaller places. All these perform the functions of hotels, and at other stations, such as Khanaqin and Diwaniyah, there are rest-rooms which are available for passengers, who however must supply their own bedding and their own food.

The railways of Iraq have never paid although they are efficiently and economically administered—Iraqi critics say that they would pay if the high-salaried British experts were dismissed. Nothing is more certain than that the removal of British technical control would be the falsest of false economy, but the Iraqis are possibly justified in arguing that the big salaries are too high having regard to the extent of the system. The Iraq Railways trouble is that the competition of road transport kills any hope they may have of showing profits. The competition of the motor-car is of the fiercest, and furthermore, an excellent motor road runs alongside the railway from Baghdad to Nasiriyah and on to Basrah. The Arab motor-owner or driver has no notion of depreciation. His budget ignores entirely the necessity of writing off a percentage of the value annually, and when his car finally falls to pieces he simply gets another on the instalment plan, being thus perpetually in debt. His fares, therefore, are low and he always carries at least twice as many passengers as his vehicle is meant to hold. The railways have thus no chance of competing with him, especially as he can do the Baghdad–Basrah run in much better time than the train. It is also the case that the camel and the river can quote, for the transport of goods, terms which the railways cannot approach. It is true that few criticisms of the railways appear in the Iraqi newspapers, but the reason for this may be the advertising which has been the railways' policy. A solution of the railways' difficulty would appear to be the formation of a Department of Transport, regulating all internal transport by road, rail and river, fixing fair scales and eliminating the present senseless individualist scramble.

Much of the visible progress made by Iraq since the war is due to the efforts of the Public Works Department, which is almost entirely a post-war creation, building construction, bridges and roads being its chief lines of activity. There are now good motor tracks stretching from even south of Basrah, right into the Kurdish mountains. Westward across the desert is a road, in places well-built and metalled, running to Rutbah and thence to Syria and Palestine. A good road runs from Mosul to Nisibin and another climbs through the Rowanduz Gorge to link up with the Persian road to Tabriz. From Baghdad to Khanaqin runs the road to Teheran and from Basrah run the roads to Mohammerah and Arabia. Within the borders of Iraq it is possible to find, between the more important towns, motoring roads that are serviceable except for about the two months of rainy weather. In all the road mileage in the country is about five thousand.

# Iraq

The rivers remain, as they always have been, through lines of communication from north to south. The river craft, like that of Noah, are "pitched within and without." The pitch is bitumen, produced in various parts of the country, the use of which as a preservative and waterproofing material has been known from the earliest times. Nor has the shape of the river craft themselves altered very much since the dawn of history. The *goofa* to be seen in Baghdad is just the early coracle. The National Museum at Baghdad contains silver models of boats made thousands of years ago, exactly the same in type as those used on the middle and lower Euphrates to-day. In this land where time stood still for so many generations, the ancient methods of river transport are still in operation. Current and wind between them make it necessary for boats to be towed upstream. Going downstream, especially in the flood season, progress is much more rapid, although in the dry season of shallow water it still takes a considerable time for boats to get from the north of Iraq down to the sea.

On the Tigris north of Baghdad flat-bottomed boats ply within the flood months. But most of the produce coming down from the north is brought in *kalaks*—rafts supported by inflated skins, on which the country produce is floated down river. On reaching Baghdad and the produce being disposed of, the raft is broken up and sold for what it will fetch, and the boatmen make their way back to their starting-point. On the Euphrates the water is too shallow, especially in the marsh areas, for steamers but small sailing craft are common. The effect of the Kut Barrage, when complete, on river navigation has perhaps scarcely been fully considered.

The confluence of the Euphrates and Tigris is known as the Shatt-al-Arab, the great Arab river. It is about one hundred miles in length and is navigable for ocean-going steamers from Basrah down to the mouth, a distance of sixty miles, for the whole of which it is tidal. The maintenance of this fine waterway is in the hands of the Port of Basrah Directorate.

Thousands of years ago Ur was close to the shores of the Persian Gulf and there was no Shatt-al-Arab, for both Tigris and Euphrates flowed separately into the sea. There must have been a time when Basrah, the town from which Sindbad set sail on his voyages, was a coast town. To-day Basrah is about sixty miles from the sea, lying

# Railway, Road and River

in the midst of date-groves on the banks of the Shatt-al-Arab. Until 1914 this silting process had gone on undisturbed for hundreds of years. The position just before the war was that the unhindered operations of nature had deposited in the bed of the river two great obstructions—thus preventing the entrance of vessels of deep draught. These two obstructions were:

(a) The Outer Bar, the major deposit swept down by the rivers and checked in its place by the tides of the Persian Gulf. Without and within this bar the water deepened, but the bar itself allowed, even at the top of the tide, a maximum draught of only nineteen feet and at the lowest tide of nine feet six inches;

(b) The Mohammerah Bar, a secondary and seasonal deposit, brought down by the flooding Karun river and piling up before the Shatt-al-Arab, whose floods occur later in the spring, comes down in sufficient volume to keep the silt moving seawards.

The formation of these two obstructions is due, therefore, to a constant factor—the carrying-down of silt, especially at flood-time, by the Shatt-al-Arab and the Karun, and its deposit at the two points where physical conditions check its free onward movement. Before the war the shoals banked up without let or hindrance. Vessels too big to cross the bar had to lie outside, often in gales or rough seas, frequently in thick weather caused by dust-storms, and unload part of their cargo into smaller craft; if outward bound, the cargo had to be taken out in lighters and loaded under similar conditions. In those days there was much talk of the *Baghdadbahn*, the great railway under German control which was to link up Constantinople with the Persian Gulf. The heavier material for the most southerly portions of this railway was to be landed at Basrah. It was found inexpedient or inconvenient to lighter this heavy stuff, and the Germans, looking round, found that at a place called Margil, a low-lying tract some four miles upstream from Basrah, the deep channel of the Shatt ran for some two miles close under the right bank. The Germans thus constructed a temporary jetty at Margil for ships up to nineteen feet draught to be brought over the Outer Bar at high water and up this deep channel to Margil.

When the war broke out Basrah became the British base for the eastern campaign against the Turks. The original Expeditionary Force consisted of one division and did not find the existing state of affairs a very serious handicap; up to the end of 1915 indeed little had been done to alter things. But the Force was growing rapidly, and with the general shipping shortage throughout the world, it was necessary to take steps at Basrah to ensure a quick turn-round of the vessels that were so urgently needed elsewhere. For a time the congestion was appalling; in the spring of 1916 twenty loaded ships lay at anchor in the stream below Basrah for six weeks before they were touched. The deep-water channel which had attracted the Germans became the determining factor in the decision to construct new and adequate wharves at Margil. The site on the "land" side was a swampy shore of low-lying date groves intersected by the usual creeks and ditches. The first thing to be done was to raise the level of the land above flood-level in order to make it available for the purposes intended. The next difficulty was that the incredible congestion of shipping made it almost impossible to get shipping-space for the bulky material needed for the wharves. And without the wharves, in a vicious circle, the congestion could not well be removed. But by the end of 1917 berths for twelve steamers, about 4,000 feet of continuous teakwood jetty, had been constructed.

With the increase in traffic, attention was turned of necessity to the two major obstructions between Basrah and the sea. The seasonal deposit at the Mohammerah bar was dealt with as occasion arose, and spasmodic attention was paid to the Outer Bar, but here no permanent deepening was achieved. Nevertheless the military authorities went ahead with their development plans, but when the Armistice came a respite was granted. Within six months the army authorities realized that the days of the port as a purely military establishment were over. Partly because they wished to pass on a share of the costs, partly because of the obvious assistance the organization could be to the commerce of this part of the world, various investigations and negotiations were carried out, and on October 9, 1919, a Port of Basrah (Provisional) Proclamation was promulgated. For six months the Port was run as a half-civil, half-military organization. Those were the spacious days of easy money and boundless optimism everywhere. The purely civil port administration came into existence on April 1, 1920, in the rosy light shed by the post-war trade boom. But it showed more than airy optimism, for it had acquired, at cheap rates, all the land likely to be needed for a century, and it inherited a port equipment second to none.

War conditions had necessitated much reduplication and waste, but the new administration set to work to trim all the redundancies away, and two main consequences ensued. One was that the properties taken over from the British Government were reduced to the minimum, the agreed valuation figure being about 72 lakhs of rupees, an extremely low capital cost having regard to the value received. The other was that the general lines of the future development were wisely decided from the start. Here the Port of Basrah has had the inestimable advantage of continuous control by a man of immense driving-force and the widest and most imaginative vision.[1]

When the Port was finally turned over to the civil authorities, the first major problem to be tackled was the problem of the Outer Bar, which seriously limited the value of the Port to ocean-going steamers, inasmuch as they could cross it only half-laden or had to remain outside and lighter, a process which caused risk, delay, inconvenience and extra expense. Early in 1920 the then Deputy Civil Engineer-in-Chief of the British Admiralty visited the Port for the purpose of investigating a scheme of dredging, and also ascertaining if any more suitable place could be discovered for shipments, particularly of oil. Among the places inspected was the Khor Abdullah, an old mouth of the Euphrates lying to the west of the spit of land on which Fao is situated and extending therefrom to the Bay of Kuwait. It was decided, however, that the cost of establishing a new Port there would be prohibitive and that the dredging of the Outer Bar offered the easiest and cheapest remedy. Borings were taken, investigations and surveys made, and complete dredging plans put up. Nearly three years elapsed when, following a report by another expert from London, negotiations were opened for financing the scheme. The Anglo-Persian Oil Company which ships its products from Abadan, on the Persian side of the Shatt-al-Arab, entered into an agreement with the Government of Iraq to provide capital up to £462,100, and to provide two dredgers of considerable capacity. Dredging dues were introduced in March 1925 on all steamers drawing over 19 feet, to meet the service and amortization of this loan. At this stage

[1] Col. J. C. Ward.

# *Iraq*

Fao began to develop. An engineering repair shop was established, and with it a medical station comprising a small hospital and dispensary. These developments were made necessary owing to the arrival of the specially constructed dredgers, whose crews required a shore base.

The first scheme provided for dredging just south of the old navigable track, but soon it became clear that to deepen the channel here was impracticable, for the nature of the bottom was such that no channel could be dredged. Casting about for an alternative, and after making fresh surveys, Colonel Ward, the Port Director, decided to drop the agreed scheme and sent the dredgers to a new channel, which seemed to be opening up. This abandonment of the earlier scheme was a bold decision, for the experts from London had come out at large fees and all the agreements were signed. The bold decision to scrap all these arrangements was amply justified. Within a few months such progress had been made that it was possible to open this new channel, the Rooka, to shipping.

To the landsman's eye, the Rooka Channel is just like any other expanse of water. Steaming out of Fao, the outgoing vessel soon finds the coasts receding on either hand; within two or three miles you are in the open sea. There are the usual beacons and buoys, as in any great waterway, among which two lines of square-topped structures stand out demarcating the Rooka Channel for ships. At night the beacons blaze like Piccadilly Circus; by day they stand like policemen, in a row nine miles long, keeping ships in the straight and narrow path. The Rooka Channel in fact is just a ditch, scooped out of the alluvial mud at the bottom, which outside this Channel has a low-water depth of about nine feet, quite insufficient to allow big ships to enter. The Rooka Channel is used only at high water and takes ships of 30 feet; it is about 300 feet wide. The nature of the bottom is such that the work must go on constantly and continuously. It is impossible to leave the Rooka Channel, for it would silt up again very soon. Thus the two dredgers remain at their station for an average of eighteen hours a day—four six-hour watches in a twenty-four day, with a complete break at the week-end. It is arduous work. These ships work out of sight of land in weather conditions which vary from the Arab winter with its bitter cold, to the Arab summer with its great heat. In summer especially, the

FISHERMAN IN GOOFA, AT BAGHDAD

MIHAILA, WITH CARGO OF GRAIN, ON THE SHATT-AL-ARAB

men are apt to get dispirited and nervy. Not even can they see what progress they are making, except for the "damned dots" on the survey charts. Their work, too, is most discouraging at this, the very worst, time of the year. For it is in the summer that the flood-borne silt sweeps down almost as quickly as it can be removed. Sometimes indeed it has happened that more silt comes down than the vessels can actually cope with, and the channel then shallows instead of deepening. It is surprising at such times to find the men of the dredgers speaking to each other. In addition to their work at the Outer Bar the men in these vessels from time to time have to work on the Mohammerah Bar to clear the seasonal deposit brought down by the flooding Karun. At other times they are called upon to do dredging by the wharves at Abadan or Basrah. The dredging in the open estuary is however their main work.

The essential difficulty of the sea work—surveying and dredging —that is based on Fao, arises from the climatic conditions. In the winter months the crews have to contend with North Sea conditions —bitterly cold weather, gales, and stormy seas. In summer they have the damp heat, sometimes reaching 130 degrees Fahrenheit in the shade, not to mention dust-storms that destroy visibility and make navigation a matter of the utmost difficulty. These dust-storms it is said, have been more frequent in recent years, and when the sand is blowing the work at the Bar must go blindly on, the sighting marks and beacons frequently being invisible for several days on end. The climatic conditions at the Bar are, indeed, as bad as anywhere in the world. When it is understood that the ships work an average of eighteen hours a day, averaging from anything between five hundred and five hundred and fifty hours a month, and during certain periods of stress have been known to put in as much as six hundred hours, it will at once be appreciated how severe is the strain on all concerned.

The dredging officers have to work in the operating room, on the flying bridge, in six-hour watches, watch and watch, day after day, either in the sun's dazzling glare or straining to pick up dredging marks miles away in dust-storms which may last for days on end and render the taking of bearings almost impossible. At night the men struggle to hold the transit lights in line in order to keep the dredgers working on the defined tracks. This too calls for a considerable amount of skill and concentration, especially in places where the tides do not run true with the channel. At the Outer Bar you will find the little *Industry*, the floating home of the Chief Marine Surveyor. It is a liberal education to put to sea with him. You report to him early in the morning—when the hot Arabian sun has scarcely touched the Shatt, which lies without a ruffle in the cool pearly dawn. You move off down the river and have breakfast. Soon you are out in the open sea and if you are really interested your host will show you his charts. They are his own, and, unlike the charts in well-ordered seas, they are constantly changing. The reason is, of course, the river silt which is the dominating factor in the whole of this complex Port of Basrah business. Day after day the *Industry* noses her way through all the channels. Soundings are constantly being taken and each reading is meticulously put down. In these charts is the ultimate proof of the success or failure of the Bar dredging scheme. Every square yard of water is mapped and the surveyor knows at once whether the dredger crews are maintaining their reputation, or the river is beating them. There is no escaping the tiny tell-tale figures on the charts.

The be-all and the end-all of all this, is the easy passage of big ships. When a big ship, bound for Basrah, reaches the top end of the Persian Gulf, she picks up a pilot—a Persian pilot! The pilot service on the Shatt-al-Arab is of very great antiquity, for since time immemorial ships from the coasts of southern India and Eastern Africa have constantly made the voyage to the date-lands of Mesopotamia. Gold would come from Ophir, frankincense from Southern Arabia, sandalwood and ivory from Africa. All these commodities and others would come up by dhow, passing on the journey the dhows sailed by Sindbad and his nameless colleagues. This traffic has gone on since the dawn of history, and with the coming of the big European ships an official pilotage service came into existence. The pilotage service, for generations, has been managed by Persians from the island of Kharag, who have long had a prescriptive right, descending from father to son, to this work. Indian naval vessels and the ships of "John Company" had used these pilots for generations, and even during the Anglo-Persian War of 1856 these men continued to serve the British vessels. As A. T. Wilson records, "In recognition of their steadfastness, the British India Steam

# Railway, Road and River

Navigation Company had agreed to use Kharag pilots only and their example had been followed by other lines." The dozen or so men thus employed at the beginning of the war, have now been increased by the enrolment of additional men, also from Kharag, and to-day these Persians have the Basrah pilotage monopoly solely because their grandfathers stood by the British in a war of eighty years ago.

The financial position of the Port of Basrah is sound. There is a substantial reserve, mainly used to finance new works, and depreciation of such works has been made annually from revenue so as to keep the reserve intact. The complaint has been made that the Port charges are too high; many have argued that the Rooka Channel, and with it the extra dredging dues, was unnecessary. The deep-water channel, however, was dredged largely to suit the convenience of the Anglo-Persian Oil Company, which was handicapped by its inability to pass fully-laden tankers over the Bar, and this Company pays the bulk of the dredging dues.[1] During the three years 1927–30 the average number of vessels arriving in a year at Basrah was 172, or a fraction over 14 a month. Those entering Abadan, almost entirely tankers, averaged in the same years a fraction over 584, or nearly 50 a month. Since the war-traffic at Basrah ended, Basrah's shipping has shrunk and the slump in grain prices has had a further depressing effect. On the contrary Abadan's traffic has shown a steady and in some ways spectacular increase since 1920.

---

[1] The official estimate of the annual saving in lightering costs on all classes of cargo is £1,000,000, while the annual dredging dues amount to little over £200,000.

## CHAPTER XV

## AGRICULTURE AND IRRIGATION

A MURDER a day in the arid summer season was the pre-war record of one of the provinces in Iraq. Water, indeed, has always been the nodal point of existence in Mesopotamia, and the employment of it has been a factor towards civilization since the beginning of recorded time. The history of Babylonia was largely one of struggles as to who should control the water supply. The central part of the country, as can be seen admirably from the air, shows a complete network of ancient canals; some parts indeed are almost, as it were, herring-boned with these obsolete irrigation works. It is certain, however, that the numerous dead channels were never in simultaneous operation, and that silt and salt between them forced the ancients periodically to abandon their canals and dig new ones. The silt has for centuries been brought down by the two rivers. Both the Tigris and the Euphrates waters contain a heavy proportion of salt and as there are (unlike Egypt) practically no drains, the land soon becomes useless. The useless areas have been extended by the hand-to-mouth methods of generations of cultivators. The Arab has got his crops by pouring water over the soil; his ignorance of irrigation principles led him to continue this watering without draining, until he could grow no more crops, when he simply moved on to another area. That is all very well when the population is small, but it is the reverse of economic and the result has been that immense areas of valuable alluvial soil are now salted and useless. Washing and draining will take time and money. No less important than the canals of old were the dykes, protecting the towns and the cultivable lands from the floods of the winter and spring seasons, whose association with Iraq has been famous since the earliest days of mankind. It should, parenthetically, be stated that the land in Iraq is not nearly so rich as has been imagined.

In Southern Iraq as the rivers approached the Persian Gulf, their courses became uncertain in direction and capacity, much water being spilt on either side in vast marshes. To-day it is largely the same. The Tigris at Amara, 120 miles from its outfall, is one-

# Agriculture and Irrigation

third the size that it is at Baghdad, 240 miles further upstream, whilst the Euphrates, in its course between Ramadi and Basrah, twice dissipates itself entirely, once in the rice-fields of the Shamiyah and once to the south of Nasiriyah. The nature of the untamed rivers, coupled with a climate that can range in temperature from 25 degrees Fahrenheit in winter to 130 degrees Fahrenheit in summer, creates a host of trials for the dweller in Mesopotamia, who for centuries past has been exposed to floods, drought, disease, locusts, civil insecurity, and foreign invasion. It is little wonder if in such circumstances he has often developed apathy and lack of patience when undertaking tedious tasks. The function of irrigation to-day is to combat not only the economic deficiencies of the kingdom, but also the psychological weakness of its people. By giving them a sense of security in their fights against floods, disease, and insect-pests, and in their division of the water supply and the cultivable lands, it is hoped to create in the people a spirit of law, order, and civilization such as has been absent from the realm for centuries.

In the programme of the State the construction of flood reduction and irrigation works occupies naturally a most prominent place, for none of the structures of the ancients remains effective to-day and nothing fresh of importance was achieved until the present century dawned. Prior to the Great War there was in Iraq but one major work, the Hindiyah Barrage, the object of which is to regulate the flow of the Euphrates from Hillah southwards. Since the British forces occupied Baghdad an irrigation department has existed in one form or another, undergoing frequent changes in its staff and its programme of immediate works. It has been required to spend much of its time and money upon matters that were momentarily of military or political importance, and its achievements have hitherto consisted much more in keeping alive or improving some existing system of canals with a population already settled upon it rather than in making "the desert blossom like the rose." Nevertheless, unobtrusively and sometimes despite discouragement from important quarters, it has managed to pave the way for a more generous future by conducting unceasingly, although of necessity slowly, that survey of the waters and the lands of the country which alone can form the basis of any sound projects; it has made a few

# Iraq

model canal systems and taught its staff to operate them, it has trained a corps of minor contractors to construct works in good fashion, and it has demonstrated in canal areas, such as that of the Yusifiyah, that the Iraq peasant can when put to it quickly learn to use his water with care, to the greater benefit of both crops and land. Under the encouraging influence of a steady water supply the sown area of many an existing canal has expanded gradually, although to an impatient observer it may have done so imperceptibly. To such a person the department's work in the Shattrah district will make more appeal, for prosperity has now been restored to this formerly distressed area, causing its tribesmen to return from their wanderings elsewhere and brigandage to become a bogey of the past. Simultaneously the numerous dykes have been strengthened or reconstructed and arrangements made to collect and distribute rapidly news of the rivers' behaviour whenever rain has fallen in the mountains of Kurdistan, Armenia, and Persia, and threatened to cause flooding in the plains. In this connection the Franco-Syrian authorities supply, by wireless, readings of the Euphrates at Jarablus and Dair-as-Zor, thus giving five days' warning to those in Iraq of what is in store for them south of Ramadi.

The Government is now coming to close quarters with some of the large works which the Irrigation Department has had in view for years. Of these the two first to be dealt with are the Habbaniyah scheme on the Euphrates and the Kut Barrage on the Tigris, each likely to cost very roughly one and a quarter million sterling. The Habbaniyah scheme provides for an off-take from the Euphrates, near the town of Ramadi. This channel will run into the great Habbaniyah depression and will be used to fill it whenever the river reaches a certain level. Thereafter in any given year one of two things will happen. If the flood proves to be exceptionally big, another channel at the south end of the depression will be opened. The further surplus water in the river, after entering Habbaniyah, will dissipate itself in another and still greater depression, the Bahr-al-Milh. In a normal year, however, the escape to the south will not be used, but in all years the Euphrates water stored in Habbaniyah itself will be kept there until the summer, when an outlet near Fallujah will be opened to allow the impounded water to run back into the river. This scheme was first propounded to

# Agriculture and Irrigation

the Turks by the late Sir William Willcocks. Its virtues are that it protects the lands of the lower Euphrates from undue floods in spring and gives the cultivators of Central Iraq the assurance of more water for their thirsty crops in the late summer, when supplies are usually exceedingly scanty. It has been criticized by Iraqis on the ground that the Machiavellian policy of Britain wants to ensure a big lake at Habbaniyah for the use of flying-boats and seaplanes.

Further to the south on the Euphrates is the Hindiyah Barrage built by a British firm before the Great War. This structure regulates the flow of the river for the benefit of the canals watering the lands to the south of Hillah. It has already performed most useful service, but before it can reach its maximum efficiency much minor work is still necessary in its subsidiary canals, although it has been difficult to make the Iraqis see this. As regards the barrage on the Tigris at Kut, the object of this work is to divert the surplus water of the Tigris into one of its ancient channels, still surviving, as often as not with a dry bed, as the River Hai (or Gharraf). Also projected is a scheme to dam the Diala river about 70 miles from Baghdad. A small canal from Fallujah eastwards to the Tigris is also being cut.

In most areas near the rivers, pumps have been set up by cultivators. But the slump in agricultural prices has in most cases prevented the cultivators from keeping up the payments—like everything else in Iraq the pumps were bought on the instalment system. The difficulties of the cultivators became so pronounced that the Government had to subsidize the purchase of oil-fuel, to exempt these cultivators from taxation, and in some cases encouraged the cultivators to put a "moratorium" into force. What Iraq needs is a paying summer crop, otherwise pumps must lose money.

Although oil has made a dramatic and highly spectacular entry upon the scene in Iraq, agriculture, as always in the past, will remain the staple industry in the country. The growing of crops and the rearing of livestock, apart from their maintaining the population, normally provide an important part of Iraq's foreign trade. Cereals form the bulk of the crops. The native wheat and barley were in the past of definitely low grade, and the prices they realized in the foreign markets were lowered still further by the flagrant adulteration that went on; the Arabs' practice was to steal grain and substitute an equal weight of dust or sand. The state of the world markets, however, has enforced reforms. The export during recent years has approximated 100,000 tons. Barley was the first to feel the international drop in commodity values in 1929–30 and cultivators were quick to change over to wheat. Many cultivators possess irrigation-pumps, but the maintenance of these pumps in commission must depend upon a rise in the prices obtained for the crops that are raised. The world slump in grain hit Iraq very hard.

In a half-hearted way the Government maintains an experimental farm, one of the ambitions of which is to supply good seed to cultivators, who in general are not interested. Most Arabs cannot be persuaded to take the trouble to maintain high-grade production even if they take the trouble to begin it, and it is not likely that the experimental work of the farm will be maintained for long at its former level or carried out with the former enthusiasm. Two big European farming estates operate in Iraq. One works on the principle of sub-letting its land to cultivators, who farm their sections in their own way; the other works on the big-scale Canadian or Australian principle, and sells its own cultivated grain and seed.

One of the troubles of the cultivator in this part of the world is the locust. Two factors help the locust in the Middle East. One is that the sparse population of the desert and the lack of quick communication prevent the early warning of threatened areas. The other is the Arab's inherent inability to combine effectively, even in his own interest. The essential of a successful locust campaign is combination between adjoining countries; in none of the Arab countries has this yet been done effectively. In the spring of the year the desert is covered with hoppers. There are millions upon millions of them, each inch of ground carrying its hopper. The desert literally appears to move; one's motor-car scrunches across and through them; the Arabs dig trenches and put sheets of glossy paper,[1] or the folded-out sides of petrol tins, against their house and garden-walls to keep the myriad swarms back. The flying swarms are also destructive; to prevent them settling on crops or

---

[1] In the locust season, back numbers of the heavier illustrated papers, i.e., those printed on art paper, sell at high prices. The lower part of the outside wall is "papered" with this, so that the hopper, jumping against it, gains no footing and falls back into a specially dug pit.

CUTTING THE RIPE DATE-CLUSTERS

BADUIN METHOD OF HOBBLING CAMELS

# Agriculture and Irrigation

gardens the Arabs bang drums and beat tins and pans, just as they do on the occasion of an eclipse to drive away the dragon that is trying to swallow the sun or moon. A few years ago the Iraqi Government spent considerable sums of money on fighting the locust. Eggs were destroyed; hoppers were poisoned in trenches; poison-bait was put down; but of late years there has been no money to continue the work on an adequate scale.

The growing of cotton has proved a failure, partly owing to the inertia of the cultivators. Immediately after the war it was thought that the prospects were of the rosiest, and the British Cotton Growing Association spent a good deal of money in setting up a ginnery and in improving the seed. The *Progress of Iraq* (page 195) says that "cotton has taken its place permanently among the staple crops of the country." This is a rash statement. At one time the outlook was promising, but of recent years both output and prices have dropped. When things looked bright, highly placed individuals invested money in a rival ginnery—the Arab is prone to kill the goose that lays the golden eggs—in spite of the fact that the British Cotton Growing Association, which is not a profit-making concern, offered to hand over its property at a fair valuation. The result is that neither is doing well, and it will not be surprising if the British concern were soon to withdraw.[1]

One of the most valuable crops is the date-crop. Iraq supplies 80 per cent of the world's dates; it is not generally known that each season ship after ship goes to French North African ports with dates from Basrah, which thus supplies all the Basrah dates on the world-market and a portion of "Tunis" dates as well. The annual export varies, according to price, from £1,500,000 to £2,000,000 in total value. The date palms are of approximately seventy different varieties. There are over thirty million palms in the great date area along the Shatt-al-Arab and each palm is fertilized separately by hand. In the spring one can see on all hands men climbing the palms, cutting open the pistil and laying within it the stamen, about the size and shape of a cricket-bat, which they carry up with them. In August and September the dates turn golden and brown and the men climb up again to cut down the bunches. The date trade

---

[1] It probably would never have been started had people in 1919–20 thought that Iraq was not to be British.

is highly organized, with world-wide ramifications. In the season, the packers and shippers import thousands of women to pack the dates in boxes and cartons. The river is crowded with ships and there is a great race to get the first dates to America for Thanksgiving Day and to England in good time for the Christmas trade. The whole river-front of the Shatt-al-Arab is dotted with packing stations, and at the height of the season work goes on day and night. The Health Department maintains a constant and strict control over the health of the packers and the conditions under which they work.

The date trade is approaching a revolution. In former times dates sold well, because they arrived in Europe and America in winter, when other fruits were scarce. To-day, however, there is an all-the-year-round supply of fruit, the different parts of the world coming in as their calendar comes round. For that reason alone the date has lost a little favour. A further reason is that the Western public are becoming more and more fastidious, and so the packing tends to come more and more costly. Much loss, moreover, is caused by date-disease. This is not harmful to human beings, but it affects the quality and appearance of the dates. A Date Research Board has therefore been set up to investigate the question with a view to improving the situation. This Board is financed by a small levy on all dates exported from the country. It is a fact that at present Basrah's capabilities of meeting a large demand are limited (*a*) by the extent of the date-growing belt and (*b*) by old and obsolete methods of cultivation. There seems little possibility of extending the date-growing area over desert lands with any immediate prospects of success, as these lands are so impregnated with salt. But the lands on the desert edge of the date-belt could be greatly improved and extended by the proper dredging of creeks and by the provision of pumps. There are also many gardens that are neglected, especially some Government-owned ones, and these with proper care could be made to give a far greater yield. In recent years agriculture, arboriculture, and horticulture in Western countries have made very great progress indeed, thanks to science. In Iraq science has not been brought into play to improve the standard of dates. Iraq, for instance, must find the origin and cure of the diseases to which date palms are addicted. Experiments with artificial manures, the best crops to grow beneath the palms and commercial usage for waste and inferior dates are other avenues be explored.

The flocks of Iraq provide other staple exports—wool, hides, and skins. The animals are poor types at present. The Veterinary Department is closely concerned with this trade, as most foreign countries require certificates of freedom from disease in the country of origin. Apart from this provision of certificates, the Veterinary Department has from time to time taken active measures against animal diseases such as rinderpest, glanders and rabies, and has done valuable research work on the diseases of animals which are transmissible to human beings; bilharzia and the Baghdad boil in particular, have been made the subject of extensive research, with satisfactory results.

Iraq lies in the great licorice belt which stretches south-east from Anatolia. The trade is in the hands of a single American firm and is remunerative to a high degree. The licorice grows along the rivers, and the roots, after storage, are sent to Basrah, where they are compressed into bales and shipped. Apart from its medicinal uses, Iraq's licorice is used in the manufacture of cigarettes and it appears as a by-product in the form of soundproof and heatproof walls for houses.

# CHAPTER XVI

## TRADE AND INDUSTRY

### I. FOREIGN TRADE

IRAQ's trade is essentially parasitic. The country has its agricultural products and (now) its oil, but its import trade has largely been an *entrepôt* trade, and its purchasing power, now that the British have gone, is sinking to something like its former low level. During the years of the Occupation, the British spent money like water. Instead of finding their houses or stores requisitioned for the incoming troops, the inhabitants found that fair and even generous prices were paid, while the purchases by the troops themselves and the high wages offered for all classes of workers led to the circulation of money on a scale of which neither Arab nor Christian nor Jew had ever dreamed. Rupees became so common that the women of the coolie classes would string them round their necks as ornaments; the fils, let alone the rupee,[1] now takes some earning. Brokers and contractors made fabulous profits, which only the wiser or luckier among them still retain. When the war ended, there was all over the world a rush to fill markets that had been starved for four years. In Iraq there was added to this a sudden boom in various mechanical devices of the West which had hitherto been unknown. Persia, too, had been starved during the war years, and with Russia so completely disrupted the only way of entry to Persia was through Iraq. Thus it happened that in the years that immediately followed the war there was unheard of prosperity among the people of Mesopotamia and the idea became prevalent that the Golden Age had returned. Politicians spoke of Iraq once again becoming the granary of the world. They saw a great country emerging out of the British conquests, with a contented peasantry, wealthy mineral resources, and prosperous trading. The old-established trading firms made profits the like of which they had not known: new concerns grew up like mushrooms. Many British traders are, to their regret, so deeply involved in business commitments in Iraq that they have

[1] A fils is a farthing, a rupee eighteenpence.

openly regretted the optimism which misled them into starting. But the early figures *seemed* to justify their optimism.

|  | In Lakhs of Rupees. | |
|---|---|---|
|  | *1912* | *1920* |
| Total exports (including re-exports) .. | 487 | 1,038 |
| Date Exports .. .. .. .. | 70 | 215 |
| Barley Exports .. .. .. | 168 | 8 |
| Wheat Exports .. .. .. | $36\frac{1}{2}$ | $\frac{1}{2}$ |
| Wool Exports .. .. .. | $45\frac{1}{2}$ | $8\frac{1}{2}$ |
| Hides and Skins Exports .. .. | 7 | 20 |
| Total Imports .. .. .. .. | 398 | 2,327 |

The figures are interesting. The drop in grain exports in 1920 is explained by the fact that the British Forces in Occupation bought up almost everything and left little surplus for export. In 1920 dates had a record year. Thus the *actual* export from Iraq in 1920 was much the same as in 1912, for the staples were still the same and what was gained on dates was lost on grain. The explanation of the huge rise in exports—apart from the changed monetary values —is the transit trade. It is clear that at least half of Iraq's export trade in 1920 was a *re*-export trade, in which no one benefited except a minority of middlemen and the Customs. This conclusion is confirmed by the import figures for the same years. In 1912 the imports were valued at Rs. 398 lakhs, in 1920 at Rs. 2,327 lakhs, some of the increase being also due to British military needs. The spirit of optimism continued for some years after 1920, but when the slump began and certain other factors began to operate figures rapidly dropped (figures in lakhs of rupees):

|  | *Exports.* | *Re-exports.* | *Imports.* |
|---|---|---|---|
| Yearly average (12 years to 1932) | 477 | 572 | 994 |
| 1920 .. .. .. .. | 1,038 | | 2,327 |
| 1912 .. .. .. .. | 487 | | 398 |

The reduction of the British military forces had a two-fold effect on the country's trade. It removed a direct market which had been profitable in the extreme and involved no risk. It also reduced the amount of money in circulation. As the years passed moreover the further factors referred to began to exercise a steadily growing influence on the trade of Iraq.

# Iraq

By 1922–23 the trade routes from Russia into Northern Persia were opening up again, and by 1924 the growth of this Russian trade with Persia was giving rise to serious misgivings in Baghdad. The Soviet policy of subsidizing their export trade and insisting on Persian contracts that favoured the Russian exporter began to hit the Baghdad *entrepôt* trade. By 1930 the Russians had regained all the ground they had lost in Persia since their Revolutions. The result was a general speeding up of transit facilities through Iraq; this has helped to retain a portion of the trade. But further severe blows were dealt by the policy adopted by Persia herself. The national revival under Riza Shah had its commercial aspect. Riza Shah wants his country to be as independent as possible. He is afraid of Russia, the only country that can seriously threaten Persia, and he would like to have direct entry into Persia from the West. These are the considerations that have led him to plan his great traffic route from the Caspian to the Persian Gulf. Some progress has been made at each end, the middle portion remaining unfinished so far as the railway is concerned. Persia already has a good port in Mohammerah, but Riza Shah has apparently decided that a Port which to all intents and purposes is in Iraqi waters is not good enough. For that reason he has pushed on the construction of Bandar Shahpur.[1] There is deep water there and it is on the sea. So it is there that the railway terminus and wharves have been built, under American supervision. It will take some years for this to develop, but if and when it does develop, Persia's transit trade through Iraq will rapidly fall away.

A further point is to be observed. In 1929 owing to the fall in the price of silver and various exchange fluctuations, the Persian Government introduced a number of exchange restrictions the effect of which, so far as foreigners were concerned, was to make it harder than ever to get money out of Persia. To these exchange restrictions were added in 1931 trade restrictions so drastic as almost to strangle business. Riza Shah decided that to balance his exchange he must balance exports and imports. He enacted that *all* foreign trade was to be a Government monopoly, operated by a system of licences. No one in Persia could import anything unless he had a licence, and these licences were obtainable only by those

[1] See p. 126.

# Trade and Industry

who exported goods from Persia. As the Persian balance of trade had been adverse—the main reason for the adoption of this policy —the immediate result was a check in Persian imports, and this once again hit the Iraqi middlemen.[1] These Persian difficulties have led the Iraqis to look further into the question of speeding up the overland route from the Mediterranean; even the French in Syria have been trying to encourage the Persian through-traffic.

It will thus be seen that the end of the period of war-conditions in the Middle East has resulted in a decline of Iraq's trade from the post-war peak towards pre-war levels. The process has been hastened by the universal fall in commodity values. After a small burst of prosperity about 1927, when the oil companies were spending some money in the country, the fall began. It no longer paid to buy stocks for holding; a man who did not, or could not, sell at once lost money and the number of bankruptcies increased. Iraq's exports—dates, grain, wool, cotton—were all faced with catastrophic declines in the prices offered, and the one redeeming feature has been that the country's needs are not complex; that Iraq's simple structure has enabled her to weather the storm better than many other countries have done. The oil agreements, too, came at an opportune time and the removal of costly British officials, although destroying a considerable purchasing power, should enable the administration to get down to a basis which they can afford.

Iraq's exports, apart from oil, are agricultural. The more purely agricultural aspect is discussed elsewhere.[2] Economically the date trade is the most important in the country. The *lowest* year since the war shows an export of Rs. 125 lakhs, whereas the *highest* grain export in any one post-war year, is Rs. 187 lakhs, grain exports in one year out of two failing to touch Rs. 100 lakhs. The date trade, as has been seen, is highly organized and, unlike most other Iraqi traders, the leading men take the trouble to go to Europe and America

[1] One curious "by-product" was the forcing down of the prices obtained by Iraq's date-growers. There are date gardens on the Persian side of the Shatt-al-Arab as well as on the Iraqi side, and a Persian date-exporter, offering the identical quality, could undersell his Basrah competitor in Europe and America. With, say, £100 worth of dates to sell, he could offer them at £80, knowing that some Persian would-be importer would be ready to pay him £20 for the £80 import licence to which his date-export would entitle him.    [2] See Chapter XV.

to study and develop the markets. So far as grain is concerned, an effort is being made to improve the qualities normally grown, but the slump in grain prices has killed much of the interest that was taken in this. "Gulf grain," as it is called, is not of very high quality and it has had a bad name because of the adulteration so freely and brazenly practised. The cultivators, too, who rushed to buy pumps in the boom-years now find that, even with the reduction in the price of oil which the Government arranged for them, they cannot make their cultivation pay. In many cases they cannot even continue the payment on their pumps, an aggregate in capital of between two and three million pounds sterling.

The wool export shows the biggest drop, largely because of the depression in the carpet industry.[1] Large stocks have been accumulated and prices are weak. Cotton has been extremely disappointing and the roseate visions of Iraq as a competitor of Egypt and the United States have vanished in the prevailing gloom.

The balance of trade is adverse, and the theories that prevail among the Arab politicians turn on increased tariffs, and prohibitions with a view to keeping imports down to the export levels. The ever-optimistic *Progress of Iraq* (p. 214) makes an effort to show that the invisible exports and imports have the effect of redressing any adverse balance. But it is impossible to get the necessary facts to justify such optimism. The invisible exports are officially given (*op. cit.*) thus:

(*a*) Disbursements by the British Government in the Embassy and the British Forces in Iraq;
(*b*) British contribution to the Iraqi army;
(*c*) Iraq's profits from Persian transit trade;
(*d*) Money spent by foreign pilgrims visiting Iraqi shrines;
(*e*) Money spent in Iraq by tourists, travellers, etc.;
(*f*) Expenditure by foreign companies in Iraq;
(*g*) Expenditure by foreign diplomatic and consular representatives in Iraq;

---

[1] This slump is due to two main factors; the inability of the West to spend as much on carpets as formerly, and the Persian prohibition of the export of silver, which compels Persian pilgrims to take with them saleable materials, usually carpets, instead of money to maintain them on their pilgrimages to the Holy Cities. Baghdad since 1932 has thus been flooded with cheap carpets.

SEA-GOING DHOW
AT THE MOUTH
OF THE
SHATT-AL-ARAB

OXEN IN PLOUGH

PRIMITIVE WATER-WHEELS AT HIT, ON THE EUPHRATES, RAISING THE
WATER IN SCOOPS TO THE LEVEL OF THE LAND

(*h*) Disbursement of charitable and educational funds from abroad in Iraq;

(*i*) Remittances to Iraq by Iraqi nationals abroad;

(*j*) Expenditure in Iraq by foreign archaeological expeditions.

The list—prepared for presentation to the League—looks imposing, but a few comments seem to be called for. The disbursements under (*a*) are being cut by the Treasury auditors wherever possible. The headings (*c*), (*d*) and (*e*) have all dwindled for reasons already shown in these pages; in any event the money brought by pilgrims goes into hoards in the Holy Cities and does not add to the country's purchasing power. Under (*f*) the foreign companies are cutting down their commitments right, left and centre; (*g*) may be regarded as of small account. The total under (*h*) cannot be accurately obtained, while under (*i*) most Iraqi nationals abroad are financed from Iraq. Under (*j*) the foreign expeditions have now less money, while the extreme Nationalist policy towards archaeology has been of the most discouraging sort.

The corresponding list of invisible imports is as follows:

(*a*) Payments by the Iraqi Government to the British Government on account of the Railways, the Port and miscellaneous charges;

(*b*) Remittances from Iraq by or for foreigners;

(*c*) Purchase of and annuities on Ottoman Debt Bonds by the Iraqi Government;

(*d*) Cost of Iraqi diplomatic and consular representatives abroad;

(*e*) Iraqi educational missions and privately incurred educational expenses;

(*f*) Amounts spent abroad by Iraqi pilgrims, tourists and travellers.

Under (*a*) the Iraqi Government cannot get these reduced further. Under (*b*) it is becoming less and less easy for foreigners in Iraq to save money. Both (*c*) and (*d*) are small; (*e*) is a fairly high item, but a considerable proportion of the money thus spent by private individuals has been received by them abroad and not in Iraq at all. Under (*f*) it is hard to get figures; the amounts in question must increase with any improvement in trade.

Iraqi "industry" scarcely exists, and the Iraqi's "get rich quick" spirit will be the main bar to Iraq's industrial development. There is nothing approaching the Persian carpet industry, for instance,[1]

[1] Except in the gaols, see p. 175.

the Arab having little or no sense of creative art and confining his activities in this direction to *gileems* of poor design and indifferent workmanship.[1] What industries there are are mostly carried on in the bazaar or in the home by medieval methods. But one or two rich men of progressive ideas have made an effort to develop these native industries on more or less modern lines, and the Nationalist elements have been quick to make political capital out of this tendency, the Government from time to time being forced to make tax and other concessions to "shelter" these nascent industries from the blasts of foreign efficiency. The tobacco, silk and liquor industries seem, however, to have established themselves. The Iraqi cigarettes look well and smoke well, and are of course much cheaper than the imported cigarettes. An attempt has been made to introduce the Virginian leaf, in order to cater for all tastes. Machine-filling is now more generally adopted, and the day of the loose hand-rolled cigarette of the bazaar is nearly over. The liquor manufacture is confined mainly to arrack, which is good, cheap and popular. There seems no reason why a good beer should not be made locally, like the excellent beers that can be bought in Turkey. It is a mistake to imagine that the Iraqi Muslim is an abstainer.

A clothing factory in Baghdad has made some progress, and its products are by no means bad, although naturally they cannot yet compete either in quality or style with European products. The brick trade flourishes and good bricks are made. Important personages in the country have been turning their minds to the making of cement, but so far little has come of this. The fact is that Iraq is not at present an industrial country, nor can she be for a long time. A big view would ensure the harnessing of the great rivers of Kurdistan and the development of cheap power throughout the land. With the low wage-rates prevailing, this would enable Iraq to enter with a favourable start upon a comprehensive industrial policy. She is in a key position, with cheap waterways and free access to the sea—a point which only very few Iraqis seem to appreciate, for none of them has seen a ship except the people of Basrah.

Imports are chiefly for the European or Europeanized communi-

[1] The Kurds, however, make artistic black-and-white rugs of goats' hair.

ties. They include beers and spirits, tobacco, luxury articles, clothes, boots and shoes, and the like. The bulk of the population are not interested in these. But there has since the war been a tremendous import of motor-cars, in which American manufacturers have had a virtual monopoly. This has closely affected the life of the Arab, for most of the cars are Arab-owned, and their general use as taxis has had much to do with the increasing civilization of the people and the opening up of the country. Regular lines of steamships ply between Iraq and India, Britain and Germany, while Soviet and other craft pay periodic calls.

Iraq's best customer is Great Britain, which takes over one-fourth of Iraq's exports, sending in return about one-third of Iraq's imports—these include plant and equipment for the oilfields and pipe-lines; that is to say, materials for capital works which cannot strictly be classed as ordinary imports. Next to Britain comes India, which is responsible for one-fifth of Iraq's imports and takes three-twentieths of her exports. The United States take about one-fifth of Iraq's exports, chiefly dates and carpets. Persia takes 13 per cent and gives 7 per cent—mostly goods in transit. Belgium, France, Holland and Germany each contribute about a twentieth of Iraq's imports, and Italy and the United States rather less.

## II. OIL

Before the war a concern known as the Turkish Petroleum Company had obtained from the Ottoman Government a concession for the exploitation of the oil resources of the Baghdad and Mosul *vilayets*. This concession was, therefore, part of the inheritance of the new Iraqi Government when it came into existence; in due course the name of the Company was changed and it is now known as the Iraq Petroleum Company—familiarly the I.P.C. In this Company (whose capital is £6,500,000) 5 per cent is held by the original concessionaire, an Armenian millionaire named Gulbenkian. The remaining 95 per cent is divided equally between British, American, Dutch and French interests. The British interests are under the control of the Anglo-Persian Oil Company. Already during the peace negotiations the question of Iraq's oil had been the subject of frequent discussion between the statesmen and experts of London and Paris.

# *Iraq*

The latter were in a position to force themselves into the picture and the San Remo agreement (April 24, 1920) not merely provided for French participation but also paved the way for the separate pipe-line terminus in Syria. By 1923 the oil interests began to come to grips with their problem. At that time the Iraqis were in the first flush of their national *ekstasis*, which was heightened by the widespread (and sedulously fostered) belief that Britain in spite of her declared policy would retain her hold on Iraq. The oil people were also suspect, and while no doubt they tried to drive as hard a bargain as they could, there is equally no doubt that for the long delays that ensued the Iraqi authorities were to blame, for they allowed their suspicions to conjure up all kinds of bogeys that were not there at all and to see themselves surrounded by traps which existed only in their imagination.

But this too clever period came to an end in due course and by the spring of 1925 it was finally agreed that the Company, after preliminary tests over the whole area, should exploit twenty-four rectangular plots, each eight square miles in area, the remaining areas divided into similar plots to be then put up for auction. By 1926 the Company had chosen ten areas for test; in 1927 (October 14th) a big gusher was struck at Baba Gurgur, near Kirkuk. The Iraqi Government then, under various pretexts, including pleas of insecure conditions in certain areas, began to put restrictions on the movements of some of the Company's officials and in 1929 the whole question of the concession was reopened. The Company meanwhile decided to concentrate on the Baba Gurgur[1] and began afresh negotiations with the Government. Agreement was not finally reached until the spring of 1931, but it was ultimately agreed that the I.P.C. concessions should be confined to the area between the left bank of the Tigris and the Persian frontier; that the "plot" system should be abandoned; that a pipe-line (carrying not less than three million tons a year) to the Mediterranean should be completed by December 31, 1935; that the Company should pay to the Iraqi Government an annual sum of £400,000 in gold, half of this to be dead rent and half to be by way of advance royalties recoverable

---

[1] By the beginning of 1934 they had over forty wells drilled and sealed down, awaiting the opening of the pipeline which was completed in the autumn and began work in January 1935.

without interest as soon as the future royalties should exceed a minimum figure; that the royalties should be at the rate of four shillings a ton on a minimum production of two million tons for each of the first twenty years.

Since then the Iraqi Government has concluded a similar agreement with the British Oil Development Company (or the Mosul Oilfields Ltd.), whose concession area lies west of the Tigris. The intention has been to earmark these revenues for capital works, but in the stress of the past two or three years they have been regarded as current revenue and used to balance the budget. The other oil concern in the country is the Rafidain Oil Company, known until 1931 as the Khaniqin Oil Company. This is a subsidiary Company of the Anglo-Persian Oil Company, set up by the latter on Iraq's insistence that if it meant to operate in Iraq it must do so by means of an Iraqi Company. The producing field is at Naft Khana in the transferred territories. These territories are on the Persian border and were allocated to Turkey by the Turco-Persian Frontier Delimitation Commission just before the war broke out.

Apart from royalty payments, the money expended by the oil companies within the country on salaries and wages, rents, transport and other contracts, are an invisible export of considerable value. Their standard of wages is high and they afford employment to considerable numbers of Iraqi subordinates who work under better conditions and enjoy much higher pay than they could hope to get under Iraqi employers.

A tribute, in conclusion, is due to the work of the Post Office, whose great efficiency has made easier the advance of trade and industry in Iraq. All modern postal services are handled expeditiously and the courtesy of the staff is noteworthy. It is, however, possible that political considerations may from time to time bring the Post Office under the Ministry of Interior so far as concerns the censorship of postal communications, and not merely in times of emergency.

# CHAPTER XVII

## ANTIQUITIES AND ANCIENT HISTORY

ALTHOUGH not so rich in its scriptural associations as Palestine is, the land of Mesopotamia nevertheless plays a great part in Biblical history and many of the more familiar and more picturesque of the Old Testament stories are concerned with its rulers and peoples. Recent excavations show strong indications that these early civilizations had trade and artistic connections with the Indus valley. The excavations in Iraq have been carried out by various archaeological expeditions. A few of these were working before the war, but it was not until the British Occupation that the country became settled enough or enlightened enough to permit foreign "digs" freely. It was not until 1924 that an adequate Antiquities Law was passed reserving to the people of Iraq the first choice among the objects discovered year by year, the remaining half going to the excavators. The foreign museums that sponsor the expeditions are clearly entitled to add to their own collections of archaeological objects in return for the skill, time and money spent on the work. The country is as clearly entitled to the first choice of remains found within its boundaries. In the result the range of historical knowledge has been immensely increased. Iraq has benefited in that she now possesses, at little or no cost to herself, the finest collection in the world of objects representing the early history of the country; the foreign museums have added to their collections of ancient remains representative objects from this important part of the ancient world.

There has been a good deal of misunderstanding over this, and a good deal of wilful misrepresentation. The expeditions pay their workmen a fixed wage for digging, *plus* a bonus for finds, *minus* fines for damage done to objects found in digging. The system works well and satisfies all concerned. But the fact that the digging is thus of necessity put on a cash basis has led to the general, but ill-informed, belief that antiquities as such have a cash value. The ignorant Arab cannot be expected to understand that the evidence gained from a scientific study of the object *in situ* is infinitely more important than whatever value it may have as a museum specimen. The curio-

222

hunter has encouraged him in his ignorance. The inevitable result has been much illicit digging, with corresponding destruction of valuable historical data. The country is embarrassingly rich in sites and it has been, and still is, impossible to stop such digging. So much for the excusable ignorance with which the foreign archaeologists have to contend. To this must be added the deliberate misrepresentation fostered for political purposes by the extremer Nationalists. In the press and in public speeches the more unscrupulous of these have in past years done much harm by their suggestions, entirely unfounded, that the foreign expeditions have swindled Iraq, and by their equally baseless suggestions that the Government has not been well served by the various distinguished Europeans, British and later German, who have held the post of Director of Antiquities. One of the first acts of the independent Government of 1932 was to appoint Arab "inspectors" at all the sites where digging was proceeding. Where these appointments were to be made out of nepotism, not much objection archaeologically need perhaps be made. But in so far as it was an attempt to put a species of detective to watch what was going on, it was both ludicrous and offensive. For Iraq has practically no one with any trained experience in such work, except the few assistants in the Baghdad museum, and they have no field experience. Within the past few years about twelve different expeditions, British, American, German and French, have been working on the Mesopotamian sites, but the work in 1934–35 was gravely endangered by the threat of a more stringent Antiquities Law dictated by ultra-nationalism. The digging season is in the winter months and the amount distributed in wages to foremen and coolies is considerable.

The kingdom of Iraq is phenomenally rich in ancient remains. The alluvial plain, in ancient times the Plain of Shinar, was studded with city-states whose sites, in many cases, have still to yield up their secrets. The average Western visitor will be most interested in those sites which have scriptural associations, although the modern archaeologists have set themselves a wider horizon in their efforts to fix the place of Mesopotamia in the history of ancient civilization and culture, and to find if possible their ultimate origins. Most of the sites are fairly easily accessible.

From Baghdad, the sites of Babylon, Kish, Ctesiphon, are within easy reach. Babylon is two or three miles from Hillah, where there is a station and a railway rest-house, or about fifty miles by road from Baghdad. It is the self-same Babylon of the Old Testament.

"And the men of Babylon made Succoth-benoth. . . ."—2 Kings xvii. 30.

"The king spake, and said, Is not this great Babylon, that I have built for the house of the kingdom by the might of my power, and for the honour of my majesty?

"While the word was in the king's mouth, there fell a voice from heaven, *saying*, O king Nebuchadnezzar, to thee it is spoken: The kingdom is departed from thee."—Daniel iv. 30 and 31.

The Germans carried out the excavations here before the war; to-day the place of Nebuchadnezzar's glory is an expanse of tumbling brickwork. The best starting-point is the Arab village of Kowairish on the Euphrates, which now flows about half a mile to the west of its ancient channel. To the north and east of this village are the ruined remains of the old riverside quays. Farther east again lies the one considerable piece of statuary that Babylon can show, the celebrated Lion—a huge basalt monument depicting a lion standing over a prostrate man. Running due south from the Lion is the Sacred Way, along which the statues of the gods were borne in annual procession. The walls on each side bore in relief figures (some of which remain to this day) of lions, winged bulls, griffins and other mythical monsters. To-day the brickwork is colourless and dull, giving no idea of the rich colouring of the ancient glazed tiles. The Sacred Way passes through the Ishtar Gate.

To the west of the Ishtar Gate is the Qasr mound, which is all that is left of the imperial splendours of Nebuchadnezzar. Here were scores of elaborate courtyards, here were the famous Hanging Gardens, one of the seven wonders of the ancient world. Here too was the great throne-room, on the walls of which Belshazzar saw his message of fate, foretelling the capture of the place by Cyrus in the fifth century B.C.

"Belshazzar the king made a great feast to a thousand of his lords, and drank wine before the thousand.

"Belshazzar, whiles he tasted the wine, commanded to bring the golden and silver vessels which his father Nebuchadnezzar had taken out of the temple which was in Jerusalem: that the king, and his princes, his wives, and his concubines, might drink therein.

"Then they brought the golden vessels that were taken out of the temple of the house of God which was at Jerusalem: and the king, and his princes, his wives, and his concubines, drank in them.

"They drank wine, and praised the gods of gold, and of silver, of brass, of iron, of wood, and of stone.

"In the same hour came forth fingers of a man's hand, and wrote over against the candlestick upon the plaister of the wall of the king's palace, and the king saw the part of the hand that wrote."—Daniel v. 1–5.

To the east of Ishtar Gate was the temple of Ishtar, and south again the temple of Marduk, one of the principal deities of the time. Ishtar was the great mother-goddess, the source of all life and reproduction. She was also invoked as the goddess of war and hunting. She was the consort of Marduk.

After the Old Testament times, Babylon's most famous figure is Alexander the Great, who made it a base in his eastern campaigns and who died there in 323 B.C. He was the builder of the Greek theatre the remains of which may still be traced about a quarter of a mile north-west of the "To Babylon" signpost on the Hillah road. Babylon was very strongly fortified. This was necessary in an era when every city might at any time be at war with its neighbour over water-supply—the chief source of those ancient wars.

In the intervals of fighting, mainly against the Assyrians in the north, Babylon developed its laws, its literature, its philosophy. For several centuries the Old Testament kings, notably the first Nebuchadnezzar, maintained the splendour of the place, until the more virile invaders from the north reduced them to impotence. The second Nebuchadnezzar, in the fifth century before Christ, did much to restore the city's ancient glories but the luxury and vice of succeeding generations soon made Babylon an easy prey of the Persians, who in their turn were defeated and ejected by Alexander the Great in his tremendous conquering progress from Macedonia to India. Babylon died soon after this, being supplanted by the short-lived Seleucia.

The great arch of Ctesiphon is one of the major relics of the past that the Middle East can show. It dominates the plain; from the air it is the one conspicuous landmark in a waste of desert. The arch is all that is left of the great banqueting hall of the Persian Kings whose winter capital Ctesiphon was twelve or thirteen centuries ago. The walls, which to-day are crumbling mud-bricks, were at that time covered with gold, silver, rubies, pearls, sapphires, jasper, chalcedony, lapis-lazuli, onyx, agate and every other precious stone and metal that the East could produce. This splendour lasted until it was overwhelmed by the rising tide of Islam.

The visitor from Baghdad can easily cover both Babylon and Kish in the same day. At Kish the great mound represents the ancient platform-tower which was a characteristic feature of the religious architecture of the land between the Two Rivers. Kish seems to have been a place of religious pilgrimage. When Babylon was at the height of her glory, Kish was a great city of temples. There still exist underground passages amid the ruins, and here and there deposits of ashes representing great conflagrations in those far-off times. Façades, colonnades, temples, stairways, palaces—all remain clearly outlined among the debris and sand. Among the more interesting discoveries here have been hundreds of ancient tablets written out by scribes and scholars.

Ur Junction is the centre from which to visit Ur of the Chaldees, the birthplace of Abraham.

"And Terah took Abram his son, and Lot the son of Haran his son's son, and Sarai his daughter in law, his son Abram's wife: and they went forth with them from Ur of the Chaldees, to go into the land of Canaan: and they came into Haran, and dwelt there."—Genesis xi. 31.

Here too is a great platform tower, or ziggurat, which forms a conspicuous feature of the landscape.

"And they said, Go to, let us build us a city and a tower, whose top may reach unto heaven; and let us make us a name, lest we be scattered abroad upon the face of the whole earth."—Genesis xi. 4.

This great tower was apparently decorated with glazed tiles. Some scholars hold that there were also great gardens of trees high up on these towers. This they regard as proof that the people who built these towers, in this treeless land, were northerners who thus did their best to reproduce the wooded mountains of their original homeland. At Ur there has been uncovered spectacular evidence of a great Flood which submerged the land. The strata clearly show civilizations progressing from the earliest times—and then suddenly there comes a great deposit of mud. This can only be explained by a great rush of water depositing a thick sediment. Upon this thick stratum later civilizations began to build themselves up. Iraq is still a land of floods. If Noah existed, and if he lived in this part of the world, he would have done what the marsh-dwellers here still do. When the floods rise they pack their belongings into boats, which are made of reeds or skins covered with bitumen[1] (Noah "pitched his ark within and without"), and float to safety. At Ur, and also at Kish, there are ample evidences of a great prehistoric deluge. At Ur the city of Abraham's time has been uncovered. It is a maze of small houses, narrow streets, and bazaars. What is left of the houses proves that they were similar in type to the Arab house which the country provides to-day—a central courtyard surrounded by a two-storied building with a flat roof, a form of architecture dictated by the climate. The ancient inhabitants of Ur worshipped the Moon-god. In the third century B.C. the place was sacked by the Elamites who thrust forward from Southern Persia. On its recovery, Ur appears to have rebelled, with no success, against the growing power of Babylon, and we find Nebuchadnezzar II rebuilding the great shrine of the Moon-god on a scale much grander and more splendid than before. The excavations at Ur are particularly interesting in that from them it has been possible to reconstruct the daily life of the people who lived in Iraq nearly four thousand years ago. They had their shops and schools, their weddings and their funerals, their trades and professions. Many valuable funerary articles have been found in the tombs of the kings and the queens, especially in the great Death Pit, where courtiers and princesses, charioteers and horses were slain and buried with the dead monarchs.

Mosul is the centre from which to visit the sites of Nineveh and Nimrud.

"Now the word of the Lord came unto Jonah the son of Amittai, saying:
"Arise, go to Nineveh, that great city, and cry against it: for their wickedness is come up before me."—Jonah i. 1, 2.

---

[1] Bitumen-fields exist in places in the north-west of the country, notably near Hit on the Euphrates.

# Iraq

Nineveh lies across the Tigris from Mosul. It was a walled city about twelve miles in circumference, the fourth and last capital of the Assyrian Empire. It was against its wickedness that the Prophet Jonah was sent to preach. Here was the capital of Sennacherib, the Assyrian who "came down like a wolf on the fold."

The remains in the north are very different from those in the southern plains. In the plains there was only sun-dried brick, the north had stone. At Nineveh, for example, there were triple-arched gates flanked by great winged-bulls with human heads. All around were sculptured bas-reliefs. The ancient Assyrian kings were ruthless in war—Sennacherib thrust towards India in the east and invaded Syria and Palestine in the west. When he was assassinated, in the sixth century B.C., his son Esarhaddon captured Lower Egypt. Esarhaddon's son extended these Egyptian conquests and also overthrew the Elamites in Southern Persia. To continue these campaigns a great military machine had to be elaborated and agriculture and the other crafts of the nation were sacrificed, with the result that the Medes and the Babylonians, in alliance against it, destroyed Nineveh, the reigning monarch, with his wives and children, condemning himself to death by burning. When Xenophon, with his Greek army, marched close by Nineveh two hundred years later, he makes no mention of it, so complete was its destruction.

At Nimrud, about twenty miles from Mosul, are to be seen what remains of the power of Shalmaneser (about 1000 B.C.). This warrior king conquered Babylon and Damascus, and his successors marched into Egypt. Tiglath-Pileser III (seventh century B.C.) received a tribute of silver and gold from Ahaz, King of Judah, as a bribe for military help against Syria.

"And Ahaz took the silver and gold that was found in the house of the Lord, and in the treasures of the king's house, and sent it for a present to the king of Assyria.

"And the king of Assyria hearkened unto him: for the king of Assyria went up against Damascus, and took it, and carried the people of it captive to Kir, and slew Rezin."—2 Kings xvi. 8–9.

Here was a great military empire: one of the most interesting and important discoveries was of a huge battering-ram, for knocking down the walls of beleaguered cities. The Assyrians' power was built on cruelty, the ancient Assyrians being a cruel race in a cruel age.

From work on these sites scholars have now put together the fragmentary early history of the country.[1] From about 3000 B.C. to 2000 B.C.[2] the history is that of Babylonia, although Babylon itself was then still an obscure village. The great cities of that time were Ur, Lagash, Eridu, Nippur, Kish, Agade and others. Under the famous King Sargon the twin-realms of Sumer and Akkad were united. This was a period of high culture. The Sumerian art is neither grotesque nor quaint; European goldsmiths could scarcely better the best of the remains that have been found. Babylon did not rise to importance until about 2000 B.C., and it was not long until Hammurabi made it mighty indeed. But Babylon soon began to decay and for the ten centuries ending 800 B.C., Babylon sank as Ashur rose until it became the great military kingdom of Assyria. Until this epoch the population was not tribal. The tribal populations did not come in until about 1200 B.C. The tribes in all the dim corners of Asia were moving in those days, starting ethnic disturbances which had their effect on the early Mediterranean civilizations. In Iraq there was a surging in of Chaldaeans and Aramaeans and the power of Assyria was threatened. But the empire was strong; indeed in the century and a half from 750 B.C., to 600 B.C., the Assyrian Empire was most powerful. In this period Babylon was destroyed, as a rival to their own stronghold at Nineveh. But Nineveh very soon afterwards was broken by the Chaldaeans and Babylon rose again, under Nebuchadnezzar, for the space of a man's lifetime. In that brief time Babylon surpassed Nineveh in its power and splendour, even Jerusalem was sacked, its people being brought across the desert to clear the canal-system of the silt constantly brought down by the water.[3] It is the remains of this Babylon that are to be seen to-day. Nebuchadnezzar was a great builder and restorer; whereas the Assyrian inscriptions tell only of wars and conquests, his tell of more peaceful achievements.

In 539 B.C., the Persians under Cyrus overthrew the native power, and Iraq began the long centuries of foreign rule. Cyrus defeated the Babylonians under Belshazzar, and in the reign of Darius, who

---

[1] See the Historical Introduction also.
[2] The dates, naturally, are only approximations.          [3] See p. 31.

made it his winter capital, the Persian influence extended to the Mediterranean in the west. It was about this time that Xenophon marched his Ten Thousand Greek mercenaries down the Euphrates, raided the province of Babylon and retreated *via* the Tigris and Anatolia to the Black Sea. At this time the great frontier between East and West was being pushed backwards and forwards between the Greeks and the Persians. It is a commonplace of history that had it not been for the Hellenic confederation and their throwing back of the Persians at the very threshold of Greece, Europe to-day would be writing from right to left and our musical modes would be Oriental. Xenophon's expedition was made possible by the close interest that the Hellenes had in Persia, and as soon as Philip of Macedon's consolidation of the city-states had established the Hellenic power, Persia naturally became the principal enemy of the young Alexander. Thus in 331 B.C. the young conqueror swept through the country, and onward into India, replacing the Persian influence with Greek. The decisive battle took place at Arbela, which is the modern Arbil, probably the oldest town in the world with its site and its name unchanged since its first appearance in the pages of history.

Having become master of the known world Alexander returned to Babylon where he died in 323, at the age of thirty-three. There was no undisputed succession, but Greek influence remained in the country through the colonizing of one of his generals, Seleucus, whose family remained at Seleucia, on the right bank of the Tigris, south of Baghdad, until the Persian power, overwhelmed by Alexander, rose again and recovered the ground that had been lost. The new Persian power was Parthian and a winter capital was built at Ctesiphon, across the river from Seleucia. The Greek power of Macedon had now completely disappeared and the Western world was dominated by Rome, whose Empire came to stretch eastwards as far as Syria. Trajan visited Babylon but the Romans decided to keep their frontier in Syria, and the Parthians found the next menace coming to them from the East, whence the Sassanids, also Persians, descended upon them and broke their power. The irrigation systems of the country were developed by the Sassanids and a comparatively big population was maintained. For four centuries the Sassanids ruled, bringing prosperity and peace to the country. The Roman power had split, and both Rome and Byzantium had their hands full with the barbarians from beyond the Danube to bother much about the provinces in Asia.

The Sassanid regime might have gone on, but a man was born in Arabia in 570 A.D., whose teachings were to exercise a profound influence upon world-history. The prophet Muhammad founded his new fighting-religion of Islam, and from Arabia he planned to carry fire and sword northwards into Syria and Mesopotamia. Both were richer provinces than Arabia, and the first Islamic movement north has from time to time been followed by others, the lean warriors from the poor country coveting the rich comforts of the fairer lands. The tendency still persists. After the Prophet's death (A.D. 632) the Arabs of the south maintained his policy and within four years they had broken the Romans in Syria and the Sassanids in Mesopotamia. From the arid central peninsula they poured north; thus Syria and Mesopotamia became predominantly Arab countries.

The effects of the great Islamic schism, which came into existence soon after the Prophet's death, are described in the chapter on the Holy Cities. When Muhammad died, he was followed by a succession of Khalifs, or Caliphs as they have come to be called in English. Within a generation there had been four, the fourth being Ali, a cousin of the Prophet, who married the Prophet's daughter Fatima. Ali's realms covered North Africa, the whole of Arabia as far north as Anatolia, and as far east as the boundaries of the Indian provinces occupied by the Hindus. He was at Medina, whence the new faith had spread, and at once moved the seat of power northwards, fixing upon Kufa, not far from Baghdad. There were many rivals and before many years had elapsed he was murdered while at prayer. There was a distant cousin called Ommaya, and on Ali's murder, the Ommayid family seized the Khalifate and moved the seat of power to Damascus. The Shiah schism came into existence in this way, and the large number, including the Persians, who believed the Ommayids to be usurpers invited Hussain the son of Ali, who was living in Medina, to come to Kufa where they promised to support his claims to the Khalifate. Hussain accepted but failed to get the promised support and was slain with all his forces, at the Battle of Karbala. Ali and Hussain now became a cult and the Shiahs in due time overthrew the Ommayids. But the family of Ali

# *Iraq*

and Hussain did not succeed to the Khalifate. This was seized by their kinsmen, the Abbassids, descended from Abbas who had been Ali's uncle. The Abbassids soon moved their capital to Baghdad, and until the time of Harun-ar-Rashid the city grew in splendour and importance. The subsequent history of the country is outlined in the introduction to this book and need not be repeated here.

In Baghdad not much attempt has been made to get together any collection of Islamic remains. The Antiquities Department has concerned itself with the purely archaeological side. There may be room for another department whose function it would be to concern itself with the more modern history. It seems impossible to mix the two, and also undesirable.

# CHAPTER XVIII

# EDUCATION AND THE EFFENDI PROBLEM

THE visitor to Baghdad is invariably struck by the smartly dressed young men who may be seen in the evenings crowding the coffee-shops and cinemas, promenading the streets, or driving about in taxis. The romantic visitor may sigh for the disappearance of the old flowing garments, but here at all events are the shaven chins, the clean linen, and the polished shoes that are the sign of Western civilization.

Until the Turks were driven from the country the young Baghdadi saw few Europeans. From 1917 onwards he saw the British in uniform; from 1920 onwards British civilians arrived, and the rising generation became accustomed to the sight of well-dressed Euro-peans. The great influx of British picture-papers and the popularity of the cinema heightened the impression. King Faisal himself dressed in European clothes except for the *sidara*, the hat which he designed as the Iraqi national hat. The Ministers and Court officials are all well-turned-out. A meeting of Parliament, except for the odd tribal member, might be a meeting of any legislative or deliberative body in Europe. The spread of European dress has been made easier by the greater ease with which the journey to the Lebanon and Europe can now be made. The huge influx of British money into Mesopotamia during and since the War increased the purchasing power of the inhabitants to a degree hitherto undreamt of. Travel to the West thus became within the reach of thousands who had never considered the possibility of going farther than a few miles from Baghdad.

In those days the country was insecure outside the towns; even within the towns the bulk of the people barred and bolted their houses at sundown, the bigger houses mounting armed guards all the night. Marauders lurked on the roads. Robber barons, as in medieval Europe, dominated the countryside, extorting money and abducting children for ransom. The journey from Baghdad to Basrah, now twenty-two hours by train or three by aeroplane, then took a week. The cross-desert journey, now a matter of twenty-four hours by fast motor-coach, was then an adventure of a month or six weeks, to be undertaken by caravan with an armed convoy. To-day the average Iraqi can get from Baghdad to Beyrouth for the equivalent of £2. There he sees a higher civilization, and every Iraqi who visits Syria comes back with new ideas. Numbers go to Europe, and it is surprising how cheaply they do it. They comprise a proportion of the well-groomed promenade to which I have referred. Their fellow-Baghdadis address them as "Effendi." An effendi is an educated person; it is assumed that anyone who is well dressed must be educated and so entitled to this form of address. Many of these well-groomed young men are Jews or Christians, who for many years have been able to attend the schools maintained by their respective communities. They are probably clerks or minor officials in Government or commercial service; a few will be teachers. But an increasing proportion of them are Muslims.

In 1913 there were one hundred and sixty schools in what is now Iraq. The attendance averaged less than forty pupils per school, which means that the actual attendance would have been even less. Moreover the language of instruction was Turkish. When the schools came under British administration Turkish was abolished in favour of the native Arabic (or, in non-Arabic districts, of the local mother tongue). The Government primary school pupils now number about thirty thousand boys and seven thousand girls. The standard of instruction is not only higher but is still rising. In addition to the Government primary schools there are non-Government schools which are subject to Government inspection and usually in receipt of grants-in-aid. The Government schools may be attended by any, regardless of religion; the non-Government are largely sectarian. Many of the latter are foundations of many years' standing.

In this production of effendis two points are to be noted. First, the educated man thinks it shameful to soil his hands or to engage in menial work. As a result the effendi is unwilling to take up engineering or mechanical work; and all the mechanics and artisans in the country are illiterate. There is in Iraq nothing approximating to a literate working class. The development of agriculture on modern lines and the opening up of the country's oil resources may in time induce a change of heart; but at present technical education is practically non-existent. The second point to be noted is the continuance of the old idea that the study of Arabic is of itself an education. The school course covers a number of subjects, but an inordinate amount of time is given to the study of the Arabic language. Whereas spoken Arabic varies from country to country and from district to district, written Arabic is a classical language that is uniform from Morocco to Iraq and from Syria to Egypt and Aden. Written Arabic, therefore, has to be learned apart from the spoken language which the pupil acquires in his home. So much time is spent on its study that sacrifices have to be made in other subjects normally regarded as indispensable to a "general utility" education.

A Government appointment is regarded by most Iraqis as the goal of their education. Every schoolboy in the country, backed by his family, is hoping to enter the Government service. The traditional jobs for educated men are in the Government, and with the achievement of independence it is now Iraqis, and not Turks or British, who will fill these jobs. A Government job enhances the dignity of the family, and it can open the avenue to petty graft and easy borrowing.[1] Other attractions are the honour and power attained and the chance of a pension.

The effendi is essentially a townsman. He likes to enjoy the company of his fellows, to talk politics in the coffee-shops, to sit in the theatres and cabarets. The reason for this lies largely in his pedigree. In Iraq there is a wide gulf between the towns and the tribes. For centuries the softer townsman has feared raids and attacks by the hardier tribesman, a born marauder. There are no effendis among the tribes; a Shaikh will have a secretary or two who will read or transcribe letters. Nowadays the sons of Shaikhs may be sent away for education, but most of them are reluctant to return to the tents. It is only in the towns that education has been possible, and the effendi hates the thought of leaving his familiar surroundings.

Why does the effendi constitute a major problem for Iraq? The answer is that most of the political and economic problems that will confront the country in the next ten years are problems which the effendi is not yet qualified to solve. The political and administrative problems might be better left in the hands of men of the Shaikh

[1] See p. 155.

type and of Shaikhly family, whether "educated" or not. This type of man comes from a governing stock and is accustomed to dealing with questions of politics or administration. The effendi in general is not yet his equal in this field. On economic questions the effendi has scarcely had time to acquire expert knowledge. The Nationalist newspapers in Baghdad keep up a constant campaign in favour of the employment of Iraqis by the oil companies and other concerns. But for some years the only possibility of employing them will be in minor grades. On the technical side of oil production, as also in the Basrah Port Directorate and the Iraq Railways, the effendi in general is not yet qualified to take over, and is often disinclined to go through the mill.

Given time, the effendi class will find its feet, and will furnish in plenty capable seniors in all the Government services. But at present the effendi, as Baghdad knows him, needs public spirit as much as patriotism (which he has in plenty). He must be made to develop a wider outlook. He must give proof that he can stick at a job through discomfort and danger. So far he has had no opportunity to do so. When he has given this proof he may conciliate the tribesmen and the minorities, religious and racial, with whom he is not so popular as he might be, and Iraq will have solved what is perhaps her greatest problem.

# THE ANGLO-'IRAQ TREATY OF 1930

TREATY OF ALLIANCE BETWEEN HIS MAJESTY IN RESPECT OF THE
UNITED KINGDOM AND HIS MAJESTY THE KING OF 'IRAQ.

*Baghdad, June 30,* 1930.

[Ratifications exchanged at Baghdad, January 26, 1931.]

His Majesty the King of Great Britain, Ireland and the British Dominions beyond the Seas, Emperor of India,
And His Majesty the King of 'Iraq.
Whereas they desire to consolidate the friendship and to maintain and
perpetuate the relations of good understanding between their respective
countries; and
Whereas His Britannic Majesty undertook in the Treaty of Alliance
signed at Baghdad on the thirteenth day of January, One thousand nine
hundred and twenty-six of the Christian Era, corresponding to the
twenty-eighth day of Jamadi-al-Ukhra, One thousand three hundred
and forty-four, Hijrah, that he would take into active consideration at
successive intervals of four years the question whether it was possible for
him to press for the admission of 'Iraq into the League of Nations; and
Whereas His Majesty's Government in the United Kingdom of Great
Britain and Northern Ireland informed the 'Iraq Government without
qualification or proviso on the fourteenth day of September, One thousand
nine hundred and twenty-nine that they were prepared to support the
candidature of 'Iraq for admission to the League of Nations in the year
One thousand nine hundred and thirty-two and announced to the Council
of the League on the fourth day of November, One thousand nine hundred
and twenty-nine, that this was their intention; and
Whereas the mandatory responsibilities accepted by His Britannic
Majesty in respect of 'Iraq will automatically terminate upon the admission
of 'Iraq to the League of Nations; and
Whereas His Britannic Majesty and His Majesty the King of 'Iraq
consider that the relations which will subsist between them as independent
sovereigns should be defined by the conclusion of a Treaty of Alliance
and Amity;
Have agreed to conclude a new Treaty for this purpose on terms of
complete freedom, equality and independence which will become operative
upon the entry of 'Iraq into the League of Nations, and have appointed
as their Plenipotentiaries:

237

# Iraq

His Majesty the King of Great Britain, Ireland and the British Dominions beyond the Seas, Emperor of India,

For Great Britain and Northern Ireland:

Lieutenant-Colonel Sir Francis Henry Humphrys, Knight Grand Cross of the Royal Victorian Order, Knight Commander of the Most Distinguished Order of Saint Michael and Saint George, Knight Commander of the Most Excellent Order of the British Empire, Companion of the Most Eminent Order of the Indian Empire, High Commissioner of His Britannic Majesty in 'Iraq; and

His Majesty the King of 'Iraq:

General Nuri Pasha al Sa'id, Order of the Nadha, Second Class, Order of the Istiqlal, Second Class, Companion of the Most Distinguished Order of Saint Michael and Saint George, Companion of the Distinguished Service Order, Prime Minister of the 'Iraq Government and Minister for Foreign Affairs;

who having communicated their full powers, found in due form, have agreed as follows:—

### Article 1.

There shall be perpetual peace and friendship between His Britannic Majesty and His Majesty the King of 'Iraq.

There shall be established between the High Contracting Parties a close alliance in consecration of their friendship, their cordial understanding and their good relations, and there shall be full and frank consultation between them in all matters of foreign policy which may affect their common interests.

Each of the High Contracting Parties undertakes not to adopt in foreign countries an attitude which is inconsistent with the alliance or might create difficulties for the other party thereto.

### Article 2.

Each High Contracting Party will be represented at the Court of the other High Contracting Party by a diplomatic representative duly accredited.

### Article 3.

Should any dispute between 'Iraq and a third State produce a situation which involves the risk of a rupture with that State, the High Contracting Parties will concert together with a view to the settlement of the said dispute by peaceful means in accordance with the provisions of the Covenant of the League of Nations and of any other international obligations which may be applicable to the case.

# Appendix A

## Article 4.

Should, notwithstanding the provisions of Article 3 above, either of the High Contracting Parties become engaged in war, the other High Contracting Party will, subject always to the provisions of Article 9 below, immediately come to his aid in the capacity of an ally. In the event of an imminent menace of war the High Contracting Parties will immediately concert together the necessary measures of defence. The aid of His Majesty the King of 'Iraq in the event of war or the imminent menace of war will consist in furnishing to His Britannic Majesty on 'Iraq territory all facilities and assistance in his power including the use of railways, rivers, ports, aerodromes and means of communication.

## Article 5.

It is understood between the High Contracting Parties that responsibility for the maintenance of internal order in 'Iraq and, subject to the provisions of Article 4 above, for the defence of 'Iraq from external aggression rests with His Majesty the King of 'Iraq. Nevertheless His Majesty the King of 'Iraq recognizes that the permanent maintenance and protection in all circumstances of the essential communications of His Britannic Majesty is in the common interest of the High Contracting Parties. For this purpose and in order to facilitate the discharge of the obligations of His Britannic Majesty under Article 4 above His Majesty the King of 'Iraq undertakes to grant to His Britannic Majesty for the duration of the Alliance sites for air bases to be selected by His Britannic Majesty at or in the vicinity of Basra and for an air base to be selected by His Britannic Majesty to the west of the Euphrates. His Majesty the King of 'Iraq further authorizes His Britannic Majesty to maintain forces upon 'Iraq territory at the above localities in accordance with the provisions of the Annexure of this Treaty on the understanding that the presence of those forces shall not constitute in any manner an occupation and will in no way prejudice the sovereign rights of 'Iraq.

## Article 6.

The Annexure hereto shall be regarded as an integral part of the present Treaty.

## Article 7.

This Treaty shall replace the Treaties of Alliance[1] signed at Baghdad on the tenth day of October, One thousand nine hundred and twenty-two of the Christian Era, corresponding to the nineteenth day of Safar, One thousand three hundred and forty-one, Hijrah, and on the thirteenth day

---

[1] Treaty Series No. 17 (1925), Cmd. 2370, and No. 10 (1926), Cmd. 2662.

of January, One thousand nine hundred and twenty-six, of the Christian Era, corresponding to the twenty-eighth day of Jamadi-al-Ukhra, One thousand three hundred and forty-four, Hijrah, and the subsidiary agreements thereto, which shall cease to have effect upon the entry into force of this Treaty. It shall be executed in duplicate, in the English and Arabic languages, of which the former shall be regarded as the authoritative version.

### Article 8.

The High Contracting Parties recognize that, upon the entry into force of this Treaty, all responsibilities devolving under the Treaties and Agreements referred to in Article 7 hereof upon His Britannic Majesty in respect of 'Iraq will, in so far as His Britannic Majesty is concerned, then automatically and completely come to an end, and that such responsibilities, in so far as they continue at all, will devolve upon His Majesty the King of 'Iraq alone.

It is also recognized that all responsibilities devolving upon His Britannic Majesty in respect of 'Iraq under any other international instrument, in so far as they continue at all, should similarly devolve upon His Majesty the King of 'Iraq alone, and the High Contracting Parties shall immediately take such steps as may be necessary to secure the transference to His Majesty the King of 'Iraq of these responsibilities.

### Article 9.

Nothing in the present Treaty is intended to or shall in any way prejudice the rights and obligations which devolve, or may devolve, upon either of the High Contracting Parties under the Covenant of the League of Nations or the Treaty for the Renunciation of War signed at Paris on the twenty-seventh day of August, One thousand nine hundred and twenty-eight.[1]

### Article 10.

Should any difference arise relative to the application or the interpretation of this Treaty and should the High Contracting Parties fail to settle such difference by direct negotiation, then it shall be dealt with in accordance with the provisions of the Covenant of the League of Nations.

### Article 11.

This Treaty shall be ratified and ratifications shall be exchanged as soon as possible. Thereafter it shall come into force as soon as 'Iraq has been admitted to membership of the League of Nations.

The present Treaty shall remain in force for a period of twenty-five years from the date of its coming into force. At any time after twenty years

---

[1] Treaty Series No. 29 (1929), Cmd. 3410.

# Appendix A

from the date of the coming into force of this Treaty, the High Contracting Parties will, at the request of either of them, conclude a new Treaty which shall provide for the continued maintenance and protection in all circumstances of the essential communications of His Britannic Majesty. In case of disagreement in this matter the difference will be submitted to the Council of the League of Nations.

In faith whereof the respective Plenipotentiaries have signed the present Treaty and have affixed thereto their seals.

Done at Baghdad in duplicate this thirtieth day of June, One thousand nine hundred and thirty, of the Christian Era, corresponding to the fourth day of Safar, One thousand three hundred and forty-nine, Hijrah.

(L.S.)                               F. H. HUMPHRYS.
(L.S.)                               NOURY SAID.

## ANNEXURE TO TREATY OF ALLIANCE.

### 1.

The strength of the forces maintained in 'Iraq by His Britannic Majesty in accordance with the terms of Article 5 of this Treaty shall be determined by His Britannic Majesty from time to time after consultation with His Majesty the King of 'Iraq.

His Britannic Majesty shall maintain forces at Hinaidi for a period of five years after the entry into force of this Treaty in order to enable His Majesty the King of 'Iraq to organize the necessary forces to replace them. By the expiration of that period the said forces of His Britannic Majesty shall have been withdrawn from Hinaidi. It shall be also open to His Britannic Majesty to maintain forces at Mosul for a maximum period of five years from the entry into force of this Treaty. Thereafter it shall be open to His Britannic Majesty to station his forces in the localities mentioned in Article 5 of this Treaty, and His Majesty the King of 'Iraq will grant to His Britannic Majesty for the duration of the Alliance leases of the necessary sites for the accommodation of the forces of His Britannic Majesty in those localities.

### 2.

Subject to any modifications which the two High Contracting Parties may agree to introduce in the future, the immunities and privileges in jurisdictional and fiscal matters, including freedom from taxation, enjoyed by the British forces in 'Iraq will continue to extend to the forces referred to in Clause 1 above and to such of His Britannic Majesty's forces of all arms as may be in 'Iraq in pursuance of the present Treaty and its annexure or otherwise by agreement between the High Contracting Parties and the existing provisions of any local legislation affecting the

Q                                                   

armed forces of His Britannic Majesty in 'Iraq shall also continue. The 'Iraq Government will take the necessary steps to ensure that the altered conditions will not render the position of the British forces as regards immunities and privileges in any way less favourable than that enjoyed by them at the date of the entry into force of this Treaty.

### 3.

His Majesty the King of 'Iraq agrees to provide all possible facilities for the movement, training and maintenance of the forces referred to in Clause 1 above and to accord to those forces the same facilities for the use of wireless telegraphy as those enjoyed by them at the date of the entry into force of the present Treaty.

### 4.

His Majesty the King of 'Iraq undertakes to provide at the request and at the expense of His Britannic Majesty and upon such conditions as may be agreed between the High Contracting Parties special guards from his own forces for the protection of such air bases as may, in accordance with the provisions of this Treaty, be occupied by the forces of His Britannic Majesty, and to secure the enactment of such legislation as may be necessary for the fulfilment of the conditions referred to above.

### 5.

His Britannic Majesty undertakes to grant whenever they may be required by His Majesty the King of 'Iraq all possible facilities in the following matters, the cost of which will be met by His Majesty the King of 'Iraq.

1. Naval, military and aeronautical instruction of 'Iraqi officers in the United Kingdom.

2. The provision of arms, ammunition, equipment, ships and aeroplanes of the latest available pattern for the forces of His Majesty the King of 'Iraq.

3. The provision of British naval, military and air force officers to serve in an advisory capacity with the forces of His Majesty the King of 'Iraq.

### 6.

In view of the desirability of identity in training and methods between the 'Iraq and British armies, His Majesty the King of 'Iraq undertakes that, should he deem it necessary to have recourse to foreign military instructors, these shall be chosen from amongst British subjects.

He further undertakes that any personnel of his forces that may be sent abroad for military training will be sent to military schools, colleges and training centres in the territories of His Britannic Majesty, provided that

# *Appendix  A*

this shall not prevent him from sending to any other country such personnel as cannot be received in the said institutions and training centres.

He further undertakes that the armament and essential equipment of his forces shall not differ in type from those of the forces of His Britannic Majesty.

### 7.

His Majesty the King of 'Iraq agrees to afford, when requested to do so by His Britannic Majesty, all possible facilities for the movement of the forces of His Britannic Majesty of all arms in transit across 'Iraq and for the transport and storage of all supplies and equipment that may be required by these forces during their passage across 'Iraq. These facilities shall cover the use of the roads, railways, waterways, ports and aerodromes of 'Iraq, and His Britannic Majesty's ships shall have general permission to visit the Shatt-al-Arab on the understanding that His Majesty the King of 'Iraq is given prior notification of visits to 'Iraq ports.

(Initialled)   F. H. H.

N. S.

------

## NOTES  EXCHANGED.

### I.

The Residency,
Baghdad, dated the 30th June, 1930.

SIR,

I have the honour to inform you, with regard to Article 2 of the Treaty which we have signed to-day, that it is intended that His Britannic Majesty's diplomatic representative at the Court of His Majesty the King of 'Iraq shall have the status of Ambassador.

I have, etc.,

(Signed) F. H. HUMPHRYS.

His Excellency Nuri Pasha al Sa'id, C.M.G., D.S.O.,
  Prime Minister and Minister for Foreign Affairs, Baghdad.

------

Ministry of Foreign Affairs,
Baghdad, dated the 30th June, 1930.

SIR,

In reply to your Note of to-day's date I have the honour to inform you that the 'Iraq Government, anxious to mark the satisfaction which the appointment of His Britannic Majesty's representative as the first Ambassador in 'Iraq affords them, intend that his precedence in relation to the representatives of other Powers shall extend to his successors. The 'Iraq Government also intend that the diplomatic representative of His

Majesty the King of 'Iraq at the Court of St. James shall have the status of Minister Plenipotentiary during the currency of this Treaty.

I have, etc.,

(Signed) NOURY SAID.

His Excellency Sir F. H. Humphrys, G.C.V.O., K.C.M.G., K.B.E.,
 C.I.E.,
 His Britannic Majesty's High Commissioner in 'Iraq.

---

II.

The Residency,
Baghdad, the 30th June, 1930.

SIR,

In connection with the Treaty signed by us to-day I have the honour to place on record that it has been agreed that all outstanding financial questions, such as those relating to the 'Iraq Railways and the Port of Basra and those which it is necessary to settle for the purpose of the operation of the Treaty and of its Annexure, shall form the subject of a separate agreement[1] which shall be concluded as soon as possible and which shall be deemed an integral part of the Present Treaty and shall be ratified simultaneously therewith.

I have, etc.,

(Signed) F. H. HUMPHRYS.

His Excellency Nuri Pasha al Sa'id, C.M.G., D.S.O.,
 Prime Minister and Minister for Foreign Affairs, Baghdad.

---

Ministry of Foreign Affairs.
Baghdad, the 30th June, 1930.

SIR,

In connection with the Treaty signed by us to-day I have the honour to place on record that it has been agreed that all outstanding financial questions, such as those relating to the 'Iraq Railways and the Port of Basra and those which it is necessary to settle for the purpose of the operation of the Treaty and of its Annexure, shall form the subject of a separate agreement[1] which shall be concluded as soon as possible and which shall be deemed an integral part of the present Treaty and shall be ratified simultaneously therewith.

I have, etc.,

(Signed) NOURY SAID.

His Excellency Sir F. H. Humphrys, G.C.V.O., K.C.M.G., K.B.E.,
 C.I.E.,
 His Britannic Majesty's High Commissioner in 'Iraq.

---

[1] See Note I, appended.

# *Appendix A*

### III.

Ministry of Foreign Affairs,
Baghdad, dated the 30th June, 1930.

SIR,

In connection with the Treaty signed by us to-day I have the honour to inform Your Excellency that in view of the close friendship and alliance between our two countries the 'Iraq Government will normally engage British subjects when in need of the services of foreign officials. Such officials will be selected after consultation between our two Governments. It is understood that this shall not prejudice the freedom of the 'Iraq Government to engage non-British foreign officials for posts for which suitable British subjects are not available.

I have also the honour to inform Your Excellency that nothing in the Treaty which we have signed to-day shall affect the validity of the contracts concluded and in existence between the 'Iraq Government and British officials.

I have, etc.,

(Signed) NOURY SAID.

His Excellency Sir F. H. Humphrys, G.C.V.O., K.C.M.G., K.B.E.,
    C.I.E.,
    His Britannic Majesty's High Commissioner in 'Iraq.

———

The Residency,
Baghdad, dated the 30th June, 1930.

SIR,

I have the honour to acknowledge the receipt of Your Excellency's Note of to-day's date regarding the engagement of foreign officials, and to confirm the statement therein recorded of the understanding which we have reached.

I have, etc.,

(Signed) F. H. HUMPHRYS.

His Excellency Nuri Pasha al Sa'id, C.M.G., D.S.O.,
    Prime Minister and Minister for Foreign Affairs, Baghdad.

———

### IV.

Ministry of Foreign Affairs,
Baghdad, 30th June, 1930.

SIR,

I have the honour to inform Your Excellency that it is the intention of the 'Iraq Government, in view of their desire to improve the efficiency of their land and air forces, to ask for a British Advisory Military Mission, the numbers of which shall be decided before the Treaty comes into force and the conditions of service of which shall be similar to those of the existing Military Mission.

I have, etc.,

(Signed) NOURY SAID.

His Excellency Sir F. H. Humphrys, G.C.V.O., K.C.M.G., K.B.E., C.I.E.,
His Britannic Majesty's High Commissioner in 'Iraq.

———

The Residency,
Baghdad, 30th June, 1930.

SIR,

I have the honour to acknowledge the receipt of your Note of to-day's date on the subject of the British Advisory Military Mission which the 'Iraq Government intend to invite to 'Iraq.

I have, etc.,

(Signed) F. H. HUMPHRYS.

His Excellency Nuri Pasha al Sa'id, C.M.G., D.S.O.,
Prime Minister and Minister for Foreign Affairs, Baghdad.

NOTES EXCHANGED WITH THE 'IRAQ PRIME MINISTER EMBODYING THE SEPARATE AGREEMENT ON FINANCIAL QUESTIONS REFERRED TO IN THE SECOND EXCHANGE OF NOTES APPENDED TO THE ANGLO-'IRAQ TREATY OF 30TH JUNE, 1930.

I.

London,
19th August, 1930.

SIR,

With reference to our conversations in London, I have the honour to propose that the following provisions shall be considered as embodying the separate agreement on all financial questions referred to in the second exchange of Notes between Your Excellency and myself at the time of the signature of the Treaty of Alliance on the 30th June, 1930.

It is understood that the agreement constituted by this note and by Your Excellency's reply thereto shall be included in the instruments of ratification of the Treaty of Alliance and shall become operative on the exchange of ratifications.

1. The Government of the United Kingdom of Great Britain and Northern Ireland shall transfer to the 'Iraq Government, within the period stipulated in Clause 1 of the Annexure to the Treaty of Alliance signed on the 30th of June, 1930, the aerodromes and encampments at

246

# *Appendix A*

Hinaidi and Mosul at present occupied by the Forces of His Britannic Majesty, and the 'Iraq Government shall accept the transfer thereof (less two "A" type steel hangars and the ice plants at Hinaidi and Mosul to be removed by the Government of the United Kingdom) at one-third of the cost price certified as correct by the Air Ministry of the Government of the United Kingdom, of the permanent buildings, plant and structures thereon, no account being taken of the mud buildings which shall be transferred to the 'Iraq Government free of cost. The 'Iraq Government shall pay this sum to the Government of the United Kingdom not later than the date upon which the aforesaid transfer is completed.

During the maximum period stipulated in Clause 1 of the Annexure to the Treaty of Alliance the Forces of His Britannic Majesty shall remain in undisturbed occupation of their present stations of Hinaidi and Mosul and at Shaiba and in the use of their existing emergency landing grounds, and the Government of the United Kingdom shall not be called upon to pay higher rental charges in respect thereof than those at present paid.

2. If upon the withdrawal of the Forces of His Britannic Majesty from Hinaidi and Mosul in accordance with Clause 1 of the Annexure to the Treaty of Alliance, the Government of the United Kingdom should decide to establish a British air base in the neighbourhood of Habbaniya, then the 'Iraq Government shall take all possible steps, at no cost to either Government, to arrange for the construction of a railway to connect such air base with the railway system of 'Iraq.

3. The leases of the sites for air bases to be granted to His Britannic Majesty, in accordance with the provisions of Article 5 of the Treaty of Alliance, shall, in so far as such sites are on waste Government land, be free of all rental charges, and, in so far as they are on non-Government land, every facility shall be given for their acquisition on reasonable terms, such acquisition being effected by the 'Iraq Government at the request and at the cost of the Government of the United Kingdom. The leased lands shall be free of all taxes and rates and the leases shall continue so long as these bases remain in the occupation of the Forces of His Britannic Majesty in accordance with the provisions of the aforesaid Treaty of Alliance or of any extension thereof. On the final termination of the leases of the said sites, or of any one of them, the 'Iraq Government shall either themselves take over the buildings and permanent structures thereon at a fair valuation, having regard to the use to which they have been put, or shall afford such facilities as may reasonably be necessary to enable the Government of the United Kingdom to dispose thereof to the best advantage.

After the expiry of the maximum period stipulated in Clause 1 of the Annexure to the Treaty of Alliance and so long as the said Treaty of Alliance remains in force the Government of the United Kingdom shall not be called upon to pay any charges in respect of the use of any of the existing emergency landing grounds in 'Iraq.

4. The following arrangements for the disposal and administration of the 'Iraq railway system shall be carried into effect as soon as possible and in any case within a maximum period of one year from the entry into force of the Treaty of Alliance:

(*a*) Legal ownership of the railway system shall be transferred by the Government of the United Kingdom to the 'Iraq Government and registered in the name of the 'Iraq Government, and simultaneously with such transfer full beneficial ownership shall be vested, by lease or otherwise and at a nominal rent and on terms satisfactory to the Government of the United Kingdom, in a special body or corporation having legal personality, to be constituted by a special Statute of the 'Iraq Legislature, the terms of which shall have been agreed by both Governments.

(*b*) The above-mentioned Corporation shall be wholly responsible for the administration and management of the 'Iraq railway system, and, subject to such limitations as may be imposed in the Statute referred to above, shall have sole and exclusive authority to raise new capital by public issue or private loan and to dispose of the revenues of that system.

(*c*) The capital of the said Corporation shall comprise:

(1) Rs. 275 lakhs of Preferred Stock, bearing interest at 6 per cent, such interest being non-cumulative for a period of twenty years from the date of the transfer of the ownership of the system and thereafter cumulative, to be allotted to the Government of the United Kingdom, of which Rs. 25 Lakhs represents the capitalized value of the debt of the railways to the Government of the United Kingdom on liquidation account;

(2) Rs. 45.85 Lakhs of similar Preferred Stock, to be allotted to the 'Iraq Government, being an amount equal to the loans which the 'Iraq Government have made to the railways on which interest charges have been waived; and

(3) Rs. 250 Lakhs of Deferred Stock also to be allotted to the 'Iraq Government.

The 'Iraq Government shall have the option to buy at any time at par the Stock allotted to the Government of the United Kingdom.

(*d*) The Board of the Corporation shall consist of five Directors of whom two shall be appointed by the Government of the United Kingdom and two by the 'Iraq Government, and the fifth, who shall be the Chairman, shall be appointed by both Governments in agreement. The first Chairman shall be the present Director of the 'Iraq Railways.

# *Appendix A*

(*e*) The Corporation shall be responsible for raising loan capital required for the reconditioning and development of the 'Iraq railway system, and neither Government shall be under any obligation to guarantee such loan capital either in respect of interest or of capital.

(*f*) Any loan capital raised by the Corporation for the re-conditioning or development of the 'Iraq railway system shall rank before the Stock allotted to the two Governments in accordance with Clause (*c*) above.

(*g*) The 'Iraq Government, as owners of the equity of the system, shall accept ultimate responsibility for any liabilities relating thereto, not devolving upon the Corporation, that may subsequently come to light and in consideration thereof the Government of the United Kingdom shall transfer to the 'Iraq Government an amount of Preferred Stock of a nominal value equal to the amount of any irrecoverable disbursements that the 'Iraq Government may have to make in the discharge of any of the aforesaid liabilities, the validity of which may have been established to the satisfaction of the Government of the United Kingdom.

(*h*) In anticipation of the transfer of the railway system and the establishment of the Corporation, the 'Iraq Government shall forthwith grant three-year contracts, on "Treaty" conditions, to such British railway officials as may be recommended therefor by the Director of the 'Iraq Railways, and shall not terminate any such contracts when granted except with the agreement of the Government of the United Kingdom. The question of granting these officials contracts of longer duration shall be left for the decision of the corporation when constituted.

5. The property in the port of Basra at present held by the Government of the United Kingdom shall be transferred to the 'Iraq Government and the port shall be administered by a Port Trust. For this purpose legislation in terms agreed with the Government of the United Kingdom shall be enacted in 'Iraq for the establishment of a Port Trust having legal personality and such legislation shall not be amended, except by agreement with the Government of the United Kingdom, so long as any part of the debt owing to the Government of the United Kingdom in respect of the port is still outstanding.

Upon the enactment of the above legislation and the establishment of the Port Trust, the property in the port shall be transferred to the 'Iraq Government in whose name it will then be registered, and, simultaneously with such transfer, full beneficial ownership shall be conferred, by lease, concession or other appropriate instrument, the terms of which shall be subject to the approval of the Government of the United Kingdom, upon the Port Trust for the period during which any part of the debt owing to the Government of the United Kingdom in respect of the port remains outstanding.

I have, etc.,

(Signed) F. H. HUMPHRYS.

His Excellency Nuri Pasha Al Sa'id, C.M.G., D.S.O.,
    Prime Minister and Minister for Foreign Affairs, 'Iraq.

---

II.

London,<br>19th August, 1930.

SIR,

I have the honour to acknowledge the receipt of your note of to-day's date setting out the provisions to be considered as embodying the separate agreement on all financial questions referred to in the second exchange of Notes between Your Excellency and myself at the time of signature of the Treaty of Alliance on the 30th June, 1930, and to confirm that your Note accurately sets out the agreement at which we have arrived.

I have, etc.,

(Signed) NOURY SAID.

His Excellency Sir F. H. Humphrys, G.C.V.O., K.C.M.G., K.B.E.,
    C.I.E.,
    His Britannic Majesty's High Commissioner in 'Iraq.

## APPENDIX B

## FAISAL'S DAMASCUS DIARY

### JULY 1920

THE following statement, dated August 25, 1920, was given by Faisal to Reuter's Cairo correspondent:

*July 8th.*—I informed General Gouraud (says the Amir) that I had decided to go to Europe, and I asked for a steamer for that purpose. The answer was that certain conditions had to be fufilled before my departure, and if I should choose any other means of leaving the country the French would be free to act as they deemed fit.

*July 10th.*—I replied asking General Gouraud to agree to the formation of a Commission composed of British, French, and Syrian representatives to settle differences according to the treaty concluded between M. Clemenceau and myself after the withdrawal of the British troops from Syria.

*July 14th.*—General Gouraud sent an ultimatum, demanding acceptance of the terms thereof within four days.

*July 15th.*—The Syrian Government asked for an explanation of certain conditions laid down in the ultimatum, and asked that the four days' time limit should commence after receipt of the explanation. General Gouraud sent the explanations asked and prolonged the time limit to July 21st.

*July 17th.*—Occupation by the French of Hasbia and Rasnia, in the Arab zone.

*July 19th.*—I informed General Gouraud that I and my Government accepted the conditions of his ultimatum.

*July 20th.*—General Gouraud sent me a letter expressing pleasure at the acceptance of his ultimatum, and asking for an official written acceptance. I postponed the sittings of the Syrian Congress, demobilized the troops, withdrew the army from the front (Majdel Anger), and gave orders to accept the Syrian currency issued at Beyrouth. At noon I gave the required official letter to the French liaison officer, stating that I had begun fulfilling the conditions of the ultimatum. In the evening of this day a riot broke out in Damascus. (The official acceptance did not reach General Gouraud until two hours after the expiration of the time limit.)

*July 21st.*—French troops occupied Majdel Anger already evacuated by Syrian troops, who left all fortified places and bridges intact, which showed our good faith in fulfilling the conditions of General Gouraud. The French liaison officer went to the front to inform the General who was leading the French Army that the French conditions had been accepted and that there was no need for any further advance, but the French General declined to acquiesce in this suggestion. The French liaison officer received a telegram from General Gouraud stating that he had received my official answer two hours after the expiration of the appointed time, and under these circumstances he could not give orders for his troops to stop.

At midnight I sent a delegate to General Gouraud, who on his way met the General commanding the troops and informed him that he was proceeding in order to conduct new negotiations, and he asked him to postpone his march until further orders from General Gouraud. The commander accepted the suggestion, setting forth certain conditions which the delegate accepted.

*July 22nd.*—The delegate met General Gouraud. His answer was that he would give orders for the suspension of the advance for twenty-four hours on the following conditions:

French commissions for various purposes: disarmament of the people; French troops to remain until all the old conditions had been fulfilled; punishment of revolutionaries; evacuation of Zabadany by Syrian troops and Syrian Gendarmerie to be placed under command of the French force in this region; and the issue of a proclamation, of his wording, by the Syrian Government.

The Syrian Government's answer was: "We refuse to make war, but your new conditions if fulfilled will cause interior riots. We guarantee to fulfil your previous conditions, if your army is withdrawn to the previous places mentioned in the original ultimatum."

General Gouraud sent a telegram stating that the French troops were marching on Meisaloon (near Damascus).

*July 24th.*—French troops made their attack on the remaining Syrian force and volunteers.

*July 25th.*—French troops entered Damascus. I organized a new Cabinet from my headquarters at Kisweh.

*July 26th.*—I returned to Damascus with the approval of all the foreign diplomats.

*July 27th.*—I was ordered to leave Damascus and went to Deraa. I stayed a few days at Deraa and then proceeded to Haifa.

## APPENDIX C

# SOME NOTES ON MARRIAGE CUSTOMS
# IN SOUTHERN IRAQ

THE ceremony of betrothal is not usually thought of in the case of a boy till he has turned seventeen. In the case of a girl she may be betrothed at the age of twelve or soon after. The two persons immediately concerned are not consulted in the matter at all.

The first claim to the hand of a marriageable maiden lies with her cousin. The majority of Arab marriages are in this way the marriages of cousins. But while the girl (especially in the aristocracy) must marry her cousin, the young man may marry outside.

In 1931 a member of one of the most influential tribal aristocracies in Southern Iraq was sentenced to penal servitude for shooting a high Government official. The family in question, the Sa'duns, maintain the rule that if a Sa'dun girl marries outside her family it can only be with an equal—and the Sa'duns have no equals, or few! The high official in question was Abdulla Beg as-Sana, Director-General of the Ministry of Interior, in Baghdad, whose marriage with a Sa'dun girl had been agreed to both by the girl and by her mother. He was a man of high integrity and ability, with an undoubted future. But he was admittedly of servile origin, and the Sa'duns felt the disgrace so much that one of them walked into his office one day and shot him dead. At the trial ministers and ex-ministers were called in defence to show that the crime was no crime according to Arab standards.

The impelling reason for these consanguineous marriages is the desire to keep property within the family. Genetically it is a form of line-breeding making for purity of pedigree if it does always make for soundness of constitution.

Once the parents of the boy have decided upon a suitable bride for him, they allow it to be known among the girl's family that emissaries are about to wait upon them. These go-betweens are elderly women, respected members of the boy's family. By convention, the girl herself and her male relatives are supposed to know nothing about this. The negotiations go on for days. The go-betweens extol the merits and riches of the prospective bridegroom, the girl's relatives are coyly hesitant, like a merchant selling a pearl of great price and holding out for the utmost he can obtain. If the offer does not seem to be sufficiently attractive, the girl's relatives conclude the negotiations by the use of the expression: "We have no girl ready for marriage." This ends everything.

If, on the other hand, an agreement is reached among the women that the marriage is not only possible but desirable, the boy's father or uncle calls upon the girl's father or uncle to arrange the details of the agreement. This includes the financial settlement.

The prospective bridegroom, in addition to making a cash payment with which his bride must provide her trousseau and certain articles of furniture for the new home, undertakes to make a settlement upon the bride providing for an agreed cash (or other) payment to her in the event of his divorcing her. The bridegroom usually pays one quarter or one third of the agreed settlement in cash, which the bride brings to the new home in the form of bedchamber and other furniture, silver, gold, etc. This remains her property. The balance of the settlement remains on the bond, to be paid over only by the bridegroom in the event of his divorcing his wife. Should the wife divorce him she must make a payment equivalent to the agreed settlement. In the case of big land-owning or merchant families, where as a rule both contracting parties are well-to-do, the amount of money involved in a marriage transaction may run into thousands of pounds. Among the poor classes it may be as low as five pounds or even less.

The financial settlement thus depends entirely upon the wealth of the contracting parties. The object of making this settlement as large as possible is to lessen the chance of later divorce, by making it more difficult to refund the amount in question. The divorce by itself is easy. But if the divorcing party is moved by caprice, then a recollection of the marriage bond that has been signed will give rise to sober reflection. Thus it happens that the marriage settlement, providing as it does legal ground for the recovery of a relatively large sum, tends towards the maintenance of marriages. If the wife divorces the husband she has to say, "I give up any right to the marriage settlement and any right to the furniture." This is a similar device to discourage divorce. Among the desert tribes similar customs prevail, in their case flocks and herds frequently taking the place of the jewels that are given among the townspeople.

All this time the prospective bride and bridegroom have not seen each other except at a distance. But after all these preliminary agreements have been reached, a day is fixed when women relatives of the prospective bridegroom go to the girl's house for the final and irrevocable acceptance. Arrangements are then made for a *Mullah* to perform the actual ceremony. Before he can do this, the *Mullah* must be in possession of a certificate from the religious courts. He then proceeds to record the terms of the settlement, which thus becomes a legal document setting forth the details of the contract between the two parties.

The actual betrothal ceremony may then take place. Standing behind a door or thick curtain in the house of the bride, the *Mullah* reads over the complete terms of the contract three times (in Basrah he reads it thirteen times), in order to prevent any doubt which might arise as the result of merely reading it once or twice. After the final reading he asks the girl if she accepts.

The girl meantime is sitting with a tray in front of her on which are placed a candle, a copy of the Koran, a piece of bread, some vegetables and a mirror. Her feet are placed in a basin of water in which float leaves of sweet-scented herbs. The *Mullah*, behind the curtain, cannot see the girl and so he has with him two witnesses, from the bridegroom's family, who confirm that the girl's reply has been audible and that it is her voice that they have heard. All three must certify this on the document.

The usual convention is that at the first time of asking the girl remains silent. She is pressed to speak up, and after the *Mullah* has repeated his question once or twice the girl will whisper her acceptance. This however is not officially audible and the *Mullah* insists on a still louder response. A "No" is impossible, things having got so far, and after the girl has said "Yes," she adds, "And I name so-and-so (a male relative) as my *wakil* (agent)."

While the girl is saying the real "Yes," she has in her mouth a sweet-meat. Her favourite slave or servant, or the woman who wet-nursed her when an infant, takes this sweetmeat from her, and puts it in a glass of sherbet which is sent to the bridegroom. This is a superstition rather than a rite, but it is believed that when he has drunk this, and duly given *backsheesh* to the serving-woman, it is a sign that everything is now irrevocably settled.

The acceptance is then recorded in legal form by the *Mullah* to the accompaniment of loud ululation by the crowds of women assembled. The slaves or serving-women bring round syrups and sherbets, and sweetmeats are passed round on silver trays. No engagement-ring is given at the betrothal, but in the case of a long engagement the bridegroom makes a present of jewellery.

From this point, the couple do not even catch a glimpse of each other, even if as may happen, they may have been brought up together during childhood.

The girl now gets her trousseau, and arrangements for the wedding are pressed on. The Arab day begins at sunset, and the day usually chosen for the wedding is that beginning on the European Thursday night, Friday being the Muslim Sunday. The ceremonies then begin on the Wednesday morning. From the bride's house are sent out many invitations to the *hammam*, either in the house, if it is a big house, or in the public Turkish baths. Women chosen from both families conduct the bride thither; all the expenses of this part of the ceremonies are paid by the groom's family.

A bride must have no hair on any part of her body except her head. The hair is not shaved, because shaved hair grows quickly. It is removed in a curious way. The part is exposed and, with an endless piece of string the barber woman slips a loop tightly around a few hairs. With each hand she pulls the string laterally; she also takes the string in her teeth, so that the endless piece of string becomes, as it were, a triangle, the angles of which are held by the two hands and the mouth. With a sharp upward wrench of the head the hair in the loop is pulled out by the root. Hair removed in this way takes a long time to grow again. The process is a painful one, and another method now adopted is to smear the parts with arsenical paste, which when removed takes the hair with it—if not removed in time it takes the skin too!

When the bridal party returns from the bath a big luncheon party is given, at the end of which the palms of the bride's hands and the soles of her feet are dipped in henna. There are special women whose calling it is to perform this particular rite in the wedding ceremonies. The henna duly applied, the bridegroom's mother or sister gives a money gift to the bride's nurse.

On the same day, at the same time, a similar ceremony takes place in the bridegroom's house. But in this case it is only the little finger of the right hand that is dipped (the whole finger) in the henna. Then follows a musical entertainment with professional dancing girls. The dances are the usual sinuous symbolic dances of the East.

On the Thursday morning the groom's relatives and best friends take luncheon in his house: there is no corresponding luncheon on the bride's side. All the company gather after the meal to attend the shaving. In the case of a wealthy family, this is done by the family's barber, who is a serving-man of the house and whose "pay" consists of the (very considerable) *pourboires* that are given as each boy grows to the age, first of circumcision and then of marriage.

The barber shaves every part of the man except the head. In the case of poorer families an ordinary barber from the bazaar is employed.

It is now time for the women to bring the bride to the *harem* of the bridegroom's house. A meal is served and there is much music and entertainment. It is now approaching sunset on the Thursday, and when the time comes for the sunset prayers all the bride's women depart except one chosen to remain with the bride—an elder married sister, aunt, grandmother or nurse.

On the same evening the closest friends of the bridegroom's family invite him to dinner: he must not dine in his own house. The party then go to the mosque for the evening prayers. All the guests depart and his father or his uncle conducts him to the *harem*. He is taken to the room where the bride is waiting and his mother takes their hands and joins them. Then he unveils his bride's face and gives her the first kiss. He then goes downstairs and kisses his male relatives. By this time the bride is alone. The bridegroom goes upstairs, and after reciting a few verses of the Koran, he goes to her.

Next morning the one female relative (who has remained in the house for the purpose) enters the room to get proof of the bride's virginity.

The sheet is put in a brocaded satchel, taken to her father's house and shown to all the near relatives. It is kept until the birth of the first baby and is then thrown away.

Later in the morning the bridegroom goes to the house of his father-in-law (now called his uncle) to kiss his hand and that of his mother-in-law. The girl's father then gives him a present, such as a ring or watch. In olden times the gift from the bride's father was usually a fine Arab horse, ready saddled and waiting. The mother-in-law's gift is usually jewels, gold or silver.

During the first seven days all the wedding gifts from friends arrive at the new house, usually on trays with sweetmeats surrounding the gifts. On the seventh day the bridegroom's mother invites the bride's mother and family to a *hammam* party and then to luncheon in her house. In the evening the bridegroom's father invites her male relatives to dinner, which is followed by music and entertainment by dancing boys and girls. To each of the girl's relatives present on this occasion is sent a tray on which is placed a candle, a little henna, some sugar and a gift. That night also, for the first time since the nuptials, the bride's father and male relatives come to see her. In olden times the bride never visited her parents' house until her first baby was born.

When the bride becomes pregnant, the seventh month sees the beginning of great activity among her relatives, who must prepare the baby's clothes, bed, bathtub, even the small commode—everything in fact that the baby will need. All this is sent to the expectant mother during the ninth month. After the baby is born, all the relatives who visit the mother leave money gifts under the baby's pillow; these gifts are for the midwife, a small present, such as a gold or silver bangle, being also left for the baby. The child's name is nowadays more freely chosen than before. But among the tribes and the older families the paternal grandfather, or the oldest member of the father's family, takes the baby on his knee and reads a passage from the Koran. He then whispers, "Allah, Allah, Allah" and (to the infant), "I give you this name . . ."

Boys are circumcised between the age of six and twelve. Circumcision is not practised in the case of girls, but an ancient superstition survives. If a woman fails to become pregnant, a slight incision is made at the top of the vagina. This is usually done by a circumcised negress and is believed to be infallible.

If the wife loses her husband's love (which is not infrequent) she calls in two of her girl friends. They take a partridge which they kill with a golden knife. The two girls, taking the dead bird, go to a cemetery and prepare a fire. They put the bird on this fire and sit back to back, with the fire between them until the bird is cooked. They must not look at it. When the bird is cooked they take the wing bones to the *Mullah*, who wraps them in Koranic texts. This they give to the wife, who wears it as an amulet between her breasts until her husband's love returns.

# *Iraq*

Another strange superstition is concerned with the birth of a baby girl. The assembled relatives watch and if they think the baby appears to pass blood the fact is noted. When such a baby grows up, her husband on the wedding night may not go to her until sunrise, and a woman of her family remains in the bridal chamber until then.

# INDEX

# Index

261

# Index

# Index

# Index

www.ingramcontent.com/pod-product-compliance
Ingram Content Group UK Ltd.
Pitfield, Milton Keynes, MK11 3LW, UK
UKHW020359010325
455677UK00021B/536